Lloyd J. Ogilvie G<

THE
PREACHER'S
COMMENTARY

1, 2, 3 JOHN, REVELATION

Earl F. Palmer

THOMAS NELSON PUBLISHERS
Nashville

The Preacher's Commentary Series, Volume 35: *1, 2, 3 John; Revela*
Copyright © 1982 by Word, Inc.

Published in Nashville, Tennessee, by Thomas Nelson, Inc.

Library of Congress Cataloging in Publication Data

The preacher's commentary (formerly The communicator's commentary).

Includes bibliographical references.
Contents: v. 35. 1, 2, 3 John;Revelation/Earl F. Palmer
1.Bible. N.T.—Commentaries—Collected works.
I. Ogilvie, Lloyd John. II. Palmer, Earl F.

BS2341.2.C65   225.7'7   81–71764
ISBN 0-7852-4810-2   AACR2

Printed in the United States of America
2 3 4 5 6 7 – 07 06 05 04

Dedicated to colleagues and friends
in three of the churches of our lives—
University Presbyterian Church of Seattle
Union Church of Manila
First Presbyterian Church of Berkeley

CONTENTS

EDITOR'S PREFACE

God has called all of His people to be communicators. Everyone who is in Christ is called into ministry. As ministers of "the manifold grace of God," all of us—clergy and laity—are commissioned with the challenge to communicate our faith to individuals and groups, classes and congregations.

The Bible, God's Word, is the objective basis of the truth of His love and power that we seek to communicate. In response to the urgent, expressed needs of pastors, teachers, Bible study leaders, church school teachers, small group enablers, and individual Christians, the Preacher's Commentary is offered as a penetrating search of the Scriptures to enable vital personal and practical communication of the abundant life.

Many current commentaries and Bible study guides provide only some aspects of a communicator's needs. Some offer in-depth scholarship but no application to daily life. Others are so popular in approach that biblical roots are left unexplained. Few offer impelling illustrations that open windows for the reader to see the exciting application for today's struggles. And most of all, seldom have the expositors given the valuable outlines of passages so needed to help the preacher or teacher in his or her busy life to prepare for communicating the Word to congregations or classes.

This Preacher's Commentary series brings all of these elements together. The authors are scholar-preachers and teachers outstanding in their ability to make the Scriptures come alive for individuals and groups. They are noted for bringing together excellence in biblical scholarship, knowledge of the original Greek and Hebrew, sensitivity to people's needs, vivid illustrative material from biblical, classical, and contemporary sources, and lucid communication by the use of clear outlines of thought. Each has been selected to contribute to this series because of his Spirit-empowered ability to help people live in the skins of biblical characters and provide a "you-are-there" intensity to the drama of events of the Bible which have so much to say about our relationships and responsibilities today.

The design for the Preacher's Commentary gives the reader an overall outline of each book of the Bible. Following the introduction, which reveals the author's approach and salient background on the book, each chapter of the commentary provides the Scripture to be exposited. The New King James Bible has been chosen for the Preacher's Commentary because it combines with integrity the beauty of language, underlying Greek textual basis, and thought-flow of the 1611 King James Version, while replacing obsolete verb forms and other archaisms with their everyday contemporary counterparts for greater readability. Reverence for God is preserved in the capitalization of all pronouns referring to the Father, Son, or Holy Spirit. Readers who are more comfortable with another translation can readily find the parallel passage by means of the chapter and verse reference at the end of each passage being exposited. The paragraphs of exposition combine fresh insights to the Scripture, application, rich illustrative material, and innovative ways of utilizing the vibrant truth for his or her own life and for the challenge of communicating it with vigor and vitality.

It has been gratifying to me as Editor of this series to receive enthusiastic progress reports from each contributor. As they worked, all were gripped with new truths from the Scripture—God-given insights into passages, previously not written in the literature of biblical explanation. A prime objective of this series is for each user to find the same awareness: that God speaks with newness through the Scriptures when we approach them with a ready mind and a willingness to communicate what He has given; that God delights to give communicators of His Word "I-never-saw-that-in-that-verse-before" intellectual insights so that our listeners and readers can have "I-never-realized-all-that-was-in-that-verse" spiritual experiences.

The thrust of the commentary series unequivocally affirms that God speaks through the Scriptures today to engender faith, enable adventuresome living of the abundant life, and establish the basis of obedient discipleship. The Bible, the unique Word of God, is unlimited in its resource for Christians in communicating our hope to others. It is our weapon in the battle for truth, the guide for ministry, and the irresistible force for introducing others to God. In the New Testament we meet the divine Lord and Savior whom we seek to communicate to others. What He said and did

8

as God with us has been faithfully recorded under the inspiration of the Spirit of God. The cosmic implications of the Gospels are lived out in Acts and spelled out in the Epistles. They have stood the test of time because the eternal Communicator, God Himself, communicates through them to those who would be communicators of grace. His essential nature is exposed, the plan of salvation is explained, and the gospel for all of life, now and for eternity is proclaimed.

A biblically rooted communication of the gospel holds in unity and oneness what divergent movements have wrought asunder. This commentary series courageously presents personal faith, caring for individuals, and social responsibility as essential, inseparable dimensions of biblical Christianity. It seeks to present the quadrilateral gospel in its fullness which calls us to unreserved commitment to Christ, unrestricted self-esteem in His grace, unqualified love for others in personal evangelism, and undying efforts to work for justice and righteousness in a sick and suffering world.

A growing renaissance in the church today is being led by clergy and laity who are biblically rooted, Christ-centered, and Holy Spirit-empowered. They have dared to listen to people's most urgent questions and deepest needs and then to God as He speaks through the Bible. Biblical preaching is the secret of growing churches. Bible study classes and small groups are equipping the laity for ministry in the world. Dynamic Christians are finding that daily study of God's Word allows the Spirit to do in them what He wishes to communicate through them to others. These days are the most exciting time since Pentecost. The Preacher's Commentary is offered to be a primary resource of new life for this renaissance.

Earl Palmer is an outstanding leader of this resurgence of expository preaching and teaching. He is the Pastor of the University Presbyterian Church of Seattle, Washington. His authentic evangelical faith coupled with his intellectual integrity won him a large following among the students and faculty of the University of Berkeley during his twenty years at First Presbyterian Church of Berkeley. He is distinguished for his penetrating analysis and lucid explanation of verses and passages of Scripture. Earl Palmer has a unique ability to get to the essence of the language, background, meaning, and message of the Bible. This has made him a model preacher who is respected and admired by clergy and laity alike. His immense gifts are channeled through a dynamic commitment to be a communicator. Rich biblical, historical, and literary material is woven together to grip the minds and hearts of his listeners or readers. This is punctuated by vivid illustrations, metaphors, and humor. He has a rare ability to communicate his own excitement about the discoveries he has made in his own studies in preparation for speaking or writing. Biblical characters walk off the page as our contemporaries and the words of a text flash like diamonds when held up to the light of illuminating research.

I am delighted that Earl Palmer has written this crucial volume in the Preacher's Commentary. His exposition of 1, 2, 3 John and Revelation introduces us to the mind and heart of the apostle John in a stunning way. The explanation of the deeper meaning of the Johannine epistles combines a scholar's research and a communicator's concern that we experience the full impact of John's message to the early church about life, truth, and love. It was Earl Palmer's goal to catch hold of the fire and joy of these letters, and he has done that in a remarkable way.

Revelation is a benchmark exposition. In it you will discover new insights into passages of the Apocalypse which are fresh to expositorial literature. The outline of the flow of thought is unique and gives the reader a distinctly different approach to understanding this pivotal book of the New Testament. Passages which previously seemed obscure or beyond the reach of the contemporary mind are explained with clarity and appreciation of life. More easily understood and popular passages are liberated from the prisons of familiarity in light of deeper wisdom about the true meaning. Revelation now becomes a rich source of inspiration for Bible study, teaching, and preaching. Earl Palmer's teaching and preaching of his insights into Revelation has stirred congregations and audiences. The result of his careful exposition now can be a primary source book for understanding and utilizing Revelation.

This volume is included in the Preacher's Commentary with gratitude for Earl Palmer's commitment to excellence.

—LLOYD J. OGILVIE

Author's Preface—1, 2, 3 John

Jesus Christ said great things so simply, that it seems as though He had not thought them great; and yet so clearly that we easily see what He thought of them. This clearness, joined to this simplicity, is wonderful" (Blaise Pascal, *Pensées*, §796).

The letters that John the apostle wrote to his friends are written in the same style of simplicity joined with clarity that John learned from his teacher. I invite you to enter into the world of these three brief letters and discover for yourself their fresh and exciting portrayal of the meaning of life and truth and love.

This commentary has been for me a very challenging task. In the history of New Testament studies, 1,2, 3 John have not received the attention they deserve. Very few expositors of John's letters have been able to catch hold of and express the fire and the joy of John the writer. The one great exception is the commentary by B. F. Westcott, 1888, which I believe still stands as the brilliant exposition of John's epistles. But most commentaries seem dry and technical. John's language is plain and direct, but there is an explosive quality that breaks out suddenly, without warning. These three letters are written to his own generation in the first century; they engage the temptations and dangers of that century without equivocation. His letters state in positive terms the meaning of daily discipleship.

John's letters are very vital to our generation, too, and I endorse them to any of you who read these words, whether you are an inquirer into the life and truth and love of which John writes or whether you are a believer who wants to grow as a Christian. I must express special thanks first of all to my family—Shirley, Anne, Jon, and Elizabeth—and then to the church, First Presbyterian Church of Berkeley, where I was serving at the time of this writing, and to my colleagues in study at New College Berkeley, during the fall term of 1981.

—EARL PALMER

INTRODUCTION TO 1, 2, 3 JOHN

There are three books in the New Testament that the early church simply entitled 1, 2, 3 John. We call them the epistles or letters of John. It was the conviction of the great majority of the early church fathers that these books were written by the same writer as the Gospel of John, namely the Son of Zebedee, John the disciple of Jesus. The book was highly regarded in the early church. Polycarp of Smyrna quotes from the Book of 1 John in his second-century letter to the Philippians. It is the distinguished apologist Irenaeus of Lyons who firmly links these books, the Book of Revelation, and the Gospel of John to the John who was the "disciple of the Lord." So also Justin Martyr, Tertullian, and Clement of Alexandria. The only other early church authorship hypothesis that we should note is that of Papias of Hierapolis, who, according to Eusebius, assigned 1, 2, 3 John to another John—a man known as John the Elder. But his view was not accepted by the early church, whose consensus clearly favors the view that John, the Lord's disciple, had written these three letters to Christians in order to share concerns with them about their life and faith and about problems they were confronting as Christians in the world. The tradition of the early Christians also assigned the Book of Revelation to the same author.

Before we make some particular comments upon these letters of John we must first focus in upon the other Johannine books, the Gospel of John and the Book of Revelation.

During the late nineteenth century and into the twentieth century there has been a great upheaval in Johannine studies. Certain scholars have been hesitant to rely upon the Gospel of John as a trustworthy historical document of the life and ministry of Jesus because of its interior nature, its reflectiveness. In his *Commentary on the Johannine Epistles,* J. L. Houlden gave this view: "Wherein lay its fault? No doubt, partly, it was simply too elaborate, too highly wrought in its doctrinal expression."[1] Rudolph Bultmann argued that John's Gospel contained within it a whole strata of basically gnostic material. For example, he treated in his *Commentary on John* the prologue of John's Gospel (John 1:1–18) as if it were a gnostic hymn. In short, by the time of the midpoint of the twentieth century many New Testament scholars had described and confined the Gospel of John as a dogmatic tract of the second-century church.

This description, for practical purposes, removed the Gospel of John from the serious attention of a reader who wanted to know what Jesus actually said and did during His life and ministry. According to these interpreters we will not find such information from John's Gospel; instead what we learn from that Gospel is the Easter faith of a part of the second-century church. For these interpreters the Gospel is the Good News of the church's faith, not the Good News of the life of Jesus Christ. A serious shift had occurred in New Testament studies, and, in my observation of this story, the results were devastating both spiritually and intellectually to those who bought into this view. The Gospel of John had been tamed and its Lion had been caged. However, the technical methods and scholarly premises by which the Gospel of John had been recast by Professor Bultmann and his followers were to have a short-lived dominance in the world of New Testament studies, because the facts of biblical research did not support the Bultmann hypothesis over the long haul.

What has in fact happened in manuscript research is that the evidence of present scholarship has moved the dates of New Testament documents earlier into the first century rather than later into the second century. This means that the Johannine literature in the New Testament is not made up of documents written down after the time of the first century, but the massive impact of manuscript studies now argues for a date of authorship at or around A.D. 70.[2] Secondly, there is no first-century evidence to support Professor Bultmann's thesis of a pre-Christian Gnosticism which becomes a thematic trajectory within the Gospel of John. John's Gospel is not a gnostic book—it is a profoundly Semitic, *Jewish* book. The prologue of John has that wonderful Jewish sense of wholeness and the exciting boldness of "Word become flesh." The whole of John's Gospel is written in simple and fluent Greek, but its profound undercurrent is the undercurrent of the Old Testament.

Within this volume is a discussion of the Book of Revelation, which in my view is also rightly to be included within the Johannine family of New Testament books. Now we come to the letters of John. When were they written? Are they perhaps earlier than the Gospel of John, or are they later? It seems likely that the traditional view of the church is correct which places these letters later than the Gospel and earlier than the Book of Revelation. I believe that we will find evidences that support this placement as we consider the text itself.

These letters are written in the same simple and yet fluent Greek as we observed in the Gospel of John. The vocabulary and writing style of the Book of 3 John and Book of Revelation is quite another matter, and I have discussed that issue in the Commentary on 3 John and in the introduction to the Commentary on Revelation.

These three letters of John are disarmingly forthright and direct. John writes in the form and philosophical frame of reference of the Old Testament Jewish wisdom and psalmic writing. Whereas Paul writes in the tradition of Greek rhetoric and argument-building—a Pauline letter is really one continuous sentence—John on the other hand writes more like the psalmist or the writer of Proverbs. He repeats; he writes with the use of parallelism and repetition of ideas.

We who are the children of Greek thought and method of argument are more acquainted with the intellectual style of Paul, but the poet and the musician is more acquainted with the style of John. Like the poet or artist, John spends much time on one detail; repetition is welcomed and embraced. We notice this attention to detail in the Gospel of John, especially in the dialogue narratives; for instance, John devotes a whole chapter to one blind youth and his encounter with Jesus (ch. 9). This is the way a poet watches a historical event unfold. This is the approach of the psalmist more than of the philosopher. John is repetitious in 1 John as certain great themes are repeated by the writer at various places within the book. But then, that is the way the wisdom literature of the Old Testament is written, too. Through Psalms and Proverbs great central themes are brought up over and over again. It will do us no good to remind our writer that he has already made that point in chapter 2; he wants to tell it to us again in chapter 5, yet with a slightly different accent and emphasis. He knows very well what he is doing, and if we watch closely and accept this way of expression, we will be deeply challenged intellectually and also poetically moved by the sheer buildup of intensity and overall design.

Let me put it in terms of an image. Think of a great quiet pond of clear water. Our writer, John, throws out into the clear plane of undisturbed water, a rock. We watch the rings move outward; the implications are spelled out. Then the author in effect says, "That's enough of that theme." He then hurls out another rock onto the water surface. A new set of rings moves outward. Some collide and intermingle with the circles of the first rock; others move out into totally new directions. Then our author will once again surprise us with another cease and will throw yet another rock. Or perhaps, since he is so expert at this art form, he will throw out onto the surface a skipping rock that connects the rings already in place.

This is the way 1 John is written. Our author has several very big rocks to throw out into the clear, glasslike water of his book. *God is life, God is light, God is love.* These are like great circles with which John confronts his readers. His two great skipping rocks that interconnect these profound circles are, first, his clear teaching about who Jesus Christ is, and, second, an antiphonal or negative connecting thread, another skipping rock that crosses over the great circles of life, light, and love. The first, which appears throughout this book as a persistent connective thread, is our author's powerful and concrete affirmation of the Person of Jesus Christ. The second, John's warning against what is false in doctrine and in lifestyle, will also course across the clear surface like another skipping stone thrown by the author to warn his readers against the dangers that he recognizes are confronting his friends in their discipleship journey.

Now let us read John's letters and listen to this beloved father in our faith as he shares Good News and warnings to us in our century. We live many years away from Ephesus in its time of Roman tyranny, but the themes in these three letters are alive and current. The great rocks in John's pond are great facts we need for living today just as much as did the men and women in A.D. 70.

NOTES

1. J. L. Houlden, *A Commentary on the Johannine Epistles* (New York: Harper, 1973), p. 11.

2. See the discussion concerning authorship in E. F. Palmer, *The Intimate Gospel* (Waco, Tex.: Word Books, 1978).

An Outline of 1, 2, 3 John

I. The Way of Life: 1 John 1:1–10
   A. From the Beginning: 1 John 1:1–4
   B. God Is Light: 1 John 1:5
   C. The Walk in the Light: 1 John 1:6–10
II. The New Relationship: 1 John 2:1–29
   A. The Advocate: 1 John 2:1–6
   B. A New Commandment: 1 John 2:7–17
   C. Abide in Him: 1 John 2:18–29
III. Truth and Love: 1 John 3:1—4:21
   A. See What Love: 1 John 3:1–18
   B. Test the Spirits: 1 John 3:19—4:6
   C. Love Is an Event: 1 John 4:7–21
IV. Discipleship: 1 John 5:1–21
   A. Not Burdensome: 1 John 5:1–12
   B. Keep Away from Idols: 1 John 5:13–21
V. Christians in the World: 2 John 1–13
   A. The Elect Lady: 2 John 1–3
   B. Tough Love: 2 John 4–13
VI. The Family of God: 3 John 1–14
   A. No Greater Joy: 3 John 1–8
   B. A Question of Leadership: 3 John 9–14

CHAPTER ONE—THE WAY OF LIFE

1 JOHN 1:1–10

Scripture Outline

From the Beginning (1:1–4)

God is Light (1:5)

The Walk in the Light (1:6–10)

FROM THE BEGINNING

1:1 That which was from the beginning, which we have
heard, which we have seen with our eyes, which we have
looked upon, and our hands have handled, concerning the
Word of life— 2 the life was manifested, and we have seen, and
bear witness, and declare to you that eternal life which was
with the Father and was manifested to us— 3 that which we
have seen and heard we declare to you, that you also may have
fellowship with us; and truly our fellowship is with the Father
and with His Son Jesus Christ. 4 And these things we write to
you that your joy may be full.

—1 John 1:1–4

The first four verses in our English text are really one long song-
like sentence from John. The atmosphere of the sentence is exciting, immediate, and intensely personal as we, the readers, are
invited into a relationship of joy with the writer John and those
brothers and sisters with him and the Lord. At the same time the
sentence is vast and historically far-reaching.

As the words begin we are reminded of the prologue to the
Gospel of John and also of the opening words of Genesis 1. "In the
beginning God created . . . and God said . . ." What is it that John
intends us to think and feel as we hear these opening words? Is he
referring to "the beginning" as seen in the more close-at-hand
sense of the beginning of the ministry of our Lord Jesus Christ

which John himself knew of personally and directly and now invites those of us who read his opening words of this chapter to experience with him? Or does John intend the more mysterious and extensive connection of these words "from the beginning" to the opening song of Genesis? In this case John connects the Jesus Christ of his personal relationship to the very source and origin of everything. John is then telling us that this Jesus Christ of our experience is the One who stands with the Father in the beginning before creation itself.

It seems the most reasonable interpretation to me that John intends both of these meanings in these opening words. The evidence that supports this interpretation is found in the obvious connection of these four verses to the great prologue at the opening of the Gospel of John. In the Gospel's prologue, the *Logos* is firmly identified with the Father in the beginning before creation. In fact John tells us "all things were made through him" (John 1:3). What we have in 1 John 1:1–4 is a practical commentary upon the mighty prologue of the Gospel of John. The great theme about life in the original prologue, "In him was life, and the life was the light of men" (John 1:4), is now made understandable and practical, totally accessible to mere human beings. John tells us in concrete terms about this wondrous *"Word of life."* His main point is that we have *seen, looked at, touched* this Word of life. Whatever the Word of life is, one thing is clear to us from John: the Word of life can be known and experienced by people. This is the contention of John, and he makes his point several different ways within these four verses so that there can be no misunderstanding.

Let us examine his vocabulary just to see how John develops his exciting affirmation. Notice the visual vocabulary that John makes use of: two vision or seeing words are used by John within these few verses. The one word *theōmai* means "to gaze" or "behold," and it contains within it a dramatic and powerful sense. It is the idea of a spectacle now seen in full power and wonder. From this Greek word we have the root for the English word *"theater."* The word *horaō* in Greek is the more common and ordinary word and means plainly and directly "to see, to catch sight of." With this word John emphasizes how real and actual was his own experience of Jesus Christ. The word offers an earthy companionship to the more dramatic sense of seeing in *theōmai.* John's experience was both a mysterious perception of the living Lord and yet it was also very basic and down to earth. Jesus was no phantom of the spiritual realm but He was Jesus of Nazareth.

The most vitally important phrase in this paragraph is made up of the three words, *"Word of life."* What does John mean by the use of the word *Logos?* "Word" within the Greek world of thought carries in it the sense of meaning, reason, purpose of it all. It is a vast word that integrates other lesser words within itself. Within the Old Testament world of thought, "word" carries the sense of authority, disclosure, decision, and action. "God *said,* 'Let there be light.'" Word is powerful, and because of it not only do things happen but disclosure of the will and character of God takes place. When God speaks we meet Him. By His Word He creates, by His Word He is known, by His Word He judges, forgives, and fulfills.

John has already proved to his readers that he is totally fluent in the Greek language. C. K. Barrett has observed that though John's Greek vocabulary is very simple, as a writer he is never at a loss for the right Greek word to express himself. John's Greek in this letter of 1 John is the simplest Greek in the New Testament. For this reason it is a very good book for the beginner in Greek studies to try out his or her language skills. This book is written in "Dick and Jane" Greek, but do not let that fact lead you, the interpreter, to a false conclusion. John is the same kind of writer Winston Churchill was a speaker. Both favor short, crisp sentences and plain, clear words. But both are fully aware of the words they are using, and that idiomatic fluency and correctness intensify the power of what is written. John is fully aware of the rich philosophical content hidden within the Greek word *Logos.* He now deliberately makes use of this loaded, awesome word, brilliantly seizing hold of it and giving it the flavor and decisive power of the Old Testament sense of "word." The more subtle Greek nuances of meaning and reason in *Logos* are not lost, but they are drawn into the larger, more primitive power of the Old Testament sense of the God who speaks and who makes Himself known, the God who creates by that very speech.

Notice in this brief prologue of 1 John the two major affirmations that John announces to his readers: first, that *life* has its origin in God's character and nature; second, that this life from God has come among us. God is the source of life. Whatever life is, we learn from John that it derives from God; *life* is not seen by John as an abstract philosophical entity. This is why John is able to add to the word *"life"* the mysterious word *"eternal."* We know from the Old and New Testament doctrine of history that the created order of both heaven and earth are not in themselves eternal (Luke 21:33). Only God is eternal and His speech is eternal—His

Word. The Word of life is eternal. John tells his readers that that Word of life has been made manifest. The Greek word John uses to describe this manifestation of the Word is *phaneroō*, which means to reveal, to become visible, plain, clear. The English word "phenomenon" comes from this Greek root. It is this sense of clarity that John wants to emphasize by the use of these words. He wants his readers to know that the decision God made which is described as the *"Word of life"* has become vivid and clear, personal and knowable. John himself and other witnesses as well had experienced a concrete personal relationship with God's speech, and now those who read his letter are assured that they too are invited to enter into fellowship with other disciples and with the Living Word.

One unusual feature in John's way of writing is that in both the Gospel of John and in his first letter, John withholds the name of Jesus Christ until the close of the prologue. It is not until verse 17 of chapter 1 in the Gospel that the name of Jesus Christ is presented to the reader. By then it has become clear that the *Logos* of which John had written is in fact Jesus Christ "The Only Son" of God. Now in this letter, as John employs the same writing method, it is at the close of the prologue that we meet the holy name of the *Logos* of life. Jesus is the Word of life. He is the eternal life that John knows so well from personal experience, and now we who read John's letter are warmly invited to have fellowship with other disciples of Christ as well as with the Father and His Son Jesus Christ.

The word *koinōnia* is used in classical Greek as a term to express the most intimate kinds of human relationship as, for example, in marriage. Its basic root *koinos* means literally "common," hence "communion." It is this interpersonal and encouraging word that John now uses. Its meanings are warm and affirming. *Koinōnia* is the word for "generosity" as in Philippians 2:1. It can be translated with the word "participation" as in Philemon 6. It may be translated in its noun form by the word "partner" or "sharer," as in Luke 5:10. We are not therefore surprised that John should conclude his prologue with a final one-sentence sigh: "And we are writing this that our joy may be complete." Manuscript evidence favors the pronoun "our" rather than "your" in his final sentence. The word "joy" is a light and whimsical word in Greek—*chara*. To this day the Greek-speaking world still makes use of this good word as a greeting. From this root the word *charis* ("grace") is developed particularly by Paul as an important word in his love vocabulary. There is the sense of surprise and acceleration within the word *chara* ("joy") and its companion *charis* ("grace")—the sense of a gift being given when no one expected it.

What has John said to us in these opening sentences of his book? And what is the significance of his prologue for our lives today? John has announced that from the beginning, before the creation itself, God who is the source of life had made His own decision to speak that eternal life into the time frame in which we human beings live out our historical existence. His breakthrough into our time has happened, and the mystery of this breakthrough is that we mere human beings have been able to understand and know the core of the mystery because at the very center of that mystery is the person Jesus Christ—not life or word as secrets to be decoded, but the Person to be known. The result of our discovery of Jesus Christ is a partnership, a sharing of our life with other human lives and with God the Father and the Son. Finally, this fellowship is so good it is fun. "Joy . . . is the gigantic secret of the Christian . . . ." (G. K. Chesterton, *Orthodoxy*, p. 160). "When the pagan looks at the very core of the cosmos he is struck cold. Behind the gods, who are merely despotic, sit the fates, who are deadly. Nay, the fates are worse than deadly; they are dead" (Chesterton, *Orthodoxy*, p. 159). But when we look at the core of the cosmos we are met by the Living God who creates, who speaks for Himself, who has surprised us by knowing our names. When this surprise sinks in, then the joyous fellowship begins.

John has thrown a great stone into the water and the rings that encircle the stone are moving out in all directions. *Here is life.* The Life has broken in!

GOD IS LIGHT

5 This is the message which we have heard from Him and declare to you, that God is light and in Him is no darkness at all.

—*1 John 1:5*

John throws another great stone upon the clear lake: *"God is light and in Him is no darkness at all."* What a sentence! It is bold and electrifying. It is written in the traditional parallel poetic form of the Old Testament prophets and psalmists. In Old Testament parallelism, a statement is made and then repeated. In some instances, the statement is parallel with a second sentence that is almost identical in tone and mood. In other instances, the first statement is followed by a sentence that is opposite yet also parallel. Psalm 46:1 is an example of the first form of parallelism: "God is our refuge and strength, a very present help in trouble. Therefore we will not fear." Psalm 55:1 is an example of the second form of parallelism: "Give ear to my prayer, O God; and hide not thyself from my supplication." Notice that in the first form of parallelism, the essential thought of the first line is repeated in the second line, though an addition is made to the original thought. In the second kind of parallelism, the first thought is stated in positive language and is then followed by the parallel statement which states negatively the essential theme of the first thought. As in the first kind of parallelism, additions are made to the thoughts of the first sentence, but the method is the method of contrasting statement rather than of rhythmic restatement.

John begins the second paragraph of his letter in the thundering language and power of the Old Testament prophets and psalmists. *"God is light and in him is no darkness at all."* The parallelism is forceful and clear. John tells us what he means and then tells us what he does not mean. Every great positive truth has its negative implication. If Jesus Christ is Lord, then I am not Lord. If God is filled with light then He is not filled with darkness. The confessing Christians in Germany at Barmen in 1934 decided to construct each of the six articles of their declaration of faith in precisely the same way as John has framed this bold sentence. Article 1 from the Barmen Declaration sounds very much like 1 John 1:5:

". . . Jesus Christ as he attested for us in Holy Scripture, is the one word of God which we have to hear and which we have to trust and obey in life and in death.

"We reject the false doctrine, as though the church could and would have to acknowledge as a source of its proclamation, apart from and besides this one word of God, still other events and powers, figures and truths, as God's revelation."[1]

The positive affirmation is announced and then the negative implications of that affirmation are also announced.

God is light. The word "light" for John in the Gospel of John and in his first letter is used interchangeably for the word "truth." (Note John 1:9, 14 and 1 John 1:6.) What is important to remember in understanding what John means by *light* and *truth* is that his teaching is rooted more in the Old Testament understanding of light and truth than in the Greek philosophical understanding of these concepts. A close examination of the way that the teaching about light and truth in both the Gospel of John and 1 John is developed will make this clear. In the Old Testament, light has to do with *finding the path.* "The people who walked in darkness have seen a great light" (Is. 9:2). "Your word is a lamp to my feet and a light to my path" (Ps. 119:105). These texts show the basic connection that is present in the Old Testament between light from God and showing His people the *way* for their feet. Light is also connected in the Old Testament to an even more fundamental discovery, and that is the discovery of the character and nature of God by His people. Psalm 27 is such a psalm. It tells of David's discovery not only of the way, but of God Himself in the midst of David's trial. He had found the face of the Lord. He begins this psalm, "The Lord is my light and my salvation; whom shall I fear?" (Ps. 27:1). So also the Isaiah 9 text moves from the pathway language to the intensely personal hope, "For unto us a Child is born . . ." (Is. 9:6).

Our Lord's summation of the great "I AM" sentences in the Gospel of John is also set into this Old Testament way of thinking about light and truth. "I am the way, and the truth, and the life; no one comes to the Father, except through Me" (John 14:6). Notice that this is the language of the *roadway* and the language of personal encounter with the Father. We find the way in the *truth* that is Jesus Christ, and because of that way we find the very source of light and life who is God Himself. Psalms 27 and 119 are now fulfilled in this encounter with Jesus of Nazareth.

John has the same roadway and interpersonal, encounter mindset in his own thinking as he tells his readers about God. As the verses unfold in 1 John 1:5–10, this will become evident.

John announces to his readers the liberating news that God is not only the source of life but also of light, of truth. John dares to commit God to the way of light. God never deceives, misleads, and distorts. There can be no strategy of "heavenly deception" on God's part, because God is Light and His own character, His own essential nature, rejects such a strategem. God is not the prince of lies but the One who *reveals* and *shows the way.* Darkness hides and confuses pathways, but light makes the faces recognizable and the outline of the roadway discernible.

But it is not John who has created this message about God. He tells us that it is the message which he heard from God's speech. John has not really committed God to the way of truth but rather he has announced like a herald this good news about God which God himself has already made known. God has spoken for

Himself, and we have learned from the first five verses of 1 John that His speech is the speech of *Life* and of *Light.*

The rings that circle out from this great rock in the pond are very impressive. From an intellectual standpoint, John has allied God with the way of truth and against the way of falsehood. God is righteous not only morally but intellectually, and this alliance is of very great importance for any development of a Christian understanding of science. There should be no fear of truth or the way of truth for the Christian, because truth of any kind does not threaten a house that is itself founded upon truth. God stands as the Author and the Genesis of all truth; therefore His truth is the foundation for both the house of faith and the house of science. He also stands as the foe of all darkness, whether moral or intellectual. As God stands against murder and adultery, He also stands against falsified lab experiments and all intellectual close-mindedness.

What does this mean for us today? John's affirmation is the promise that God's self-disclosure is on the side of truth, and therefore when Jesus Christ is Lord of our life, then we see the road more clearly. Jesus Christ not only shows us who the Father is, He also shows us who we are and where we are. We better see our own faces and we better see the landscape. He is the Light who makes the roadway upon which we live and move and have our being come into focus. "We believe that the sun is in the sky at midday in summer not because we can clearly see the sun (in fact, we cannot) but because we can see everything else" (C. S. Lewis, *Miracles,* p. 133).

One way to test the worthiness of a world-view or religious claim is to ask the question: Does this world-view bring all of the parts of the puzzle of my life and world together? Are the separate pieces that make up normal existence integrated so that each is meaningful and in clear focus when seen through the lens of this world-view? Jesus Christ as Lord and center of our lives makes sense of the parts just as He makes sense of the core. This is the characteristic of light. It is like a lamp unto our feet.

TO WALK IN THE LIGHT

6 If we say that we have fellowship with Him, and walk in darkness, we lie and do not practice the truth. 7 But if we walk in the light as He is in the light, we have fellowship with one another, and the blood of Jesus Christ His Son cleanses us from all sin.

26

[8] If we say that we have no sin, we deceive ourselves, and the truth is not in us. [9] If we confess our sins, He is faithful and just to forgive us our sins and to cleanse us from all unrighteousness. [10] If we say that we have not sinned, we make Him a liar, and His word is not in us.

—*1 John 1:6–10*

The language of the roadway and the language of fellowship are now drawn together by John in a few simple and direct sentences. God's truth is not an abstract philosophical ideal to be honored and held up for respectful admiration, but a relationship to be lived. It immediately becomes clear that God's truth is a dynamic roadway upon which we are to walk, and on a day-to-day basis. We are to experience God's light upon our own existential pathway, and this makes all the difference. For John, Christian faith is not a matter of spiritual speculation or the mastery of secrets and code words. John continues to write with the same freshness and lack of pretention that has marked his opening sentences as he now sketches in how a person can live in fellowship with God and with God's people.

We are to *"walk in the light,"* and this means to walk in the way of disclosure. First we discover God in the way of light (v. 6); we also discover ourselves in the way of light (v. 8). What is it that we discover about God? And what do we discover about ourselves? Within these four verses we make these discoveries: (1) God is on the side of truth and openness. Therefore, in order for us human beings to have common relationship with God, we must stand before God in the way of openness and light. (2) John shares a surprise with his readers. We are told an amazing good news at the very moment that we could not dare to expect it. The way of light is dangerous, and its disclosure is threatening to every human being because the light shows up our own inadequacies and, what is worse, our own wickedness. We have walked the way of harm. Now, in the presence of the light, that distorted way is in full view. We are warned not to attempt any cover-up.

But, what is it that will happen now as the way of our lives becomes apparent and exposed because of the light of God's justice and truth? We have walked so much of our lives in darkness, more than we want to admit, and therefore John's command to us that we enter upon a totally exposed and brilliantly illuminated roadway is hardly good news. In theory we respect light but to step out into its sheer spotlight intensity is frightening. Then the surprise comes. "Right in the middle of all these things stands up an enormous exception. It is quite unlike anything else. It is a thing final like the trumpet of doom, though it is also a piece of good news; or news that seems too good to be true. It is nothing less than the loud assertion that this mysterious maker of the world has visited his world in person" (G. K. Chesterton, *The Everlasting Man*, p. 271). We make the greatest discovery of all. The Lord who is the Light for the roadway is also our Companion on the roadway. This is the enormous exception for which we had no right to expect or hope. Jesus Christ is on the road with us as the Light who reveals our sinfulness so that we dare not play games with that fact: "If we say we have not sinned, we make Him a liar." But Jesus Christ is also the Lord of Life who enables us to resolve injustice and sin and the tragedies of darkness. The resolution of the human crisis is a person who comes alongside us in the middle of the road.

John tells us that if we walk in the light the *"blood of Jesus Christ his Son, cleanses us from all sin."* The word "blood" is crude and definite for a Greek reader; it is profoundly rich and significant for a Jewish reader or any person grounded in the Old Testament. For each reader the word implies *death,* but within the background of the Old Testament the word also means *life.* It is the life of Jesus Christ that is given by which we are resolved and made right for the road of light. John makes use of the strong Greek word *katharizō* to express the result of this encounter. The word means to "clean out." The English word "catharsis" comes to us from this Greek root. John's message to us is very basic. We are able to do only one thing ourselves and that is to step out into the light. The tragic confusion and anger and hurtfulness that the light reveals in our lives is too much for us to handle and to resolve by ourselves. God Himself who brings the light also brings the help; that help is the Person Jesus Christ who gives His own life in our behalf. At just the right moment, we discover the enormous exception that God does not destroy the wanderers He finds upon the road. Rather He cleanses them and qualifies them for the way of light.

John is insistent with his readers on one very important point. To walk in the light does not mean that a human being is sinless and flawless; rather to walk in the light means that a human being as a sinner is, in the light, fully aware that he or she is a sinner. That is the point! The surprise of this passage is that just such a sinner is not a lost cause, beyond help, but that at just the right moment the companion of our road—who himself is the source of the light which makes us recognize our guilt—now becomes the means of our help which resolves our guilt. The answer to the human tragedy therefore is not a secret to be learned, not an escape from the road into a more spiritual atmosphere, and not the denial of the problem, but the man Jesus Christ alongside.

John presents a classic summary sentence in verse 9. *"If we confess our sins, he is faithful and just, and will forgive our sins . . ."* The Greek word that is translated in our text by the word "confess" is the word *homologeō.* This word means to agree or to declare alike. It is made up of two Greek words, the prefix *homo,* which means literally "alike," and *logos,* "word, speech." We are told by John that our responsibility is to agree with God about the nature of our crises. This openness and vulnerability on our part is what firmly plants our feet upon the pathway of light. There are no special code words to learn or special incense formulas to master, or elaborate rituals to perform!

How unlike the mysticism and religiosity of the first century and our own day are John's words. They are simple, direct, and real. Come into the light where Jesus Christ is; here you will meet yourself and here you will meet Him. Then stand in the open position and admit who you are, agree with God and receive cleansing and forgiveness. The word "forgive" in Greek means "to *leave behind,"* literally "to abandon." The promise to us from John is that God will forgive, will leave behind our sins. He who is righteous will cleanse us from our anti-righteousness.

We learn from John by his use of one single word that forgiveness is a costly gift. That one word is the word "blood"; John will have more to say about the meaning of this awesome fact later in his book. Jesus Christ has won for humankind the right to the way of light and life because of the event of his own lifeblood spent on our behalf. Forgiveness is not a transaction in a courtroom but the event that happens at a cross.

John Bunyan in his book *Pilgrim's Progress* has caught both the costly intensity and the wonder of this event. "Now I saw in my dream that the highway up which Christian was to go was fenced on either side with a wall, and that wall is called salvation. Up this way therefore did burdensome Christian run, but not without great difficulty, because of the load on his back. He ran thus till he came at a place somewhat ascending, and upon that place stood a cross, and a little below in the bottom, a sepulcher. So I saw in my dream, that just as Christian came up with the cross, his burden loosed from off his shoulders, and fell from off his back, and began to tumble, and so continued to do, till it came to the mouth of the sepulcher, where it fell in, and I saw it no more."[2]

One final part of John's affirmation has to do with the fellowship of those who are on the roadway together with Jesus Christ. John teaches that the openness before God that enables our forgiveness also enables our fellowship. Fellowship is not founded upon deception and never has been. It is the common or shared crisis that the disciples experience together when the light of the road first confronts us, and that common crisis is resolved in the common forgiveness that comes when we recognize our sinfulness and our need for the Savior.

This means that the kind of fellowship that John is describing in this chapter is the fellowship of brokenness. The people we meet on the roadway of 1 John 1 are too wrung out by the experience of God's sheer honesty and light to play games about moral superiority or mystical one-upmanship. These folk have met the good light, the enormous exception, and the main feelings that they have are gratitude and joy. John had promised it, and now we are able to feel it in this great chapter.

There is no cause for the acceleration of joy that can match the shock of recognition that "I am loved for who I really am." It is not a religious leader or wealthy contributor or revolutionary zealot who by courage and performance has won the respect of God. It is instead a mere person who, like all other human beings, is in need of God's life and God's light. I cannot make it alone without both the light of the Creator and the resolution of the Redeemer. The fellowship that emerges between such persons is not superficial but substantial. We have discovered the brokenness of each other and because of the broken healer we are drawn together into a fellowship of grace. It is a fellowship that is created by the act of God.

Dietrich Bonhoeffer describes it well: "Christian brotherhood is not an ideal which we must realize; it is rather a reality created by God in Christ in which we may participate. The more clearly we learn to recognize that the ground and strength and promise of all our fellowship is in Jesus Christ alone, the more serenely shall we think of our fellowship and pray and hope for it."[3]

NOTES

1.   Barmen Declaration, Article I, *Book of Confessions,* 2nd ed. (United Presbyterian Church in the U.S.A., 1970), p. 8.08.

2. John Bunyan, *The Pilgrim's Progress* (London: J. M. Dent & Sons, 1954), p. 39.

3. Dietrich Bonhoeffer, *Life Together* (New York: Harper & Bros., 1954), p. 30.

CHAPTER TWO—THE NEW RELATIONSHIP

I JOHN 2:1–29

Scripture Outline

The Advocate (2:1–6)

A New Commandment (2:7–17)

Abide in Him (2:18–29)

THE ADVOCATE

2:1 My little children, these things I write to you, so that you may not sin. And if anyone sins, we have an Advocate with the Father, Jesus Christ the righteous. ² And He Himself is the propitiation for our sins, and not for ours only but also for the whole world.

³ Now by this we know that we know Him, if we keep His commandments. ⁴ He who says, "I know Him," and does not keep His commandments, is a liar, and the truth is not in him. ⁵ But whoever keeps His word, truly the love of God is perfected in him. By this we know that we are in Him. ⁶ He who says he abides in Him ought himself also to walk just as He walked.

—1 John 2:1–6

In *"My little children,"* John makes use of a diminutive form of the word *teknion,* the word for "child" in Greek. The force of the use of the diminutive is represented in the English translation with the insertion of the word *"little."* John's intent is probably not so much to imply the young age of his audience but rather to express affection; this is the real linguistic purpose of the diminutive in such a context as we have here in 1 John 2:1. We have the same literary device in English by our addition of "ie" or "y" at the end of nouns. For example dad—daddy and Bill—Billy.

We are able to sense from this greeting something of the warm relationship that exists between the writer and those to whom he sends this letter. At this point in our consideration of 1 John we must ask some questions about the possible recipients of this letter. We assume that 1 John is a general letter designed to be circulated by Christians from church to church. Unlike the letters of Paul and the Book of Revelation, this letter from John does not identify any particular church or city location.

The sense of authority that resides with the author is clear throughout the letter. The author does not identify himself, but he writes this letter with an unmistakable autograph. That autograph is the briefer but obviously similar prologue that opens this letter and unites it with the prologue that opens the Gospel of John. We know from the Gospel of John that the author of that book has consciously chosen to indicate his identity by means of an indirect autograph, namely the several restrained and unusual references to the disciple John, son of Zebedee. In this first letter, our author John the son of Zebedee preserves his original style.

One interesting historical validation of the apostolic authorship of this letter is a psychological-sociological observation. Only a person with immense personal influence within the first-century Christian church would write such a letter as this letter: general, authoritative, and definite, while at the same time fatherly in tone. Such a letter would be unlikely and strained were it the work of a young leader in the church. Only a person of established reputation and stature writes without personal autograph, and only an elder statesman would say *"my little children."* Very few writers could write such a greeting appropriately. If the apostle John is not the author of this book, then we have the highly improbable fact that there is a towering figure in the early church of which the early church fathers have nothing to say. The evidence strongly points to the disciple John, and he writes to Christians that he knows personally. Church tradition favors the view that John was resident in Ephesus for a long period of his ministry, and there are interesting supporting evidences for that contention which we will note later when we consider the third letter.

John warns against sin. The verb "sin" is the Greek word *hamartanō*, which throughout the New Testament is the most common word choice for sin. It means to fall short, to do wrong. John counsels strongly against sin; however, he is realistic about the needs of his readers. Therefore he decides to emphasize the source of their common help more than to warn them of their common crisis. He tells them of their Lord; Jesus Christ the righteous one is the advocate. The Greek word that is translated by the word "advocate" is the word *parakletos;* this is a very interesting word in the New Testament. It is made up of two elements: *para* and *kaleō. Para* as a prefix for various verbs and nouns means "along the side of" or "from." *Kaleō* is the verb "to call." Therefore the verb *parakaleō* means to call to one's side, to summon as in Acts 28:20 and 2 Corinthians 12:8. The noun *parakletos* means one who comes alongside, one who appears in another's behalf, a mediator, a helper. Our Lord uses this as His word for the Holy Spirit in John 14:16–26; 15:26; 16:7. The RSV translates the word in these passages with the English word "counselor," while the King James Bible made use of the English word "comforter." The literal sense of the word is that of one who comes alongside as our helper.

The word offers us one more important linguistic connection between the first letter of John and the Gospel of John. The word is a roadway word, and by its use John continues the pathway imagery of the first chapter. The advocate who helps us is personal, not ideological, and this is a vitally important point for Christian faith. The Christian hope is not rooted in fate or in ideological affirmation; the Christian hope is rooted in the personal intervention of God's Son—He is the enormous exception.

John continues his sentence with these words: *"And He Himself is the propitiation* [expiation] *for our sins.* " The Greek word that John uses in this sentence, which is translated by "propitiation" (KJV), or "expiation" (RSV), is one of a family of words that are used in only a few places in the New Testament. *Hilasmos* is the word used here and also later in 1 John 4:10. Other uses of this family of Greek words in the New Testament are in Hebrews 2:17 where the verb form is used, ". . . to expiate the sins of the people"; in Luke 18:13 in the parable of Jesus in which the publican cries out, "God be *merciful* to me a sinner"; and in Hebrews 8:12 where the sense of the root is also used: "For I will be *merciful* toward their iniquities." Still other uses of this root word are in Romans 3:25, ". . . whom God put forward as an *expiation* by his blood" and also Hebrews 9:5 in which the writer describes the temple of Israel: "Above it were the cherubim of glory overshadowing the *mercy seat.*"

This final citation is the most important key to our understanding of the word in its New Testament usage. When the seventy Hebrew scholars translated the Old Testament into Greek at about the year 100 B.C. in the textual version we call the Septuagint, they set the tone for much of the New Testament vocabulary by the word choices that they made to translate Hebrew words into

Greek. When they chose a Greek word to translate the Hebrew word *kippur,* the covering or mercy seat of the Old Testament ark, they made use of this Greek root *hilasmos.* This is therefore also the root word used to translate the Old Testament "atonement" and "mercy" vocabulary.

Our best understanding of John's intention in his use of this word thus is to recognize its origins in the Old Testament understanding of *kippur* or covering. The blood of the sacrificed animals was sprinkled upon the mercy seat. Leviticus 16:15–16 gives to us the worship practice which employs this word: "Then he shall kill the goat of the sin offering which is for the people, and bring its blood within the veil, and do with its blood as he did with the blood of the bull, sprinkling it upon the mercy seat and before the mercy seat; thus he shall make atonement for the holy place, because of the uncleanness of the people of Israel."

As noted, *kippur* is the Hebrew word for mercy seat and the word for atonement. Within the practice of Leviticus, a substitution is made in behalf of the people, and this word *kippur* expresses that substitution. The life of an animal is sacrificed in behalf of the people. This substitution is what atonement means. A covering is placed between the people and the righteous Lord which recognizes the sinfulness of the people and also which represents the forgiveness that is God's gift to the people. What John is teaching by his use of the word *hilasmos* is that Jesus Christ has identified himself with us. The identification is total, costly, and universal; *"And not for ours only but also for the sins of the whole world."* The One who has come alongside us on the road has taken our place at a deadly moment.

But Jesus Christ is not like the trapped animals of Leviticus which are sacrificed as victims to satisfy a drama of reconciliation. Jesus fulfills that ancient drama, but His fulfillment is not ceremonial. Rather, it is the real and ultimate battle scene of all time in which Jesus Christ disarms the power of sin and death and the devil once and for all by taking death and sin upon Himself. "I am the good shepherd, I know my own and my own know me, as the Father knows me and I know the Father; and I lay down my life for the sheep . . . No one takes it from me, but I lay it down of my own accord. I have power to lay it down, and I have power to take it again" (John 10:14–18, RSV). Here we have no victim but the Lord, who conquers through the way of brokenness.

There is no other way for such terrible foes as death and sin and cosmic evil to be overcome. This is a key passage in 1 John, and its theological significance is crucial in the development of our whole understanding of the atoning ministry of Jesus Christ. The commentator B. F. Westcott stated the central question clearly and helpfully in his classic work: "The scriptural conception of *hilasmos* is not that of appeasing one who is angry, with a personal feeling, against the offender; but of altering the character of that which from without occasions a necessary alienation, and interposes an inevitable obstacle to fellowship."[1] It is not that we propitiate God with sacrifices or somehow win His love by the act of the Levitical sacrifice. Our Lord Jesus Christ does not stand alongside us to somehow win for us the love from God as if God were hardened and bitter toward us. "The love of God is the same throughout; but he 'cannot' in virtue of His very nature welcome the impenitent and sinful; and more than this, He 'cannot' treat sin as if it were not sin."[2]

But now in the fulfillment of Jesus Christ's act the sacrifice has been finally made. The one overwhelming difference between Leviticus and 1 John is in the fact that we know the Lord of our atonement, unlike the priests of the ancient rite: "The union between the offerer and the offering was conventional and not real. The victim was irrational, so that there could be no true fellowship between it and the offender."[3] But our *kippur* is our advocate, the one who comes alongside us. John wants to impress upon his readers this fellowship of the believer with Jesus Christ by his next sentence, *"And by this we know that we know him . . ."* (v. 3). John has good news for his readers. Atonement is not a matter of heavenly bookkeeping in which a mark is placed in the ledger in our behalf. If this were the case, then our main goal in life would be to find the secret of our personal salvation. Our main concern would be to be sure of a ledger entry, or to find the gift of atonement as an end in itself. The giver or provider would be quite secondary, much like the pitiful animals used in temple sacrifice. What are they to me, apart from the drama that is acted out with their blood? It all then becomes so religious and one step removed from where I am really living.

It is my observation that this kind of religious captivity of the atonement event of Christian faith can happen today too when a Christian becomes more interested in the gifts that God gives to us than in the Lord who gives the gifts. When forgiveness is turned into a general truth or religious principle, then we no longer have our eyes upon the One who comes alongside us on the road but instead upon the religious benefits we seek to possess.

This also means that atonement is not a status of things that can be administered by the church as if it were a quantity of merit. Atonement is the event that happened once and for all on the road just outside the city wall in Jerusalem by the man Jesus Christ. And this event is to be received and known and lived.

The event of our atonement is so important that nothing can be the same for us again. We must live in daily relationship with our Advocate. We show our love for Him, and our love is itself fulfilled (this is the sense of the word "perfected," v. 5) as we obey His self-disclosure. We must walk with Him. John will have very much more to say of this.

"Cheap grace means grace as a doctrine, a principle, a system. It means forgiveness of sins proclaimed as a general truth, the love of God taught as a Christian 'conception' of God. . . . Cheap grace is the preaching of forgiveness without requiring repentance. . . . Cheap grace is grace without discipleship, grace without the cross, grace without Jesus Christ, living and incarnate. . . . Costly grace is the gospel which must be sought again and again, the gift which must be asked for, the door at which a man must knock. Such grace is costly because it calls us to follow, and it is grace because it calls us to follow Jesus Christ" (Dietrich Bonhoeffer, *The Cost of Discipleship*, pp. 35–37).

A NEW COMMANDMENT

7 Brethren, I write no new commandment to you, but an old commandment which you have had from the beginning. The old commandment is the word which you heard from the beginning. 8 Again, a new commandment I write to you, which thing is true in Him and in you, because the darkness is passing away, and the true light is already shining.

9 He who says he is in the light, and hates his brother, is in darkness until now. 10 He who loves his brother abides in the light, and there is no cause for stumbling in him. 11 But he who hates his brother is in darkness and walks in darkness, and does not know where he is going, because the darkness has blinded his eyes.

12 I write to you, little children,
Because your sins are forgiven you for His name's sake.
13 I write to you, fathers,
Because you have known Him who is from the beginning.
I write to you, young men,
Because you have overcome the wicked one.

I write to you, little children,
Because you have known the Father.
14 I have written to you, fathers,
Because you have known Him who is from the beginning.
I have written to you, young men,
Because you are strong, and the word of God abides in
you,
And you have overcome the wicked one.
15 Do not love the world or the things in the world. If
anyone loves the world, the love of the Father is not in him.
16 For all that is in the world—the lust of the flesh, the lust of
the eyes, and the pride of life—is not of the Father but is of the
world. 17 And the world is passing away, and the lust of it; but
he who does the will of God abides forever.
—1 John 2:7–17

"Brethren, I write no new commandment to you." Agapē is a
word that John will use in various forms many times as this letter
continues, and he will define its meaning by the way he makes use
of the word. The use of this word is extremely rare in classical
Greek. Its extensive use in the New Testament is the result of the
fact that the Septuagint translators of the Old Testament employed
it consistently to express the love vocabulary of the Old Testament.
Later in this commentary we will consider this word in more detail
as we trace John's own definition of *agapē* in his great love statement of 1 John 4:7–21.

It is with a form of this good word that John now addresses his
readers: *Agapētoi,* "Beloved," as the RSV has it. He acknowledges a
prior fact about those who will now hear his counsel. They are
loved. Does John intend this word to express his own love for his
readers or is the author expressing the even larger truth that he
recognizes the inclusion of these friends in the love of God? We
shall need to watch the future use of this exciting word by John
in order to answer that question.

He tells his readers that the commandment of which he now
writes is *not new* and yet *it is new.* How can a great fact or
commandment be both at the same time old and new? It becomes
clear what he means by this "old, new" riddle within this paragraph. John develops his argument that the will of God has
remained steady and unchanged throughout all time. God's *logos*
of light and life is from the beginning and has never changed. The
commandment, that is to say, the holy will of God, is permanent.

What then is new? The new fact has to do with us and with our setting, the age in which we live; we are changed; we are new because of the fulfillment in history of God's will. Because of Jesus Christ there is a radical newness, not in God's character, but in our character. Secondly, the age in which we live is new because the decisive battle against evil has been won by Jesus Christ. *"The darkness is passing away and the true light is already shining"* (v. 8). This shift in balance against the power of darkness is new in that the dramatic turning point is so close to us. Therefore the commandment is in these two senses new—new first of all because we have been forgiven and therefore we obey the commands of God from a new standpoint.

What John is describing is an evangelical ethic—we love out of fullness; we follow God's will because of his prior act in our behalf. Second, we are not afraid of our age as if there might not be hope for the survival of the good and the true. John here describes an eschatological ethic. The critical balance has already shifted away from the power of despair for us. Evil is powerful but its power is bounded by a greater authority. God's decision, His Word, is more permanent, more powerful than the power of darkness. We will notice in the last book of the Bible, the Book of Revelation, that the theme John has introduced here in this letter will become a major focus for John's final work. His theology will be the same as he expands the scenario to include the whole of cosmic reality.

What does this teaching mean for the reader of 1 John and for us today? John has presented to us the ethical, interpersonal mandate that flows out of our relationship with Jesus Christ, and also our recognition of Christ's lordship over history. At this point John is crystal clear—the commandment is the commandment to love. In this letter John is presenting a commentary upon the greatest commandment. Our Lord Himself settled this question once and for all in His discussion with the scribes, "'Which commandment is the first of all?' Jesus answered, 'The first is, Hear, O Israel: the Lord our God, the Lord is one, and you shall love the Lord your God with all your heart, and with all your soul, and with all your mind, and with all your strength.' The second is this, 'You shall love your neighbor as yourself'" (Mark 12:28–31, RSV).

Later in this letter John will probe the meaning of our love for God, but now at this point in his letter he forcefully insists upon the commandment that we love our neighbor. John does not use the noun "neighbor"; he uses throughout this book the even more personal word: "brother," *adelphon.* In the light of the total biblical setting of this teaching it would be an incorrect conclusion to assume that by the use of "brother" John only has in mind the obligation of a Christian to love his immediate biological family, or even the extended family represented by the church, the brothers and sisters of faith. Rather, John's approach, as we have already observed in this letter, is to make use of the most personal and close-to-life vocabulary. John would agree with Paul that every human being holds me in debt to love not because he or she has won my love but because Jesus Christ loves. We do not have the command to love so much as we have experienced in Jesus Christ the love that commands, "Owe no one anything, except to love one another; for he who loves his neighbor has fulfilled the law" (Rom. 13:8 RSV). It is this broader sense of neighbor that John intends by his use of the very personal word "brother."

The point that John makes is this: the way I treat my brother will show whether I am walking in the light or in the darkness. John has provided a concrete test of my journey and of my convictions. When I go the way of hatred, I am walking in the way of darkness. The word translated here by the word "hate" means to detest, to abhor. When I love my brother, I am walking in the light.

Notice that two tests of our journey situation have been presented by John within this book. We are walking in the light when we confess our sins (1 John 1:7–9); we are walking in the light when we love our brother. The two tests are related to each other. The first reaches out to the love of Jesus Christ toward me the sinner in my need of help. The second test reaches out to my neighbor with the love that I have received from Jesus Christ. In both cases the love has its origin in Jesus Christ. In both cases I am a recipient and in both cases I share of myself. In confession I open myself toward the Lord and my neighbor; in love I open myself toward the Lord and my neighbor.

John cautions his readers that the way of hatred is inevitably the way of confusion. The one who hates *"does not know where he is going because the darkness has blinded his eyes"* (v. 11). The tragedy of hatred is always twofold. First, there is the harm it does to the neighbor; second, there is the harm it does to the person who hates. Hatred, according to John, blurs vision and sets into place a basic disorientation and confusion. Love clears the head; hatred confuses the head. There is even a greater danger: we become like that which we do. When we choose the strategy or tactics of darkness we inevitably end up under the control of darkness.

Martin Luther warns us of the danger of the form of hatred we always tend to justify for ourselves, namely, retribution toward those who first harm us. Luther warns, "See to it that he who hurts you does not cause you to become evil like him . . . for he is the victor who changes another man to become like himself while he himself remains unchanged."[4] This is the double tragedy of the way of darkness; the person who adopts the methods of evil for whatever reasons, experiences the result of which Luther warned. His life is changed and his roadway is changed; therefore the person or situation which first hurt him wins a twofold victory.

At this point John assures his readers of the faithfulness of the way of light. John's approach continues to be fatherly as he writes to the *"little children," "fathers," "young men."* He assures his readers of the reality of forgiveness, the reality of their relationship with Jesus Christ, and of the fact that because of the Word of God which abides within them they have overcome *"the evil one," tou poneron.* This term, "the evil one" (*"the wicked one,"* NKJV) used to refer to the devil in the New Testament. (Note also Matthew 6:13, "but deliver us from the evil one," and John 17:15, "that You should keep them from the evil one.") Here John uses this term to identify the source of the darkness—the devil.

What we must note in this letter up to this point is that John has portrayed the Christian journey with strong and vivid freedom language. We are invited into fellowship but the decision is ours to make; we are challenged to choose for ourselves the way of light, to confess our sins, to keep God's commandments, to love our brother. John has not in any way diminished the authority or provision of God in our behalf but he has insisted that we have decisions to make and our right to make those choices is preserved by God's decision. God has made His own sovereign choice and our freedom is the result of God's decision. It is His will that we should have an authentic journey experience of authentic freedom. It is His decision that preserves for us the right to make good and also bad choices.

God is so sure of Himself that He is not threatened by our freedom. The mystery of the existence of *"the wicked one"* shows that even at the heavenly order of creation God has allowed that same freedom, and when the New Testament mentions the devil, it refers to the real existence of moral, personal will against the will of God at the heavenly order of creation. John warns his readers of the existence of this evil, but the warning is notably without any sense of panic or terror; he is not afraid of the evil (wicked) one. Because of the Word of God that dwells within the disciples we have overcome the evil one. Jesus Christ is our authority and power over all evil, even the devil. This word translated "overcome" is the Greek verb *nikaō*, which will become a very decisive word in the Book of Revelation as it was also in the Gospel of John. (Note John 16:33; Rev. 2:7.)

"Do not love the world. . ." (v. 15). What does John mean by this sentence? We are at first surprised by the sentence because it reminds us immediately of the most famous of all Johannine sentences, "For God so loved the world that he gave his only begotten Son that whoever believes in Him should not perish but have everlasting life" (John 3:16). We know that God loves the world, *kosmon,* and yet we are now challenged by John not to love the *kosmon.* John clarifies what he means as his sentences continue. John is describing not so much the created earth itself but a worldly perspective toward life which he explains by the use of two further words: "lust" and "pride." The root word for lust is *thumos,* which means passion or strong desire and which also is used as a word for anger. (Note Rev. 14:8; Rev. 12:12.) The word translated "pride" is a word that means pretense, arrogance. Note its use in James 4:16, ". . . you boast in your arrogance." Runaway desire and arrogance toward life are not from God but they are in fact what John means by his reference to the world; they are worldly values. John's point is that we are not to crave the world nor love it from its own standpoint. We are to love the world from God's standpoint. The world and all desire and arrogance pass away, but the one who does the will of God abides forever. The Greek reads literally "into the aeon, the time, the age." This is the word used in the New Testament for the idea of age or eternity. It is this word that our Lord uses in His promise to the disciples in Matthew 28, "Lo, I am with you always, to the close of the age" (28:20, RSV). What lasts is that which is rooted in the will of God—that is John's point. Therefore our motivation and our perspectives should be rooted in what God has shown to us about life, not in ourselves and our desires.

The character Rubashov in Arthur Koestler's novel *Darkness at Noon* reviews the result of his life as he lived it by his own inner revolutionary criteria.

> We were the first to replace the nineteenth century's liberal ethics of "fair play" by the revolutionary ethics of the twentieth century. . . . Our minds were so tensely

charged that the slightest collision caused a mortal short-circuit. Thus we were fated to mutual destruction. I was one of those. I have thought and acted as I had to; I destroyed people whom I was fond of, and gave power to others I did not like. . . . We have thrown all ballast overboard; only one anchor holds us: faith in one's self. . . . Mine has worn thin in the last few years. The fact is: I no longer believe in my infallibility. That is why I am lost.[5]

Rubashov writes as one who has discovered the terrible collapse of the ethics of anger and desire. But Rubashov is nearer to finding the true way than he imagines. Pascal put it this way: "It is good to be weary and worn out . . . so that we may open our arms to the Redeemer."

ABIDE IN HIM

18 Little children, it is the last hour; and as you have heard that the Antichrist is coming, even now many antichrists have come, by which we know that it is the last hour. 19 They went out from us, but they were not of us; for if they had been of us, they would have continued with us; but they went out that they might be made manifest, that none of them were of us.

20 But you have an anointing from the Holy One, and you know all things. 21 I have not written to you because you do not know the truth, but because you know it, and that no lie is of the truth.

22 Who is a liar but he who denies that Jesus is the Christ? He is antichrist who denies the Father and the Son. 23 Whoever denies the Son does not have the Father either; he who acknowledges the Son has the Father also.

24 Therefore let that abide in you which you heard from the beginning. If what you heard from the beginning abides in you, you also will abide in the Son and in the Father. 25 And this is the promise that He has promised us—eternal life.

26 These things I have written to you concerning those who try to deceive you. 27 But the anointing which you have received from Him abides in you, and you do not need that anyone teach you; but as the same anointing teaches you concerning all things, and is true, and is not a lie, and just as it has taught you, you will abide in Him.

44

28 And now, little children, abide in Him, that when He appears, we may have confidence and not be ashamed before Him at His coming. 29 If you know that He is righteous, you know that everyone who practices righteousness is born of Him.

—1 John 2:18–29

"It is the last hour." The word *eschaton* is translated here by the English word "last." In Greek *eschaton* means last or final. The word is used extensively in Revelation, e.g., in 1:17, "Fear not, I am the first and the last." It is a boundary word that points to the future in the sense that God Himself bounds history with the beginning and the end, first and last, alpha and omega. Think of it! We have been living in the last days since the time of this letter at about A.D. 70! John lives on the road *from* the center who is Jesus Christ alongside us on the road, and John lives *from* the end, the *eschaton,* because he follows that same Jesus Christ who is at history's beginning, its center, and its fulfillment. All Christians from John's time onward have continued to live in that very same hour.

"Antichrist." The only place in the New Testament where this Greek word *antichristos* appears is in 1 John and 2 John. The ordinary meaning of the word *anti* in Greek is "against," or "opposite." It is interesting, however, to note that the preposition also carries within it the meaning of "instead of," "in the place of" as in the case of Matthew 2:22, *"in place of* his father Herod." Note also in Jesus' parable in Luke 11:11, ". . . a snake instead of a fish." It is reasonable to recognize that John may intend by this word *antichristos* not only those false teachers who are adversaries of Jesus Christ but also the more subtle possibility of those who are counterfeit christs, perhaps very much like the *pseudo* christs our Lord warned us of in Matthew 24:24. I agree with Dr. Stott that, "Perhaps both ideas are present in the word."[6] We are here contending with the problem of an adversary and also the problem of a counterfeit. The second challenge is the more dangerous because it is more easily masked as we shall soon discover.

John's warning gives one more item of evidence concerning the Antichrist challengers: "They went out from us . . ." It is possible that there are teachers at large within the Christian community who were themselves once a part of the fellowship, or at least it appeared that way. But though they claim a historical connection with the fellowship, John warns that "they were not of us . . ." This warning causes us to suspect that John must cope with false teachers who claim their connection to the church and perhaps even with John himself, but in fact they are fraudulent.

Before John continues his warning in a more definite fashion, he interrupts himself to once again assure his readers of their own relationship to God: "But you have been anointed by the Holy One . . ." The word for "anointing," *chrisma,* used in the Greek syntax, is an interesting word made the more so because of John's repetition of it in this passage. Three times in close succession he employs this word (1 John 2:20, 27a, 27b). The verb form of this root word is used in Acts 4:27 when Peter and John sing praises to God's son: ". . . Your holy Servant Jesus whom You anointed . . ." Paul uses the word with reference to Christians in 2 Corinthians 1:21, 22: "Now He who establishes us with you in Christ and has anointed us in God, who also has sealed us." This word is also interesting because of its Old Testament significance. The word in classical Greek means to "smear" or "spread," "rub over," hence "anoint." From this root comes the very title of our Lord, *Christos,* literally "the anointed one."

Now John makes the promise to us that we are anointed by God Himself. God is the one who has confirmed and sealed His people and therefore these Christians do not need to seek out other anointings in order to be equipped for their age. I believe that John has consciously and wisely confronted the most pernicious temptation of the false teachers to the young Christians who are now in danger. The false teachers will offer to the Christians a new and different "anointing" which is only available to those who will submit to the secrets and special teaching of the teachers. The young Christians are tempted because almost everyone wants more spiritual authority or strength if there is more to be had. The Greek-Roman mystery cults had many special anointings to offer, and now what these Christians face is the temptation of special anointings but from a supposedly Christian source.

John confronts this temptation positively rather than negatively. He reminds the Christians of the anointing that they already have in Jesus Christ, that that anointing is not from a movement or guru but from the Holy One Himself, from God. John wants the Christians to know the resources that they already have as a preparation against the false promises they will meet from the antichrists. The best protection against a cold is to stay healthy. C. S. Lewis says, "The best safeguard against bad literature is a full experience of good; just as a real and affectionate acquaintance with honest people gives a better protection against rogues than a habitual distrust of everyone."[7]

I am convinced that the best protection against cults is first of all a robust and healthy relationship with God and His people. It is also important to have accurate information. John offers both protections, but first things first: he assures the Christians of their relationship with the Lord and with each other. Now he is ready to continue with particular informational warnings about the nature of the false doctrines which his friends will encounter: "he who denies that Jesus is the Christ." The false teachers will deny that the Jesus of history and the Christ of faith are the same person. This is of central importance to John, and this false teaching leads inevitably to the denial of God the Father and the Son. The critical theological question is this: Who is Jesus of Nazareth and what do you think of him? This question is still the central question twenty centuries later. "Tell me how it stands with your Christology and I will tell you who you are," said Karl Barth. John writes clearly and plainly; he who agrees (homologeō) with the Son has the Father also. The issue is now openly before the reader. The false teachers in one way or another have diminished the importance and the person of Jesus Christ.

Once again John returns to his positive assurance. In verse 28 he invites his brothers and sisters to abide in the relationship with the Father and the Son with which they began their Christian walk. The result is eternal life. The word "abide," menō, is a very important word in the Gospel of John. It means to "dwell" or "rest in." This is the word that Jesus uses in the promises He makes in the deeply personal Thursday evening discourse: "Abide in me and I in you" (John 15:4). The word is practical and warmly personal; it is definite and understandable; it is too common a word for the religious or ideological elite. It is the word for amateurs who may not know the ways of ritual or of avant-garde privilege but who know how to settle into a genuine relationship and enjoy the fellowship and the view. John invites his young friends in the faith to enjoy their faith and put their weight down upon the faithfulness of God: "And now, little children, abide in him . . ."

It seems to me that John's counsel is as good and as wise for our own high-speed generation as it was for a people pulled in this direction and that direction during the era of Nero. Keep your weight down upon what is the center of the boat. From that center you will be able to stretch out in response to the various pitches of the wind. Most people who go adrift in their lives do so because they lose a living relationship with the living center of life, and they throw away the ballast. Then it is that superficial and secondary themes take over and the counterfeit looks appealing—not because it is good but because we are confused. John's word is not superficial. It is good news: "Abide in him."

NOTES

1. B. F. Westcott, *The First Epistle of John* (Grand Rapids: Eerdmans, 1952), p. 35.

2. Ibid., p. 87.

3. Ibid., p. 35.

4. Martin Luther, *Lectures on Romans* (St. Louis: Concordia Press, 1972), p. 466.

5. Arthur Koestler, *Darkness at Noon* (New York: Macmillan, 1941), p. 99.

6. J. R. W. Stott, *The Epistles of John* (Grand Rapids: Eerdmans, 1960), p. 105.

7. C. S. Lewis, *An Experiment in Criticism* (New York: Cambridge University Press, 1961), p. 94.

Scripture Outline

See What Love (3:1–18)

Test the Spirits (3:19—4:6)

Love Is an Event (4:7–21)

SEE WHAT LOVE

3:1 Behold what manner of love the Father has bestowed on us, that we should be called children of God! Therefore the world does not know us, because it did not know Him. ² Beloved, now we are children of God; and it has not yet been revealed what we shall be, but we know that when He is revealed, we shall be like Him, for we shall see Him as He is. ³ And everyone who has this hope in Him purifies himself, just as He is pure.

⁴ Whoever commits sin also commits lawlessness, and sin is lawlessness. ⁵ And you know that He was manifested to take away our sins, and in Him there is no sin. ⁶ Whoever abides in Him does not sin. Whoever sins has neither seen Him nor known Him.

⁷ Little children, let no one deceive you. He who practices righteousness is righteous, just as He is righteous. ⁸ He who sins is of the devil, for the devil has sinned from the beginning. For this purpose the Son of God was manifested, that He might destroy the works of the devil. ⁹ Whoever has been born of God does not sin, for His seed remains in him; and he cannot sin, because he has been born of God.

¹⁰ In this the children of God and the children of the devil are manifest: Whoever does not practice righteousness is not of God, nor is he who does not love his brother. ¹¹ For this is the message that you heard from the beginning, that we should love one another, ¹² not as Cain who was of the wicked

one and murdered his brother. And why did he murder him? Because his works were evil and his brother's righteous.

13 Do not marvel, my brethren, if the world hates you.

14 We know that we have passed from death to life, because we love the brethren. He who does not love his brother abides in death. 15 Whoever hates his brother is a murderer, and you know that no murderer has eternal life abiding in him.

16 By this we know love, because He laid down His life for us. And we also ought to lay down our lives for the brethren.

17 But whoever has this world's goods, and sees his brother in need, and shuts up his heart from him, how does the love of God abide in him?

18 My little children, let us not love in word or in tongue, but in deed and in truth.

—1 John 3:1–18

In this chapter John continues his message of assurance. The way in which John continues to emphasize the basic relationship of these Christians shows how deep is the problem they face. Something has eroded their self-confidence. As we look closely at John's teaching in this third chapter, we are able to discover the two main directions that the false teaching takes. First the false teachers seek to create an overwhelming feeling of inadequacy on the part of the Christians. This self-depreciation will then prepare them for a receptive attitude toward the special promises of the new movement. The second false direction occurs as the actual teaching becomes established with the initiates. It consists in the new theology of the movement which contradicts the teaching of the faith of the gospel.

As we have already observed, the first and most fundamental feature in false doctrine has to do with the teaching about the Person and ministry of Jesus Christ. But when there is distortion concerning the center, there will always be distortion at the edges. To put the issue in another way, when the theological center is shifted, the result always has an ethical implication. John's teaching in this third chapter will grapple with the two false directions.

"Beloved, now we are children of God. . . ." John's message is basic and uncluttered. He refuses to become entrapped by details concerning the future, either of our future nature or of the countless possibilities of eschatalogical details about which restless minds are able to wonder. His approach is pastoral and authoritative. We are beloved children of God because of the love that the Father has for us. As for the future, we leave it in His hands with

hope and confidence, knowing that the key reality for the future is that His love lasts and our relationship with Him lasts, too. We shall know Him there as we walk in His love here. Our motivation toward purity is because of that hope and that assurance.

"Whoever commits sin. . . ." Beginning with verse 4, John takes on the ethical distortion that inevitably evolves from the faulty theological center. *"Little children, let no one deceive you . . ."* (v. 7). The false teaching to which these young Christians have been exposed has broken their sense of self-confidence in their beloved-ness; it has substituted a counterfeit understanding of Jesus Christ in place of the true Lord. Now we discover that the teaching has deceived them ethically. (Later in this commentary we will examine in some detail the evidences we have from second-century sources about the nature of the protognostic movements that John is here in all probability challenging. But for now, let us confine our observations to the text as it has thus far developed the argument.) The false teachers have confused these young Christians about the nature of sin and about the commandment of love. They are confused about these two ethical implications of faith because they are confused about the center.

John makes two major points. First he challenges sin. He defines it as lawlessness, that is to say, a disregard for the commandments of God. He goes on to make the point that a Christian can never be at peace with sin. His verb tense usage is instructive for us; the sense of the verb is, "No one who abides in him continues in sin." We are engaged in a warfare with sin and therefore we cannot live comfortably with sin.

John is not saying that Christians do not sin. The first and second chapters have made his teaching clear on that point. What he is probably challenging here is the false teaching that those who are "spiritually" ascendant are not as responsible to obey the ordinary and clear teachings of the commandments of God as are other people who have not been initiated into this new and higher state.

John could not be clearer with his reply to this false doctrine. Sin is evil to its core, and in fact the devil is the author of sin. Therefore when we sin, we submit our wills to the power of the devil. The word *diabolis* means literally "the slanderer." John Calvin puts the situation as follows: "Man, by making a bad use of free will, lost both himself and his will."[1] The slanderer has taken us captive when we abide in sin. It has always been this way and it still is. The human crisis is precisely this crisis, that when we ethically choose to do what is harmful there is a double result:

first, the actual harm, and second, our captivity to the way of harm. We become what we do.

John is now warning his young friends of this double danger. Our only hope is to confess our sins and then to be released from their domination of our roadway and of our life.

John now throws another great rock into the water for which he has been preparing his readers. "This is the message which you have heard from the beginning, that we should love one another." The infection of bad doctrine has made these young Christians unable to love. They have become interested in the secrets and slogans to know and say, and they have gone adrift from the relationship with Jesus Christ that is to be lived in and lived out. It is interesting to consider one Old Testament example John presents. In the narrative concerning the murder of Abel by his brother Cain, note that it is because of Cain's inner confusion and distortion about his own relationship with God that his dreadful deed is worked out at the ethical boundary, that is, in his relationship with his neighbor and brother, Abel.

But we have a belovedness from which we derive both our own sense of self-worth and also our ethical motivation toward those who are around us. That belovedness is not a grand statement or "spiritual" reality, but it is the actual event of the love of Jesus Christ who gave His own life for us. From this centerpoint John draws out a major theological conclusion: "Little children, let us not love in word or in tongue (speech) but in deed and in truth" (v. 18). Once more John's approach helps us to understand a little better the nature of the false teaching. These young Christians have been turned toward a theoretical kind of faith in the place of the realistic and concrete faith that they had first discovered in Jesus Christ. John draws together the theology and the ethics of true Christian faith; that united whole is the inseparable mixture of word and work. Jesus Christ did not speak the word of forgiveness to humanity; Jesus Christ is in Himself that very forgiveness; it was not salvation by mimeograph but salvation by costly love. Our Lord always combined within His ministry what he said and what he did so that the two are inseparable. This is why we cannot develop an elaborate theology about the words of Jesus and His teaching apart from the events of Jesus. The Cross and the empty tomb are essential to our faith because Jesus is both what He said and what He did. Otherwise we are in danger of developing a theology of Christian ideology and theory, and when that happens the truly radical nature of Christian faith has been totally subverted. But Christian faith is radical. God has spoken for Himself, the Word become flesh.

Because this Word and work reality is absolutely essential to our theology, it then follows that our ethics must also be the ethics of Word and work, inseparable. Because of Christ's journey upon the very roadway that we live upon, then we too must live our lives within that same roadway where the people are, where the ethical issues become relevant and where we meet brothers and sisters who need our love.

We now can see how a spiritualized theology will produce a spiritualized and vaporous ethic. We also see how the rugged and concrete love of Jesus Christ on the road produces a concrete ethical mandate for those who discover the love.

C. S. Lewis, through his clever and devilish Screwtape, has put the matter into focus for us in one of the Screwtape letters. The senior devil, Screwtape, gives the following advice to the junior temptor, Wormwood, in the matter of how Wormwood should attempt to undermine the faith and repentance of a young Christian.

> It remains to consider how we can retrieve this disaster. The great thing is to prevent his doing anything. As long as he does not convert it into action, it does not matter how much he thinks about this new repentance. Let the little brute wallow in it. Let him, if he has any bent that way, write a book about it; that is often an excellent way of sterilizing the seeds which the Enemy plants in a human soul. Let him do anything but act. No amount of piety in his imagination and affections will harm us if we can keep it out of his will. As one of the humans has said, active habits are strengthened by repetition but passive ones are weakened. The more often he feels without acting, the less he will be able ever to act, and, in the long run, the less he will be able to feel.[2]

TEST THE SPIRITS

[19] And by this we know that we are of the truth, and shall assure our hearts before Him. [20] For if our heart condemns us, God is greater than our heart, and knows all things. [21] Beloved, if our heart does not condemn us, we have confidence toward God. [22] And whatever we ask we receive from

Him, because we keep His commandments and do those things that are pleasing in His sight. 23 And this is His commandment: that we should believe on the name of His Son Jesus Christ and love one another, as He gave us commandment.

24 Now he who keeps His commandments abides in Him, and He in him. And by this we know that He abides in us, by the Spirit whom He has given us.

4:1 Beloved, do not believe every spirit, but test the spirits, whether they are of God; because many false prophets have gone out into the world. 2 By this you know the Spirit of God: Every spirit that confesses that Jesus Christ has come in the flesh is of God, 3 and every spirit that does not confess that Jesus Christ has come in the flesh is not of God. And this is the *spirit* of the Antichrist, which you have heard was coming, and is now already in the world.

4 You are of God, little children, and have overcome them, because He who is in you is greater than he who is in the world. 5 They are of the world. Therefore they speak *as* of the world, and the world hears them. 6 We are of God. He who knows God hears us; he who is not of God does not hear us. By this we know the spirit of truth and the spirit of error.

—1 John 3:19—4:6

John continues to assure his readers of their relationship with God. That assurance, according to John, is not dependent upon our own perception of ourselves and of our worthiness before God. The point of John's teaching is as follows: even though our hearts condemn us the fact is that God is greater than our hearts. In other words, our relationship is not finally qualified or disqualified by our own assessment of the relationship. There is an objective ground that stands beneath the subjective perception of the relationship, and that ground is God's decision.

Very often in human relationships the same dynamic situation occurs that John is describing here. As a pastor I have often counseled persons who are suffering emotional depression. Such persons sometimes will assess the quality of his or her relationships and for them the result is totally pessimistic; but the negative assessment is very often not a true representation of the real situation.

John is aware that his young friends have been under assault from false teachers who have in various ways succeeded in diminishing the self-confidence of these young Christians at this most

54

fundamental level. From this text we discover what is the difference between the temptation of the devil and the conviction of the Holy Spirit. The temptation of the devil always erodes our confidence in the relationship we have with God. The goal of temptation is to make an individual feel so bad about the failures of life that the person concludes there is no help from God for such complicated failure. That is the temptation to despair.

The temptation to pride has the same goal but employs a different tactic. In this case a person is convinced of personal greatness or the promise of greatness to the end that the same utter loneliness results. In both instances the objective of temptation is to draw a human being away from the love and truth of God toward a false understanding of the self and toward a counterfeit hope. The purpose of conviction of the Holy Spirit is to draw a person toward the Lord and toward a healthy understanding of the self.

The Greek word for condemn in these sentences, verse 20–21, is an interesting one. It is made up of two words: *kata,* "against," and *gnoskō,* "to know." The word literally means to "know against myself." By the use of this word John shows that he has in mind self-condemnation more than objective condemnation, as would be the case if the word *katakrinō* "to pass judgment upon," had been used (cf. Rom. 8:34).

John has shifted the ground of our assurance away from ourselves and has established it upon God's faithfulness. Now it will be proper and helpful for John to speak of the sense of assurance which we then feel: *"We have confidence toward God"* (v. 21). The word that is translated by the English word "confidence" is the Greek *parrēsia.* This word in its root form means openness, plainness, frankness. It is the word used in John 10:24: "If you are the Christ, tell us *plainly."* It is also used in John 11:14: "Jesus told them *plainly,* 'Lazarus is dead.'" It is also the root word for the word used in 1 Thessalonians 3:13 to refer to our Lord's Second Coming and appearing: ". . . at the *coming* of our Lord Jesus Christ." *Parousia* means grand appearance, grand openness. It is from this root word that John decides to describe the result of our assurance. John's meaning is that when we know the basis of our assurance, then we are able to stand in the open toward God, toward ourselves, and toward each other.

John now draws together the threads of the commandment theme of the second chapter and announces the object and goal of the commandments. *"And this is His commandment, that we should believe in the name of His Son Jesus Christ and love one another"* (v. 23). The word "believe," *pisteuō,* is here used for the first time in 1 John. Since its meaning is rooted in the Old Testament understanding of faith, we will find our definition there and in closely watching its use in the New Testament rather than in searching through the Greek lexicon. Faith in the Old Testament means to "put our weight down" upon the faithfulness of God (Hab. 2:4). Faith is a response to the evidence of faithfulness. It is a total response and has to do therefore with the whole self. It is not a leap of bold carelessness in which the mind is shut down so that the heart may believe. Faith in the Bible is our response to the character of God that has been revealed to us as trustworthy. When I am convinced of the trustworthiness of Jesus Christ, then it is that I trust in that integrity. John invites his readers to make that very choice on the basis of the evidence.

The final sentence of assurance in the third chapter introduces yet another new word to the book of 1 John. *"By this we know that He abides in us, by the Spirit whom He has given us"* (v. 24b). *"The Spirit"*—we may wonder why it is that John has waited so long into his book before he has mentioned the Third Person in our triune faith. It is not that John has neglected Holy Spirit theology within this book. All conviction of sin and assurance of the love of God in Jesus Christ is by the express ministry of the Holy Spirit. This is John's clear teaching here in 3:24. We know of the abiding presence of Jesus Christ in our lives because of the inward confirmation of the Holy Spirit. The fact is that—and John has demonstrated the fact—the Holy Spirit is the quiet member of the Trinity. The Holy Spirit never points toward Himself but always toward Jesus Christ and toward our relationship with Jesus Christ, our relationship with the body of Christ, and our mission toward the world. Therefore the ministry of the Holy Spirit is to assure, strengthen, and enable our relationship with Jesus Christ and with all of the implications that flow from that relationship. When I am able to say that Jesus Christ is my Lord and that I am assured of His love, it is because the Holy Spirit has convinced me of that good news. God Himself has authenticated Himself.

One very interesting thing to note linguistically is that John in his New Testament books does not in any instance make use of the whole and full term "Holy Spirit." When John refers to the Holy Spirit he always uses the simple term "the Spirit" or such a phrase as the "Spirit of God." The text of 1 John 5:7 in the King James Version which includes the term "Holy Spirit" is not a reading supported by manuscript evidence. This is a distinctive mark in John's writing that further linguistically connects the Gospel of John, the Letters of John, and the Book of Revelation.

"Beloved, do not believe every spirit, but test the spirits, [to see] whether they are of God" (4:1). Now John uses the word "spirit" in its generic word sense. The word *pneuma* literally means wind, and with this meaning of the word in mind, John counsels his friends to test the various winds of their generation. The word "test" is a strong and exciting word. Its root, *dokeō*, means to think, to examine closely. it is this word that Paul uses in Romans 12:2 when he promises that "you may *prove* what is the will of God. . . ." Paul also uses the word in 1 Thessalonians 2:4 as he remembers that he wants "to please God who *tests* our hearts."

Here in chapter 4 John calls upon his young Christian friends to use their heads and to examine closely the theologies and doctrines of all their teachers. There are no benefits to ignorance or to sloppy thinking. Christians are given by John the mandate to be mentally wide awake and to be growing Christians intellectually, as well as morally and spiritually. They need to discern what is sound and then to test the winds to see where those winds really come from. The question for these Christians is this: What are the criteria by which the winds may be tested? There are many pseudo prophets; therefore these young believers need to think clearly and to think for themselves. John decides to endorse only one central criterion at this point, though in chapter 3 he also introduced two other criteria: the test of obedience to the law and the test of love. At this point he centers upon the one crucial issue from which the others derive. *"Every spirit that confesses that Jesus Christ has come in the flesh is of God, and every spirit that does not confess that Jesus Christ has come in the flesh is not of God* (4:2b—3a).

It is now clear what these young Christians are up against. They face false teaching that has denied the full humanity and full deity of our Lord. They have been offered another theory. Who are these false teachers and what is it that they teach? The evidence from John's letters and the Book of Revelation points toward what New Testament scholars have termed proto or incipient gnosticism. We are up against this false teaching in these letters of John and the Book of Revelation.

The most helpful way to understand this phenomenon is to understand the setting from which it emerges. The Mediterranean world of the first century was not an empty stage when the Good

News of Jesus Christ was first preached by the original apostles, Paul, and the other early Christians. The philosophical atmosphere was hellenistic (Greek), and this atmosphere accounts for some of the feelings and yearnings that people brought with them when they first were to encounter the Christian message. Greek philosophy has within it a profound respect and longing for truth and for reason; the question of meaning has longstanding honor in the Greek world of thought.

We know from first-century evidence that large numbers of people who were deeply influenced by Greek philosophy became Christians. We have the evidence of this acceptance from within the New Testament documents themselves, but there is also a growing body of evidence that points to the fact that the first-century church was growing at a rate much faster than scholars at first had estimated. One fascinating Roman document written at the opening of the second century from a Roman official in Bithynia is a very significant indication as to the universal appeal of the gospel in that region. Pliny the Younger wrote to Trajan with reference to the persecution of Christians,

> The matter seemed to me to justify my consulting you, especially on account of the number of those imperilled; for many persons of all ages and classes and of both sexes are being put in peril by accusation, and this will go on. The contagion of this superstition has spread not only in the cities, but in the villages and rural districts as well; there is no shadow of doubt that the temples, which have been almost deserted, are beginning to be frequented once more, that the sacred rites which have been long neglected are being renewed, and that sacrificial victims are for sale everywhere, whereas, till recently, a buyer was rarely to be found.[3]

What was it that drew these folk away from the sacrificial rites of the Greek-Roman mystery cult religions and the temples of Greek religion? It was the sheer size of the Christian affirmation that won them. Paul's words at Athens give us some sense of that strong appeal. "The God who made the world and everything in it, being Lord of heaven and earth, does not live in shrines made by man" (Acts 17:24, RSV). When the Greeks heard this expansive and integrating word, it made sense to them. We also sense that vastness in the prologue to John's Gospel and the shorter prologue to 1 John: ". . . the word was with God, and the word was

God" (John 1:1). Jesus Christ makes sense to the great quest for meaning; He alone integrates the parts into a totality. The city gods and demigods seem so trivial in comparison.

But there are other yearnings and dispositions within Greek thought that by their nature are set in a collision course with the Christian gospel. There is the platonic distinction between appearance and reality in which physical, concrete reality is downgraded, whereas the spiritual, ideological realm of ideas and pure idea is glorified. This Greek viewpoint denies existence which the Old Testament and New Testament embrace. The result of this platonic conviction is the development of a disdain for tangible and concrete physical existence and as a replacement an infatuation with everything mystical and spiritual.

The problem that the early Christians encountered was that as the gospel of Jesus Christ was presented throughout the Mediterranean world there were people who were fascinated by the message but who then sought to draw the message about Christ into their own philosophical framework. In effect they would take possession of the name and some of the teaching of Christ, but then redefine and recast these Christian elements so that they would harmonize with the point of view into which these persons were already settled. The result was a domesticated Christianity. It would be as if a person who had already decided upon the main motivational influences of his life then reached out to the Christian faith in order to support the position he already held. Jesus Christ would be incorporated insofar as He agreed with the previously decided position; where disagreements arose He would be either ignored or redefined. For example, this is what happened in the first century at Galatia with the Jewish party; we have Paul's New Testament Letter to the Galatians which challenges that legalistic captivity of the gospel.

But the more serious threat to the integrity of the gospel was occurring from the Greek side of the Roman world. It posed the danger of the spiritualization of the Christian faith. Many in the Greek world wanted to escape from what they saw as the inferior physical existence of the earth and the body into the superior spiritual realm of reality. They were basically elitist in outlook; they were basically escapist in goal. Both of these outlooks are on a collision course with the realism and the universality of the gospel. But the most fundamental collision point has to do with the understanding of the center of the gospel, Jesus Christ Himself. They want a form of salvation that is not salvation at all; they want their "redeemer" to assist them toward a spiritual escape from the real world; they want to be dazzled by overwhelming spiritual experiences. They are yearning for the ecstasy of *eros,* but the gospel offers the freedom of *agapē* They want to tame the lion but, "Aslan is not a tame lion" (C. S. Lewis).

The discovery in 1946 of an extensive library of gnostic documents at Nag Hammadi in Egypt has been of great assistance to New Testament scholars in better understanding the direction that these protognostic teachers were to move as they established the counter movement to Christianity called *gnosticism.* From the church fathers of the second and third centuries we were already aware of these gnostic movements, but the extensive discoveries at Nag Hammadi give to us the kind of primary documentary evidence that greatly strengthens our confidence in the church fathers and what they wrote. We know now, for instance, that such ancient writers as Irenaeus, Ignatius, and Hippolytus are precise and accurate in their discussions of these movements.

What we find in the documents of the gnostic movements is the logical result of the false turns in the road they made at their first encounter with the gospel. They sought to bring it safely into their philosophical house, and the result of their work was a movement cut adrift from the Old Testament and New Testament gospel.

Let me give some examples. The teaching in the gnostic book *The Apocryphon of John* teaches that the beginnings of human life have a perverse origin. Woman is not created by God but by the figure Jaldabaoth, which has the appearance of a serpent and a lion and who creates without God's approval. As we can see in this elaborate doctrinal teaching, the physical existence of the earth and of human beings is contaminated not because of sin but because of creation. The very creation itself is chaotic.[4]

Irenaeus, in his argument against the gnostics, makes extensive use of the Gospel of John, 1 John, and the Book of Revelation as his major documentation against the false teaching. Listen to Irenaeus as he describes the central mistake in gnostic teaching: "Now according to them neither was the word made flesh, nor Christ, nor the Savior. . . . For they allege that the word and Christ never came into this world, and that the Savior was neither incarnate nor suffered, but that he descended as a dove upon that Jesus who was made by higher dispensation."[5] This means that the Christ of gnosticism is a phantom Christ, superpersonal, superphysical. There is throughout gnostic teaching a preference for the secretive, spiritual realm but at the same time a consistent rejection of human concreteness and particularity. Notice this feature in a supposed dialogue between Jesus and Peter in the gnostic book *The Gospel of Thomas.*

> Simon Peter said to them: Let Mariham (Mary) go away from us, for women are not worthy of life. Jesus said: Lo, I will draw her so that I will make her a man so that she too may become a living spirit which is like you men; for every woman who makes herself a man will enter into the kingdom of heaven.[6]

It is clear from this saying that the sexual identity and concreteness of the woman is not only downgraded, it is obliterated in the gnostic fascination with the elitist spiritual state. When Jesus Christ is redefined and spiritualized, the results are therefore psychologically chaotic for us. The church father Ignatius put it simply and directly:

> Turn a deaf ear therefore when anyone speaks to you apart from Jesus Christ, who was of the family of David, the Christ of Mary, who was truly born, who ate and drank, who was truly persecuted under Pontius Pilate, was truly crucified and truly died. . . . But if, as some Godless men, that is, unbelievers, say, he suffered in mere appearance (being themselves mere appearances), why am I in bonds?[7]

The ethics in gnosticism are highly adaptable to the particular preference of the group. Since physical life is not real and only the spiritual is real, there is no concrete touchstone or roadway upon which our lives and our actions are held accountable. What matters the most for us is to know *(gnosis)* the secrets, and if a person is privileged to know the secrets, then that person is therefore above the common restrictions or accountability of law or gospel.

But the gospel of Jesus Christ has interpersonal and social ethics deeply etched within its essence because of Jesus Christ who was Word and event inseparably united. This is why the Christian gospel is a better hope for the world, because it does not take the world lightly. Suffering is real, and Jesus Christ really suffered. Death is real, and Jesus Christ really died. Life is real, and Jesus Christ has really conquered death. Therefore we suffer, we die, and, because of Christ, we live not only now in the present, but in the resurrection we will live in the fulfillment of time after the end as well.

"Since men are real, they must have a real existence, not passing away into things which are not, but advancing among things that are."[8] Father Irenaeus, who made this comment, has understood the road language of John. The Jesus Christ who is the *Logos* is the Jesus of our journey. He is not the phantom, the unlimited idea, the limitless number. He is our atonement, our friend, the Lord.

LOVE IS AN EVENT

[7] Beloved, let us love one another, for love is of God; and everyone who loves is born of God and knows God. [8] He who does not love does not know God, for God is love. [9] In this the love of God was manifested toward us, that God has sent His only begotten Son into the world, that we might live through Him. [10] In this is love, not that we loved God, but that He loved us and sent His Son to be the propitiation for our sins. [11] Beloved, if God so loved us, we also ought to love one another.

[12] No one has seen God at any time. If we love one another, God abides in us, and His love has been perfected in us. [13] By this we know that we abide in Him, and He in us, because He has given us of His Spirit. [14] And we have seen and testify that the Father has sent the Son as Savior of the world. [15] Whoever confesses that Jesus is the Son of God, God abides in him, and he in God. [16] And we have known and believed the love that God has for us. God is love, and he who abides in love abides in God, and God in him.

[17] Love has been perfected among us in this: that we may have boldness in the day of judgment; because as He is, so are we in this world. [18] There is no fear in love; but perfect love casts out fear, because fear involves torment. But he who fears has not been made perfect in love. [19] We love Him because He first loved us.

[20] If someone says, "I love God," and hates his brother, he is a liar; for he who does not love his brother whom he has seen, how can he love God whom he has not seen? [21] And this commandment we have from Him: that he who loves God must love his brother also.

—1 John 4:7–21

These two paragraphs make up some of the most profound and exciting teaching in the whole of the Bible. In a very real sense John has drawn together into one great set of sentences the whole theology of his letter.

Agapē is the word which John will make use of twenty-eight times in these sentences from verses 1 through 21 of chapter 4. The word in classical Greek is not a strong or precisely anchored word. "Its etymology is uncertain, and its meaning weak and variable. . . . It is indeed striking that the substantive *agapē* is almost completely lacking in pre-biblical Greek."[9] This Greek word which is colorless in meaning in classical Greek was taken over by the Septuagint translators of the Old Testament in order to translate the Hebrew words for "love" in the Old Testament. What happened is that the rich Old Testament love meanings, particularly in the word *ahab* (Deut. 7:13; Lev. 19:18, etc.), imprinted upon the mild word *agapē* a new content and a new excitement. Professor Stauffer observes of the Septuagint writers, "*Eros* and *philia* and derivatives are strongly suppressed. The harmless *agapē* carries the day, mainly because by reason of its prior history it is the best adapted to express the thoughts. . . . But the true victor in the competition is the ancient *ahab* which impresses upon the colorless Greek word its own rich and strong meaning."[10]

Therefore in order to understand what the word *agapē* means, we should first of all observe its Old Testament underpinning. Second, we should watch closely as New Testament writers define the word as they make use of it in the texts of the New Testament. It is the same situation linguistically that we are in as we listen to subcultures within our English language system make use of the words of our language. Teenagers are particularly expert in the coining and the capture of words. The more vague or colorless a word is the more easily it is adapted. For example, during the 1960s the mild and inobtrusive word "cool" was captured by teenage speakers of English. Another capture took place with the word "neat." Since both of these words have the advantage of vacuousmildness, they are therefore most easily redefined. The New Testament and Septuagint writers have done this very thing with the word *agapē*. Now let us watch closely as John defines the word for us by the way he uses it in this great text.

"Beloved." Love is granted toward a person. *"Let us love one another."* Love is a freedom word about which we make decisions; it involves our will. *Love is of God.* The syntax is possessive in this sentence. The meaning is clear that love has its origin from God; He is its source. *"He who loves."* John now tells his readers that the experience of God's love is an integral part of our essential relationship with God. He then repeats that

sentence in negative parallelism to make the point; if we do not experience love we are not experiencing God, *"for God is love."* He continues the affirmation of the earlier line. Love has its origin from God. As the context of this paragraph from John will make clear, John does not invite his readers to reverse the sentence and conclude that *love is God.* John is not teaching that our theory about love is divine but rather that God is the one who gives to us the meaning of love. Our love or our conception of love does not define God; rather it is God who is the source of love.

In his study *The Four Loves,* C. S. Lewis makes a very thoughtful theological reflection upon this text.

> St. John's saying that God is love has long been balanced in my mind against the remark of an author (M. Denis de Roegemont) that, "Love ceases to be a demon only when he ceases to be a god." Which of course can be restated in the form, "begins to be a demon the moment he begins to be a god." This balance seems to be an indispensable safeguard. If we ignore it the truth that God is love may slyly come to mean for us the converse, that love is God.[11]

"In this the love of God was manifested toward us, that God sent his only begotten Son. . . ." Love is the event in which God spoke for Himself in human history by His Son. This sentence and its parallel sentence are at the theological core of John's definition of love: "Not that we loved God but that He loved us and sent His Son to be the *one who takes our place. . . ."* Love, for John, is what God has done in our behalf. Love is the person Jesus Christ alongside humanity on the road as Savior of the world.

"If we are so loved then we ought to love." John now comes back to his opening sentence, *"Let us love one another."* But what has been shared with us in the sentences in between has granted a rugged and solid foundation for the ethical imperative. John has presented to his readers what may be described as an evangelical ethic. We are to love out of the fullness of God's prior love. There is no confusion in John's order; we do not earn God's love by our acts of love, but rather it is our experience of God's love that provides the inner motivation toward love. It is the kind of love we ourselves received; the love that forgives our sins and identifies with us in our journey. Therefore we have that experience of love as the "en route" training in love to enable us to express its implications with those around us.

The point is, we are not mandated to create or develop a quantity of love. Rather we are to love outwardly toward others what we received personally in our belovedness from God. We learned it at the Cross. We continue to learn love en route in our Christian discipleship on a day-to-day basis, with ups and downs. Love in the New Testament thus is not an ideal; it is a relationship. If love were an ideal, then it could be described by a list of attributes. But love is a dynamic and growing result of a relationship with Jesus Christ.

God's love abides and is completed as we "exercise ourselves in grace" (Luther). This is the sense of John's final imperative in the first paragraph. Love is a dynamic word, not a static word. We must then decide to live in its living presence and grow in its full implications or else we will grow cold and go adrift. When we lose a living relationship with God's love it is not that God leaves us; it is that we leave Him.

John begins his second paragraph, verse 13a, with a restatement of the assurance of the Holy Spirit in our lives. These sentences are like great regathering summary sentences by which John once again keeps the Christocentric focus clear. We have already observed throughout this letter that one of the writing style features of John's letter is his delight in restatement and repetition. He writes in the spirit of the authors of Old Testament Wisdom literature. Much of this book has the feel of Proverbs. John has no hesitation about repeating a theme which he has previously discussed.

"In this is love perfected with us, that we may have confidence (boldness) for the day of judgment" (v. 17). Once again the word *parrēsia* is used. We have openness before God as His love matures within our lives even in the face of the day of judgment *(crisis)*. The word for judgment is the word *krinō*, from which we derive many very important New Testament words. The basic meaning of the word *krinō* is to separate, to distinguish. *Katakrinō* is the strong word translated in the New Testament by the word "condemn," literally, "to judge against" *(kata)*. The noun *krisis* is the word used here in 1 John 4:17—"judgment" or "moment of distinguishing." Our English word "crisis" comes from this word. The word *kritikos* is the person able to judge; hence the English "critical." The word *kritērion* is the word for tribunal or law court in Greek; hence the English word "criterion." The word *krima* in Greek is the word for decision or verdict; hence, the cognate for the English word "crime." John makes the promise that as we claim God's love for us in Jesus Christ, the result is an openness on our part toward even so vulnerable a moment as the moment of distinguishing, the moment of judgment.

John's point is both psychologically and theologically profound. The basis of our openness theologically is the faithfulness and love of God. Psychologically, the openness is possible because the love I received was discovered at the moment of my deepest need and vulnerability ("If we confess our sin . . ."); therefore once I know I am loved when I am empty-handed, this sets me free from the depressive self-doubt about my future acceptability. God has already seen me completely and has loved me in that total vulnerability and in that stark light; therefore the light of further judgment *(crisis)* is not really a new reality with which I must cope. The Christ I met on the road as my redeemer is the Christ I meet in judgment as my Lord.

John seals this point with the reminder that the Jesus Christ we meet in the light of *krinō* is the Christ who himself understands and knows our daily journey: ". . . as He is, so are we in *this world"* (4:17).

"Perfect love casts out fear." *Phobeomai* is the word John uses for the verb "fear." It means to be frightened, in the sense of alarm, fright, terror. John makes a remarkable promise to his readers. As love matures in our lives on a day-to-day basis, the result is that fear is cast out. The reason that John gives is that fear has to do with our worry about torture or punishment. *Kolasis* carries that very harsh sense in the Greek. Every human being worries about the problem of pain and the threats of punishment or torture. John places even such dreadful fears as these within a larger boundary, a larger framework. All dangers are surrounded by God's decision, and therefore their cruelest power to intimidate has been greatly reduced.

"We love . . . because he first loved us." This one electrifying sentence is a classic one-line summary of the historical basis of Christian ethics. It is combined with the eschatological basis of the previous few sentences in which we have a love in the present because our hope for the future is sure in Christ. Then we must add to this our present assurance of Christ's abiding presence because of the ministry of the Holy Spirit in our lives. We recognize a threefold basis for the Christian's life and relationship. It might be seen more clearly by the following line model.

In the Present
Because of the Holy Spirit we have
"known and believed the love
God has for us" (v. 16).

From the Past
"Because He first
loved" we now love
(v. 19).

From the Future
We have confidence
for the day of
judgment: because
love casts out fear
(vv. 17, 18).

From these three sources of assurance we live our lives in the world. And we are to live in the real world; the world where the neighbor also lives. John concludes this incredible passage with that neighbor on his mind. We must love the real people in the real places where we live. There is not one ounce of escapism here, but, instead, a fully involved, definite lifestyle in daily companionship with Jesus Christ.

NOTES

1. John Calvin, *Institutes* (Grand Rapids: Eerdmans, 1953), 1:229.

2. C. S. Lewis, *Screwtape Letters* (New York: Fontana Books, 1942), pp. 69–70.

3. Pliny the Younger correspondence to Trajan, quoted in H. Bettenson, *Documents of the Christian Church* (London: Oxford University Press, 1943), p. 5.

4. W. C. Van Unnik, *Newly Discovered Gnostic Writings* (London: SCM Press, 1960). See discussion of Apocrypha of John, pp. 69ff.

5. Irenaeus, "Against Heresies," in *Early Christian Fathers*, ed. C. C. Richardson (New York: Macmillan, 1970), p. 379.

6. *Gospel of Thomas*, trans. William R. Schroeder, Saying 112 (New York: Fontana Books, 1960), pp. 18–26.

7. Ignatius, "Against Heresies," quoted in *Documents of the Christian Church*, ix, x.

8. Irenaeus, in *Early Church Fathers*, p. 396.

9. Ethelbert Stauffer, in *Theological Dictionary of the New Testament,* ed. Gerhard Kittel and Gerhard Friedrich (Grand Rapids: Eerdmans, 1964), 1:36.

10. Ibid., p. 39.

11. C. S. Lewis, *Four Loves* (New York: Harcourt Brace, 1960), p. 17.

Chapter Four—Discipleship

Scripture Outline

Not Burdensome (5:1–12)

Deep Away from Idols (5:13–21)

NOT BURDENSOME

5:1 Whoever believes that Jesus is the Christ is born of God, and everyone who loves Him who begot also loves him who is begotten of Him. 2 By this we know that we love the children of God, when we love God and keep His commandments. 3 For this is the love of God, that we keep His commandments. And His commandments are not burdensome. 4 For whatever is born of God overcomes the world. And this is the victory that has overcome the world— our faith. 5 Who is he who overcomes the world, but he who believes that Jesus is the Son of God?

6 This is He who came by water and blood—Jesus Christ; not only by water, but by water and blood. And it is the Spirit who bears witness, because the Spirit is truth. 7 For there are three that bear witness in heaven: the Father, the Word, and the Holy Spirit; and these three are one. 8 And there are three that bear witness on earth: the Spirit, the water, and the blood; and these three agree as one.

9 If we receive the witness of men, the witness of God is greater; for this is the witness of God which He has testified of His Son. 10 He who believes in the Son of God has the witness in himself; he who does not believe God has made Him a liar, because he has not believed the testimony that God has given of His Son. 11 And this is the testimony: that God has given us eternal life, and this life is in His Son. 12 He who has the Son has life; he who does not have the Son of God does not have life.

—1 John 5:1–12

"Everyone who believes." Our faith in the character of God is the doorway that opens up our lives toward God. The result of faith is our relationship with God as His children. John teaches that this relationship is really a fourfold relationship. It might be described by the following model:

There is an upward vertical relationship toward God as our Lord. There is the inner self-understanding that the believer has toward himself or herself, the knowledge that he or she is a child of God. There is the love that the believer has toward the persons around his or her life. The persons closest to us are those who share our relationship with God, and the love flows beyond that inner circle of the *koinonia* toward the world around the fellowship. There is, finally, the relationship of our life to the whole created order around us.

John then repeats a mandate which by now has become a recurrent theme in 1 John, *"For this is the love of God, that we keep His commandments."* The Greek word translated by "keep" is a word that carries the idea of "guard," "keep watch over." We are to be careful to carry out God's commands because so much is at stake. God's very love is involved in His commandments.

God's commandments have been made clear by John; they are deeply related to the fourfold relationship: (1) a true understanding of who God is and that He has spoken in His Son Jesus Christ. (2) God's commandments have to do with our inner self and walk. We are meant to walk in the light and to be assured of our forgiveness in Jesus Christ. (3) The third relationship of our lives according to John's anthropology has to do with our relationship toward the neighbor closest and farthest. We are to live out God's love toward our brother and sister in Christ and also the neighbor. (4) There is still a fourth relationship, and that is the relationship of the person to heaven and earth that surround our existence. We are to obey God's commandments in this relationship too. We are to gain the meaning of our life from God's decision and not from the created order of heaven or earth. We are to worship God alone. The created order does better when it is not worshiped.

Verse 4: "And his commandments are not burdensome" ("grievous"). The word *baros* means literally "weight," "burden." It is this word that Paul uses in 2 Corinthians 1:8 when he writes, ". . . for we were so utterly unbearably *crushed* that we despaired of life itself." The sense of the word is crushing, fierce weight. In one use of the word, in fact, the word is translated by the RSV translators with the word "fierce" (Acts 20:29). The will of God for our lives is not a crushing weight. God does not build His greatness upon our smallness; He is in no sense threatened by our joys and our fulfillment. God's will is challenging because it goes crossgrain to the expectations of our age and generation. But God's will is not burdensome, because our lives thrive in the way of His Righteousness, whereas they are stunted and confused in the way of unrighteousness. Adultery, fraud, selfishness, murder, gossip, fear—these are not the attributes that build up a human personality and encourage human relationships or social justice.

The way of righteousness that John has sketched in for his readers is plainly a better way. It is honest, vulnerable, open, alive from the center, and it has the living daily experience of God's love at its core. Because there is the admission of sin, the ulcer-producing games that people play are not needed here. This way of righteousness is a roadway that has the Savior-Lord Jesus Christ as the companion, and this makes all the difference. We are yoked with Christ; therefore the burden is easy.

John once again makes use of the powerful word "overcome" *(nikaō)*, and again he affirms the fact that because of our faith in Jesus Christ we have won the victory over the world. The power that the Christian has over the world is not a power or force that we control. It is our confidence that Jesus Christ has the authority. His boundary is greater than either the terrors or the temptations of the world. This boundary theology will become the central theme in John's final great work, the Book of Revelation.

"This is he who came by water and blood." John has previously explained his use of the word "blood." The term refers to the death of Jesus Christ in our behalf. What does John mean by the term "water"? The water may be a reference to the baptism of Jesus Christ by which our Lord made clear His identification with humanity. In Jesus' dialogue with Nicodemus (John 3:1–21), our Lord tells Nicodemus, "Unless one is born of water and the Spirit, he cannot enter the kingdom of God" (John 3:5). It appears from

the context of John 3:1–21 that Jesus means by "water" the *faith* of Nicodemus and by "Spirit" the mighty act of God in Nicodemus's behalf. Now we are told by John of three witnesses that agree in reference to Jesus Christ: the *water,* the *blood,* and the *Spirit.* From the context of this book and the New Testament, we conclude that John means first the water of baptism, therefore faith; the blood refers to the Cross; the Spirit refers to God's own validation of His Son, and His assurance in our lives of Jesus Christ. The KJV includes a quite different reading for 1 John 5:7: "For there are three that bear record in heaven: the Father, the Word, and the Holy Ghost; and these three are one." This sentence does not belong in the text since it is not found in any Greek manuscript earlier than the 15th century nor in Jerome's Latin text.

John concludes this section with the strong claim for the centrality of Jesus Christ for the life of the Christian. The eternal life we have from God comes through our faith in His Son. This positive affirmation is followed in the tradition of Old Testament parallelism with the statement stated negatively. There is no eternal life apart from the Son of God. Jesus Christ is not one of several possible saviors, or a shepherd among the shepherds; Jesus Christ is the Savior, the true shepherd. God has spoken in His Son, and we must listen to that speech. Karl Barth says:

> When we pronounce the name of Jesus Christ, we are not speaking of an idea. The name Jesus Christ is not the transparent shell, through which we glimpse something higher—no room for platonism here! What is involved is this actual name and this title; this person is involved . . . so we confront God. God really encompasses us in Jesus Christ "on every side." Here there is no escape. But there is also no drop into nothingness. In pronouncing the name of Jesus Christ we are on the way. "I am the way, the truth, and the life." That is the way through time, the center of which He is . . . .[1]

John does not make the Christian church the center nor is the life a reward for the mastery of secrets. Eternal life is in Jesus Christ. That is the Good News—not a burden but an adventure.

I have been a Christian long enough that I have seen proven to me the daily truthfulness of these unforgettable sentences of John. Our lives work better when we live from the true center, Jesus

Christ. It is also true that the more we grow in loving people around us, the more love we experience. Love is so durable and powerful that its resources or resourcefulness never wear out. I have also discovered that the more I grow as a Christian the better I feel about myself. I don't mean in the sense of hollow pride but in the substantial sense of knowing and watching the daily verification of God's grace at work in my own life day-by-day. It is true that His love is better each morning. "We grow old but our Father is younger than we are" (G. K. Chesterton).

Screwtape was right when he wrote to Wormwood this warning about our God: "When he talks of their losing their selves, he only means abandoning the clamour of self-will; once they have done that, He really gives them back all their personality, and boasts (I am afraid, sincerely) that when they are wholly His they will be more themselves than ever" (Letter 13).[2]

KEEP AWAY FROM IDOLS

[13] These things I have written to you who believe in the name of the Son of God, that you may know that you have eternal life, and that you may continue to believe in the name of the Son of God.

[14] Now this is the confidence that we have in Him, that if we ask anything according to His will, He hears us. [15] And if we know that He hears us, whatever we ask, we know that we have the petitions that we have asked of Him.

[16] If anyone sees his brother sinning a sin which does not lead to death, he will ask, and He will give him life for those who commit sin not leading to death. There is sin leading to death. I do not say that he should pray about that. [17] All unrighteousness is sin, and there is sin not leading to death.

[18] We know that whoever is born of God does not sin; but he who has been born of God keeps himself, and the wicked one does not touch him.

[19] We know that we are of God, and the whole world lies under the sway of the wicked one.

[20] And we know that the Son of God has come and has given us an understanding, that we may know Him who is true; and we are in Him who is true, in His Son Jesus Christ. This is the true God and eternal life.

[21] Little children, keep yourselves from idols. Amen.

—1 John 5:13–21

John teaches the young church to pray. Prayer is the natural breath of a genuine relationship with God. John does not make use of the word "pray." However, he uses a verb that we find in Jesus' teaching about prayer (Matt. 7:7–12) "ask." John invites his readers to *"ask anything according to his will . . ."* John has advocated throughout this book an open style of life. We are to continue that openness before the Lord as we bring before the Lord the concerns that well up in our lives.

Within the context of this teaching on prayer John has written some counsel which has been baffling to interpreters through the centuries: "If anyone sees his brother committing what is not a mortal sin, he will ask . . ." The word translated by the English "mortal" is the Greek *thanatos* and simply means "death"; thus the meaning of the word in this text would be "a deadly sin." But what does John mean by this distinction between deadly sin and sin that is not deadly? F. F. Bruce has suggested that the text quite possibly is best interpreted in its most literal sense: "I suggest that it is, quite literally, a sin which has death as its consequence. . . . What John is doing, in that case, is to make it plain that he does not advocate praying for the dead."[3]

John's teaching makes one point very clear to us, and that is that we cannot take too much responsibility upon ourselves and upon our prayer mandate. There are tragic possibilities that are beyond our responsibility. This does not mean that these situations are beyond God's responsibility, but John wants to set certain limits for the Christians to whom he writes.

The problem for the interpreter still remains, however, in attempting to understand the original distinction that John has portrayed between deadly and nondeadly sin. J. R. W. Stott suggests that John's readers may have been familiar with the expression, which explains why John does not offer more about the concept. But that still does not solve our interpretive problem.

I believe that the most basic rule for biblical interpretation is the rule "Lean is better than luxurious." In a teaching such as we have here in I John 5, that rule requires that we as interpreters stand back from the passage with respectful caution and restraint. What is made clear in the teaching is that our prayers have efficacy, but that there are boundaries beyond which we cannot intrude. God's authority and saving power have not been diminished by this limitation, but our authority is under a greater authority than our own. We are not the Savior, and this text certainly makes that fact evident. But the text is still good news.

Though it sobers us with the seriousness of life and life choices, yet the Lord is Lord and it is He whom we must trust even with this apparent riddle.

We do not need to fear the evil one, because God keeps us and the evil one cannot *"touch"* us. The strong word *haptetai* is used in this instance. That same word is used in John 20:17 in the resurrection narrative; "Jesus said to her, 'Do not hold me.'" The word means to lay hold of or hold on to. The evil one cannot cling to us. He has no hold on us. The world is contested territory, and John does not make light of the power that the evil one exercises over the world. But the interpreter of this passage must not misunderstand John's statement. This one sentence does not cancel out the even stronger statement of Jesus Christ in John's Gospel. "In the world you will have tribulation; but be of good cheer, I have overcome the world" (John 16:33). John's statement in 1 John 5 is a description of the tribulation and of the serious extent of the contest, but there is no question that the world is God's beloved domain (John 3:16) and that the devil's power does not rival the authority of Christ for us in the world. "For He who is in you is greater than he who is in the world" (1 John 4:4).

We must also remember that John has been making use of the word *kosmon* in a special way, as we observed in 1 John 2:15–17. In that text, the word "world" is used in the sense of worldly values. The fact is clear, however, that there is a battle underway. The battle is wholesale and critical, but there is no sense of panic in John; indeed, he has powerfully taught us that God's love drives out fear. John is not so alarmed by the contest or by the antagonist that he turns toward some form of escapism or survivalism.

The final affirmation in John's first letter points us toward Jesus Christ as the one who is the truth and who has already come in the flesh to this world. He is the one who grants to us the understanding of His victory and the gift of eternal life.

"Little children, keep yourself from idols" (v. 21). The Greek word for "idol," *eidōlon,* in classical Greek has the meaning of "shadow" or "phantom." John now hurls at his readers one final challenge. Do not set your affection upon shadows and phantoms. At the very core of gnosticism there is an affection for the pure spirit and the reality of the spirit. This yearning runs from top to bottom in gnosticism, and John now dares to describe its fundamental error. The gnostics have chosen shadowy idols in place of the true and living God. They have gone against the command of God (Deut. 5:8–10); they have exchanged the reality of

Jesus Christ with a phantom Christ who has been fashioned according to the desires and requirements of their highly spiritualized preferences. But the result is nothing less than idolatry. The challenge is like a last shout to a youngster as he or she leaves home on a trip, "Watch out for idols!" Idols are the more serious threat because they look so much like the real thing. In that fact is their special kind of deadly peril.

This last challenge is one more Johannine freedom sentence. It calls upon the readers to be resourceful and clear-headed, to think things through and test the options with which they are confronted. The Christian life is not a sheltered existence in which there are no temptations or perils, because Jesus Christ does not take away the freedom of the believer. Discipleship is a thoughtful, freedom journey; it is not the experience of being overwhelmed in which the human senses are put into the frenzy of spiritual ecstasy.

This desire for overwhelming experience is the yearning in Greek mythology and in much of gnosticism, but not in the New Testament. (Note Paul's warning in 1 Cor. 12:1–2.) The New Testament world of thought is more basic and wholistic. The human personality is understood in total terms of body, spirit, and soul, inseparably united. The biblical hope is not the immortality of the soul but the resurrection of the body; it is the whole of me that is beloved by Jesus Christ. This respect for wholeness runs throughout Christian faith and is why John insists upon the real Jesus Christ who became flesh. This is also why John insists upon real love: "*for he who does not love his brother whom he has seen, how can he love God whom he has not seen*" (1 John 4:20).

The Christian fellowship is real too; it is, as Barth says, not the "*civitas platonica* or some sort of cloud-cuckooland in which the Christians are united inwardly and invisibly; while the visible church is devalued. . . . The first congregation was a visible group, which caused a visible public uproar."[4]

But the incipient gnosticism of which John is so deeply concerned wants nothing of the concrete reality of Christian faith, and instead it has fallen in love with shadows and phantoms. John will express this shadowy nature of idols in his Book of Revelation with the following description; ". . . idols of gold or silver and bronze and stone and wood, which cannot either see or hear or walk" (Rev. 9:20).

The God of Abraham, Isaac, and Jacob who has spoken for Himself in Jesus Christ can see and hear and walk, therefore little children, keep yourselves from idols!

NOTES

1. Karl Barth, *Dogmatics in Outline* (New York: Harper, 1959), pp. 69–70.

2. Lewis, *Screwtape Letters,* p. 68.

3. F. F. Bruce, *Answers to Questions* (Grand Rapids: Zondervan, 1972), p. 134.

4. Barth, *Dogmatics in Outline,* p. 142.

CHAPTER FIVE—CHRISTIANS IN THE WORLD
2 JOHN 1–13

Scripture Outline

The Elect Lady (1–3)

Tough Love (4–13)

THE ELECT LADY

1:1 The Elder,
To the elect lady and her children, whom I love in truth, and not only I, but also all those who have known the truth, ² because of the truth which abides in us and will be with us forever:
³ Grace, mercy, and peace will be with you from God the Father and from the Lord Jesus Christ, the Son of the Father, in truth and love.

—2 John 1-3

"The elder to the elect lady and her children." This letter is noticeably different from First John in that the term "elder" *(presbuteros)* is used to describe the author. The writer assumes that no other identification is necessary. The linguistic style of the letter unites this book to 1 John. We can only speculate that as it is written later than the first letter, and because of the more personal and direct identification of the recipient, our author decided to identify himself simply as "Elder."

Who is this elect lady? Alexander Ross in his commentary (Eerdmans, 1954) argues that the letter is written to a person and her family who probably live in Asia Minor. This would mean that the letter therefore addresses her personal situation. J. L. Houlden (Harper, 1973) in his commentary has observed that the word *kuria* ("lady") is an equivalent to the name Martha in Aramaic, a well-attested proper name.

The most common view of interpreters is that the term "elect lady" refers to a church in Asia Minor. The final verse of 2 John offers some support to this view: *"The children of your elect sister greet you."* This greeting appears to sound like the greeting of members of one part of the church toward members in another part of the church. But if this letter is a directed letter with a particular church in the mind of the author, the question that we must then ask is why John has not named the city within which the church is located. In the Book of Revelation, John will identify the seven cities which are to receive that book.

I find it hard to agree with the church theory. It makes better sense in my view to interpret this letter in its most obvious sense, as a letter written by John to an esteemed friend and her family. The fact that no city designation is made also supports this view.

TOUGH LOVE

4 I rejoiced greatly that I have found some of your children walking in truth, as we received commandment from the Father. 5 And now I plead with you, lady, not as though I wrote a new commandment to you, but that which we have had from the beginning: that we love one another. 6 This is love, that we walk according to His commandments. This is the commandment, that as you have heard from the beginning, you should walk in it.

7 For many deceivers have gone out into the world who do not confess Jesus Christ as coming in the flesh. This is a deceiver and an antichrist. 8 Look to yourselves, that we do not lose those things we worked for, but that we may receive a full reward.

9 Whoever transgresses and does not abide in the doctrine of Christ does not have God. He who abides in the doctrine of Christ has both the Father and the Son. 10 If anyone comes to you and does not bring this doctrine, do not receive him into your house nor greet him; 11 for he who greets him shares in his evil deeds.

12 Having many things to write to you, I did not wish to do so with paper and ink; but I hope to come to you and speak face to face, that our joy may be full.

13 The children of your elect sister greet you. Amen.

—2 John 4–13

There are not to be found in this letter any themes which are not more fully expressed in 1 John. Therefore the value of 2 John to the New Testament does not rest in the doctrinal teaching of the letter since each doctrinal theme has already been more fully explained in the first letter. The importance of the letter is precisely in the fact that we who read it are able to see how deeply John felt about the themes of his first letter.

John's concern for the concreteness of Jesus Christ over against the phantom christ of incipient gnosticism is once again affirmed in strength. John's concern about Christians obeying the commandment of God concerning love is once again emphasized forcefully. John's concern about the false teachers is once again stated. The word for "deceivers" in verse 7, *planoi,* has the same root as the verb *planaō* that John uses in 1 John 1:8—*"we deceive ourselves."* The noun appears again in 1 John 4:6—"... by this we know the spirit of truth and the spirit of *error."* The verb form literally has the meaning to *"lead astray,"* to *"wander from the path."*

John dares to share with his friend and her family some pastoral advice concerning those false teachers who are traveling among the churches: *"Do not receive him into your house"* (v. 10). This pastoral counsel gives us some insight into a special problem with which the early Christians were faced. We have substantial evidence within the New Testament that the Christians traveled extensively throughout the Mediterranean world of the first century. One dramatic evidence of this is chapter 16 of Romans, which contains a long list of people who are living in Rome and who are now hearing by letter from their friend Paul. Yet Paul himself has never been to Rome! Traveling Christians stayed as guests in the homes of the Christians from city to city. The inns in most Roman cities were dangerous places. W. M. Ramsay tells us that "the ancient inns . . . were little removed from houses of ill fame. . . . The profession of inn-keeper was dishonorable, and their infamous character is often noted in Roman laws."

The Christian tradition of hospitality was therefore a beautiful and important ministry within the first-century church community, but now we hear John warn against its exploitation by persons who masquerade as Christians and then take advantage of the generosity of Christian hospitality. The worst part of this exploitation is that these pseudo prophets then make use of the offered hospitality to spread a chaotic and false teaching.

We see in this pastoral warning the first hints of what will be a very serious problem for the Christians by the beginning of the second century. This is the delicate question of balance between openness and hospitality on the one hand and on the other the wisdom to protect a family or a church from the kind of sophisticated cunning which intends to exploit the very kindness that grows out of the gospel. If such exploitation occurs, then the elect lady's family has been taken advantage of and, also, false seeds of impure doctrine have been planted.

The early second-century Christian document the *Didache* contains some very interesting teaching in this regard.

> Now, you should welcome anyone who comes your way and teaches you all we have been saying. But if the teacher proves himself a renegade and by teaching otherwise contradicts all this, pay no attention to him. . . . Now about the apostles and prophets: Act in line with the Gospel precept. Welcome every apostle on arriving, as if he were the Lord. But he must not stay beyond one day. In case of necessity, however, the next day too. If he stays three days, he is a false prophet . . . if he asks for money, he is a false prophet *(Did.* 11.1–6).

Notice that there is a threefold test: Does the prophet teach the truth? Does he try to stay more than two days? Does he ask for money? The *Didache* helps us to understand some of the kinds of exploitation that the early Christians faced once the first-century world made the discovery that Christians were generous.

John is advocating a balance. He advocates a zeal for truth, a vigorous and active tough love, and a wise and discerning approach to people and situations. The con man or con woman is not helped in his or her own spiritual journey if he or she is enabled to exploit us. In the same way, we have done no favor to a psychologically confused person when we allow our own lives to be woven by that person into a confused and distorted tapestry. Such meekness is not love and is not just. John is advocating the healthy mixture of law and gospel, of truth and grace, of wisdom and tough love.

NOTES

1.   W. M. Ramsay, quoted in Stott, *Epistles of John,* p. 198.

CHAPTER SIX—THE FAMILY OF GOD
3 JOHN 1–14

Scripture Outline

   No Greater Joy (1–8)

   A Question of Leadership (9–14)

NO GREATER JOY

1:1 The Elder,
To the beloved Gaius, whom I love in truth:
2 Beloved, I pray that you may prosper in all things and be in health, just as your soul prospers. 3 For I rejoiced greatly when brethren came and testified of the truth that is in you, just as you walk in the truth. 4 I have no greater joy than to hear that my children walk in truth.
5 Beloved, you do faithfully whatever you do for the brethren and for strangers, 6 who have borne witness of your love before the church. If you send them forward on their journey in a manner worthy of God, you will do well, 7 because they went forth for His name's sake, taking nothing from the Gentiles. 8 We therefore ought to receive such, that we may become fellow workers for the truth.

—3 John 1–8

This letter is written *"to Gaius."* Who is this man? In Acts 19:23–41 we have the narrative of Paul's terrifying and very close call at Ephesus when he was opposed by the silversmiths and the worshipers of Artemis. In that text we hear of a Macedonian named Gaius who was identified as a companion of Paul. There are two other possibilities, however—the Gaius in 1 Corinthians 1:14 and the Gaius of Derbe in Acts 20:4. The name Gaius is a common first-century name; in fact, according to Barclay, "in the world of the New Testament Gaius was the commonest of all names."[1]

As this letter opens, we are immediately struck with the fact that John is employing a more formal letter-writing style than that which we noted in 1 and 2 John. The familiar vocabulary word choices of John are used, but the compositional style is more highly structured and precise.

The crisis concerning hospitality that was the concern of 2 John is a matter of concern also in 3 John. If 2 John states the mandate on the negative side, then 3 John states the mandate on the affirmative side. If we place the two texts together, we have a very wise and encouraging counsel in the matter of hospitality toward strangers.

A QUESTION OF LEADERSHIP

⁹ I wrote to the church, but Diotrephes, who loves to have the preeminence among them, does not receive us. ¹⁰ Therefore, if I come, I will call to mind his deeds which he does, prating against us with malicious words. And not content with that, he himself does not receive the brethren, and forbids those who wish to, putting them out of the church.

¹¹ Beloved, do not imitate what is evil, but what is good. He who does good is of God, but he who does evil has not seen God.

¹² Demetrius has a good testimony from all, and from the truth itself. And we also bear witness, and you know that our testimony is true.

¹³ I had many things to write, but I do not wish to write to you with pen and ink; ¹⁴ but I hope to see you shortly, and we shall speak face to face.

Peace to you. Our friends greet you. Greet the friends by name.

—3 John 9–14

Diotrephes is a name for which we have no other New Testament evidence. From the context of this letter it appears that this man is a leader in the Christian fellowship but that he has taken a stand against John's authority. The word translated in the NKJV by "does not receive us" is a rare word in New Testament usage. The RSV translates it with the English word "authority." Besides 3 John 9 and 10, where it is used in the sense of "receive," it is used in only one other place in the New Testament, and that is Acts 15:40. The word is *epidechomai* and it means to "receive someone" or "take along someone," "recognize someone." Here it is accompanied by the negative, of course. The King James translation is truer to the sense of the word than the RSV. The Jerusalem Bible translates it "refuses to accept us." Since there is another word for "authority," I favor the more literal translation of this unusual word choice that has been adopted by the King James Bible and Jerusalem Bible.

John does not choose to describe specific issues and deeds with which Diotrephes is involved, though he does make the charge that Diotrephes is "prating against me with evil words." The word "prating" is a form of the verb *phluareō* which means "to talk nonsense, to gossip." Its use in the New Testament is limited to this single passage. The noun form is used also, by Paul in 1 Timothy 5:13 but only once: "and not only idlers but *gossips* and busybodies." We have then in this word another rare word choice evoked by John in his description of Diotrephes.

John also says of him that he "likes to put himself first" *("to have the preeminence,"* NKJV). Here again John makes use of an unusual word, *philoprōteuōn.* This word is made up of two words—*phileo,* "to love instinctively," and *prōteuōn,* which is from the root word "first." This is the only place the word is used in the New Testament. Another interesting linguistic feature in this book is John's use of the word *ekklēsia* for "church." Only here and in the Book of Revelation is this word used by John, though it is used extensively in Paul's writings.

How do we explain these unusual linguistic features? John's approach, as we have earlier observed in the Gospel of John and in 1 and 2 John, has been to employ the simplest and most common of Greek terms and expressions. Now our author has adopted a different approach to his language selection. The most logical explanation is the hypothesis that John has dictated this letter to a secretary who in transcribing the letter for John has made the unusual vocabulary choices. Another possibility is that John first wrote this letter in his native dialect of Aramaic, and then at a later date the letter was translated into Greek. These two suggestions have also been advanced in explanation of the distinctive vocabulary of the Book of Revelation. We know that Paul made use of secretary assistants in the writing of his letters (Rom. 16:22), and it is reasonable to assume that John would also take advantage of such assistance, especially if he were attempting to express the more complicated thoughts involved in the Revelation and in this difficult interpersonal church crisis in 3 John.

Diotrephes refuses to receive John, and he also refuses to receive the brothers and sisters. He "puts them out of the church." The text suggests that this church leader has taken onto himself the right to divide away and expel members of the church. We have no reasons offered or other evidence that can help us really to understand the specific reasons for his actions. All we have is John's concern about the arrogance of a church leader, an arrogance that is having a devastating effect upon the fellowship. Diotrephes is evidently a very powerful leader who has succeeded in ruling the church by his own self-contained standard. But now a check-and-balance counterforce is put into the picture. John has written this letter to call into question the runaway authority of Diotrephes.

It is always healthy when this kind of earnest dialogue can take place within the Christian church. Because of the sinfulness that we must always battle within ourselves as well as within the world, we are not surprised to find arrogance in the Christian church. In fact, if we are to stay true to the Bible, what we must not do is to imagine that it does not exist. John faces it squarely and in fact plans a personal trip to visit the church so that the issue may be resolved. Harm can be done to people's lives in the Christian church, and that harm is especially devastating when there is no voice raised for justice, for repentance, and for renewal.

In the RSV, verse 11 reads: "Do not imitate evil but imitate good." This word for "imitate," *mimeomai*, from which we have the English word "mimic," is a favorite root word of Paul's, but only in this place is it used by John. John does not want the church to follow the arrogance of Diotrephes, but to imitate good, *"agathos,"* which means literally "kindness." A severe spirit has infected the church, and that severity has crowded out love.

"Demetrius has testimony from everyone." Who is this Demetrius? One suggestion is that he may be the carrier of the letter. However, John's very strong endorsement of him seems too extensive for an individual who is simply the carrier of the epistle.

It seems more likely that Demetrius may be a person in the church who has felt the wrath of Diotrephes. Perhaps he is the person who has been punished by this powerful leader in the church.

The name Demetrius appears in Acts 19 in that same scene in which we find the name Gaius. It was Demetrius the silversmith who stirred up the city against Paul. It is also true that the name Demas (Col. 4:14; Philem. 24; 2 Tim. 4:10) is a short form of the name Demetrius.

We have no way to be certain who this man is. I find it intriguing, however, to read closely the speech of the angry Demetrius at Ephesus as he speaks out against Paul and the gospel (Acts 19:25–27). That speech is like Ivan's angry parable in the lunchroom scene of *The Brothers Karamazov*. Demetrius has sought to condemn Christ, but he has really honored Him. Listen to that angry Demetrius: "Men, you know that from this business we have our wealth. And you see and hear that not only at Ephesus but almost throughout all of Asia this Paul has persuaded and turned away a considerable company of people, saying that gods made with hands are not gods." This last sentence is fascinating because Demetrius is almost persuading himself against his own business. Once he realizes the vastness of the goodness of the God who does not need our idols, then this angry businessman will become a believer. Is it possible that this very Demetrius became a Christian and, as John was resident for much of his ministry in Ephesus, also became his friend? Now the apostle endorses to the church this convert who has such a notorious past. John stands with this friend against a tide of opposition and personally supports the integrity of Demetrius's faith and life.

"Our friends greet you" (v. 14). The Christian church is a fellowship, and friendships are made in the church that exist upon the foundation of God's love. Charles Colson's book *Life Sentence* is a powerful contemporary affirmation of the real meaning of that friendship. "In the year and a half since I had made the most important decision of my life, I had learned that Christian fellowship did not mean light-hearted fraternal gatherings but caring men and women 'bearing one another's burdens.'"[2]

It is with this note of friendship that John concludes his third letter. We have come full circle to the joy and fellowship of 1 John 1:4. The fellowship in Jesus Christ is not burdensome but joyous.

"I hope to see you soon." C. S. Lewis was right in his final shout across High Street in Oxford to his young friend Sheldon Vanauken.

> "At all events," he said with a cheerful grin, "we'll certainly meet again, here or there.". . . We shook hands, and he said, "I sha'n't say goodbye. We'll meet again." Then he plunged into the traffic. I stood there watching him. When he reached the pavement on the other side, he turned round as though he knew somehow that I would still be standing there in front of the Eastgate. Then he raised his voice in a great roar that easily overcame the noise of cars

and buses. Heads turned and at least one car swerved. "Besides," he bellowed with a great grin, "Christians *never* say goodbye!"[3]

"Name," *onoma,* is the last word in our Greek text. *"Greet everyone by name."* Because God has a name, we have names too, and our names are important because of the decision of God by which He made us, He redeemed us, and He meets us. This note of human worth and belovedness is the final stroke of the book.

NOTES

1. William Barclay, *The Letters of John* (Edinburgh: St. Andrew's Press, 1958), p. 171.

2. Charles Colson, *Life Sentence* (Lincoln, Va.: Chosen Books, 1979), p. 23.

3. Sheldon Vanauken, *A Severe Mercy* (New York: Harper & Row, 1977), p. 125.

Author's Preface—Revelation

The first attempts I made to read and understand the Book of Revelation were only partly successful. What happened to me was that my feelings and my understanding were so startled by the sights and sounds of John's vision at Patmos that I found it difficult to relate to the book. But if the Book of Revelation is a hard book to understand, it is also a hard book to put down.

Now after several years of the study and reading of the Revelation, it continues to startle me, but my understanding of it has gradually taken form, and I now am able to relate to its themes and songs and visions. This book has been very helpful to me in my own discipleship as a follower of Jesus Christ.

What will you find as you read the Revelation of John? The book opens at the prison work-camp of Patmos. John has a vision on the Lord's Day. It is a grand and stately vision of Jesus Christ as the Eternal Lord of History, and the Companion of His Church. The Seven Letters to the Seven Churches are clearly addressed to congregations of believers in the first-century Roman province of Asia (in our century, Turkey). In each of the letters there is a hiddenness of style that makes the reader aware of the pressures and intensity of persecution that threatened the Christian congregations at the time of John's writing. The songs of chapters 4 and 5 form a dramatic focal point for the Book of Revelation. They are the great high towers upon which every other theme and truth is dependent. It is something like the two towers of the Golden Gate Bridge in San Francisco Bay; the cables, steel network, and roadbed of that bridge are totally dependent upon the two mighty towers from which the whole bridge sways and stays.

The remaining chapters of Revelation are like a symphony of four vast movements followed by a postlude. Or they can be thought of as an adventure, a journey through a mysterious and dangerous terrain of sheer outcroppings and sudden downward chasms. The traveler encounters at one valley the peril of monstrous adversaries, and then the surprise of the safety, joy, and wonder of a new and promised place.

The book is about power. It is about battle. It is about freedom. It is about faith. It is about evil. It is about hope. The Book of Revelation is supremely a book about the meaning of the lordship of the Redeemer Jesus Christ. The book is a nourishing and encouraging letter, not only to seven first-century congregations, but also for us who read it two thousand years later.

I appreciate the encouragement I have received from class situations where I have taught Revelation at Union Church of Manila, First Presbyterian Church of Berkeley, and New College for Advanced Christian Studies, Berkeley. My wife, Shirley, who typed the original manuscript, and my children, Anne, Jon, and Elizabeth, have warmly encouraged me during the writing of this commentary. I also thank my secretary, Miss Dorothy Gilroy, for her assistance in typing the early chapters, and Mrs. Ruth Roderick, who typed the final revision.

Do not be afraid of a careful reading of the last book of the Bible. As with the whole of the Bible, it is God's Word for us.

—EARL PALMER

INTRODUCTION TO REVELATION

There is a choral-symphonic nature about the Book of Revelation which stirs up our feelings as much as it does our ideas. It is dramatic, forceful, yet surprisingly tender and comforting. The result is that this remarkable book is both hard to understand fully and impossible to forget. This is why the last book of the Bible must be felt as well as read. And yet this book is a thoughtful book. As hidden and mysterious as are many parts of it, nevertheless, we are able to follow its paragraphs from theme to theme. We may not understand each sentence, but there is a sense of careful order and progression throughout the twenty-two chapters, and at no time does the book trail off into nonsense or chaotic jumble.

This book is solidly anchored into the Old Testament; in fact, the Book of Revelation has more allusions to the Old Testament than any other New Testament book.[1] But the Book of Revelation in the early centuries of the church had an uneasy relationship with parts of the church. Up until A.D. 500, it was not included in the Syriac version of the New Testament; yet, on the other hand, The Revelation is attested to by more sources in the ancient church than any other New Testament book. The most ancient evidences we have from the early church show a broadly based support for the Book of Revelation and a confidence in it as a part of the canon.[2] The second-century discipleship tract *The Didache* quotes from the Revelation as do all of the church fathers.

This book has probably been understood in the deepest sense by those who have suffered the most because the book is about the victory of the Word of God in the very face of terror and evil. I believe it is significant that one of the most meaningful twentieth-century expositions of this book was written by Hans Lilje, a German Lutheran who wrote his commentary while imprisoned during the Nazi era.[3] Nevertheless, because of its unique hidden character, Revelation has also been subjected to frivolous and often arrogantly contrived interpretations throughout the history of the church. This book, which should be read and understood in its own terms, has been used by many religious movements as a textual source for selective quotation but without obedience to its own central affirmation of the gospel of Jesus Christ. In some instances, these specialized and imaginative uses of the texts of the Book of Revelation have been so alarming to ordinary Christians that they have been frightened away from this important and very good book. This may be because they were too quick to conclude that the Book of Revelation belonged to the realm of strange doctrines and cults. The fact is that throughout the history of the church, Christians have insisted that the Book of Revelation belongs to the Lord Jesus Christ to whom it bears faithful witness, and it belongs to the church, the whole church, as a vital part of the New Testament. Let us now see how important and significant this, the last book of the Bible, really is both for its place within the New Testament and as a book for our lives.

The book is unique in several ways.

1. Its Greek usage and vocabulary are so different from that of the other books of the New Testament that it has been necessary for textual scholars to develop a special grammar in order to grapple adequately with the text. The very special Greek usage of the book was first noticed by the ancient church father Dionysius of Alexander, who called it "utterly different." The book is written in Hebraic Greek, and some interpreters have speculated that it was possibly translated into Greek from an Aramaic original form. The language is poetic, and that fact also contributes to its uniqueness. Certainly the Revelation language is far different from the simple and flawlessly idiomatic Greek of John's Gospel, and 1, 2, 3 John. But at the same time, there are striking linguistic similarities to the Johannine books which we will observe within this commentary.[4]

2. The name of our Lord Jesus Christ only appears in this book in eight places. This is a noticeable contrast to other New Testament books. For example, the apostle Paul names the name of Jesus Christ nine times in Philemon, his briefest letter, which contains only twenty-five verses. It is also true that specific references to the Holy Spirit are very limited within the Revelation. The word "spirit" appears especially in chapters 1 through 3 and chapter 22, but at no place does the full New Testament term the "Holy Spirit" appear. It is interesting to note that though these two factors set the book apart from the other New Testament books, they tend to unite the book with the Gospel of John and the letters of John. John never once uses the term *"Holy* Spirit" in

1 John, but always the term "Spirit" alone. Also, John has shown in both the Gospel and 1 John that he favors a writing method which holds back from the early mentioning of the name of Jesus Christ until he has first described his Lord with other terms and phrases. Notice that in the prologue to John's Gospel the name of Jesus Christ does not appear until verse 17, and the same method of writing is used in 1 John as well.

What do we make then of this remarkable Book of Revelation? What kind of book is it?

Within the opening three sentences of Revelation, two words are used by the author himself to describe the book he is writing, and both are essential clues to its meaning. The first word is the word *"apocalypse,"* and the second is the word *"prophecy."* What exactly do these words mean? Consider first of all the very opening word in the Greek text of the book, and hence the title of the book: *"Apocalypse."* This book stands in the Old Testament—New Testament tradition of apocalyptic writing. The nature of apocalyptic literature is distinguished by the threefold mixture of hiddenness, of vast upheaval, and of decisive divine act. There is often a heavy pessimism on one page, which is then surprised by the sudden breakthrough of God's mighty act on the next page. These are marks of apocalyptic writing. Some examples of Old Testament apocalyptic writing are found in the vision passages in Ezekiel, Daniel, Isaiah, and Jeremiah. For example, listen to the words of the Book of Isaiah.

> In the year that King Uzziah died I saw the Lord sitting upon a throne, high and lifted up; and his train filled the temple. Above him stood the seraphim; each had six wings: with two he covered his face, and with two he covered his feet, and with two he flew. And one called to another and said: "Holy, holy, holy is the LORD of hosts; the whole earth is full of his glory." And the foundations of the thresholds shook at the voice of him who called, and the house was filled with smoke. And I said: "Woe is me! For I am lost; for I am a man of unclean lips, and I dwell in the midst of a people of unclean lips; for my eyes have seen the King, the LORD of hosts!"
>
> Then flew one of the seraphim to me, having in his hand a burning coal which he had taken with tongs from the altar. And he touched my mouth, and said: "Behold, this has touched your lips; your guilt is taken

away, and your sin is forgiven." And I heard the voice of the Lord saying, "Whom shall I send, and who will go for us?" Then I said, "Here am I! Send me." And he said, "Go, and say to this people: 'Hear and hear, but do not understand; see and see, but do not perceive.' Make the heart of this people fat, and their ears heavy, and shut their eyes; lest they see with their eyes, and hear with their ears, and understand with their hearts, and turn and be healed." Then I said, "How long, O Lord?" And he said: "Until cities lie waste without inhabitant, and houses without men, and the land is utterly desolate, and the LORD removes men far away, and the forsaken places are many in the midst of the land. And though a tenth remain in it, it will be burned again, like a terebinth or an oak, whose stump remains standing when it is felled." The holy seed is its stump (Is. 6, RSV).

Notice the mixture of gloom and impossibility, which demands the inevitability of severe judgment. Then in a profoundly hidden way the Lord gives to Isaiah a glimpse of sudden hope out of utterly dry and burned ground. "The holy seed is its stump." This sentence is totally apocalyptic—hidden, mysterious, wondrous. Jeremiah contains the same kind of apocalyptic message:

"See, I have set you this day over nations and over kingdoms, to pluck up and to break down, to destroy and to overthrow, to build and to plant."
And the word of the LORD came to me, saying, "Jeremiah, what do you see?" And I said, "I see a rod of almond." Then the LORD said to me, "You have seen well, for I am watching over my word to perform it."
The word of the LORD came to me a second time, saying, "What do you see?" And I said, "I see a boiling pot, facing away from the north." Then the LORD said to me, "Out of the north evil shall break forth upon all the inhabitants of the land" (Jer. 1:10–14, RSV).

The prophet is called into his ministry by the Lord. He is told of the fearsome cauldron but also, by surprise and in a hidden fashion, Jeremiah hears of the sign of the almond branch. On the one hand are dreadful events and on the other is the springlike hope of new life.

There are examples of apocalyptic teaching in the New Testament as well. A good example is in 2 Thessalonians 2:1–12, in which Paul writes very much in the same veiled and mysterious style as found in Revelation. Our Lord often speaks with these same elements of hiddenness. For example, consider the prediction Jesus makes of His own death and victory in John 2:19: "Destroy this temple, and in three days I will raise it up." When our Lord speaks these words during His first visit to Jerusalem, He says them in response to a request from the people for a sign. But none of those persons who hear His answer really understand what He is saying. In fact, they totally misunderstand Him. Even in the final hours of the Cross, the crowd will shout out to the suffering Jesus the taunt, "You who would destroy the temple, save yourself." The sentence that Jesus speaks is apocalyptic in the great tradition of Jewish apocalyptic preaching.

The theme is hidden and yet its truth is present in the saying, though it will take the breakthrough and unfolding of the hiddenness before it becomes finally clear. It is very much like the message given in the mysterious words of Jesus in John 12:31–32: "Now is the judgment of this world; now the ruler of this world will be cast out. And I, if I am lifted up from the earth, will draw all peoples to Myself." Both of these texts are very significant examples of apocalyptic teaching. The words of Jesus, recorded in Luke 21, are still another example of apocalyptic preaching. Some of the parables that Jesus tells are also apocalyptic. Note especially the parable of the shepherd as recorded in John 10.

We have as well many examples of apocalyptic writing outside of the Old Testament and New Testament. The two centuries before Christ and the two centuries afterward offer many examples—some Jewish, some Christian, some gnostic; books like the Jewish *Testaments of the Twelve Patriarchs,* or the Christian second-century tract *The Didache* (especially chapter 16), or the gnostic *Apocalypse of Peter.* In other words, it is clear and very important for us to remember as we read the Revelation that the apocalyptic way of writing was not unfamiliar to the people of the first century. The first-century Christians who were to receive the Book of Revelation were, therefore, very familiar with the sharp and bold contrasts of apocalyptic literature. They would not be either confused or surprised to receive such a book; they had already had experience with the cadences, the rhythms, and intense colors that go along with apocalyptic writing. They respected apocalyptic writing and understood some of the inner rules that must be followed when a person reads such a book.

It is a little like what happens in the realm of music. That person who has developed an understanding of the complex and subtle inner relationships of harmony, rhythm, and sound that are present in the music of rock or jazz is prepared to hear with appreciation, discernment, and joy a musical performance that another person is not able to hear with understanding, much less enjoyment! The second person may write of a rock sound: "It is too loud," or, "It all sounds the same," when, in fact, there were musical puzzles present within the music which, if only that person understood the idiom and respected some of the rules being observed within the art form, the listener would have discovered.

We must make the same sort of observation about the kind of literature that makes up so large a part of the Book of Revelation. Be sure not to forget that the very first word of the Greek text of the book is the word "apocalypse." This kind of preaching at first may sound very strange to our ears, and that is why we, as readers in the twenty-first century, need patience and care in our reading of the book. By all means, we must not avoid the imagery and colors and sounds of the Revelation any more than we should avoid the music that at first seems different and strange. We must respect the apocalyptic writing-preaching in the New Testament by listening closely to what is said and by waiting for the pieces of the puzzle to come together within the text as a whole. We must do what our Lord's disciples did with the strange words at Jerusalem, "Destroy this temple, and in three days I will raise it up." They heard what Jesus said; they did not understand its meaning; they waited until the symbolic parts of the mysterious quotation were made clear to them in the total and fulfilled context of our Lord's life, death, and victory. They waited!

Prophecy. The Book of Revelation is also called a *prophecy*. Prophetic writing is even more common in the Jewish and Christian tradition than is the apocalyptic. The largest part of the Old Testament prophets is prophetic writing. Such writing, which is theological, evangelistic, and ethical by nature, intends to call people to repentance. The prophetic message emphasizes the decision-making freedom of the people before God, whereas the apocalyptic message emphasizes the freedom of God. Prophetic preaching calls out and affirms the implications of the will of God to the people here and now and, therefore, has a more present-tense cutting edge; its meaning is not as mysterious and hidden as in the apocalyptic. The mark of the prophetic word is its clarity and its immediacy.

The New Testament preaching of Peter at Pentecost (Acts 2) is both prophetic and apocalyptic. He narrates the mysteries of the apocalyptic vision of Joel, and he also plainly tells the crowd about the ministry of Jesus and what the lordship of Jesus Christ means for them here and now as the fulfillment of the prophetic visions of the Old Testament. Then he calls upon the people to decide. Both elements are present in Paul's writings as well, though there is more of the prophetic than the apocalyptic. We shall find both forms of preaching present in the Book of Revelation, too.

3. Another important question we must ask has to do with the identity of the author. The ancient church fathers were almost universally of the opinion that the beloved disciple John was the writer of this book. (Dionysius and Eusebius were exceptions who suggested a different John as the author.) I believe that the recent experience of New Testament scholarship has taught us to weigh very heavily the witness of the ancient church, and to be cautious about developing elaborate authorship hypotheses for New Testament books that counter the early church traditional understanding.

Modern scholars have made various suggestions as to the author of this last book of the Bible. The most recent is the contention of J. M. Ford that chapters 4 through 22 are documents from John the Baptist and his followers, while chapters 1 through 3 and the close of 22 are the work of later Christian redactors. I commend J. M. Ford for the extensive research she has done on the background of Jewish and Christian apocalyptic literature, but her "John the Baptist" hypothesis is in my opinion both reckless and unwarranted in light of the internal evidence of the documents, or in view of the history of textual criticism of the text itself, or from the evidence of language usage; nor is there any support in the ancient church for such a view. The hypothesis of authorship by accumulation and by a later editorial committee is not supported by the evidence. In the end, I conclude that her thesis is as novel as it is mischievous.

Jacques Ellul has put it very well in his own commentary:

> Another current tendency to which we are also opposed
> . . . is that of fragmentation of the text. As I have
> already indicated, it is now a tradition to cut texts up

into fragments in order to discover the sources. This is a possibility not without interest, but which rarely explains anything. I do not deny that the author of the Apocalypse could possibly have used one or another text already written, but that provides us with absolutely nothing. . . . We must consider the text in its final state, because that has a value as such completely superior to the bits and pieces that compose it.[5]

I believe that the strongest evidence of all sources and from within the document points to John the son of Zebedee as the author of the book, language difficulties notwithstanding. We shall need to puzzle and wonder as to why so much of the linguistic form of the book is in stark contrast to the rest of the New Testament. It may be due to the poetic necessity, or because of the Aramaic-Hebraic background of John himself which comes to the surface as he writes this book about dreams and visions, or the writing style may be the result of a secretary (amanuensis) who may have written down John's vision. We know such secretaries aided Paul with his letters (Rom. 16:22). The similarities in theme, style, and theology to the other books of John are very impressive, so that I chose for these reasons to agree with the early church on this question.[6]

4. Now one last question: when did John write the book? The most recent research on the texts of the New Testament has brought increasing pressure toward the earlier and earlier dating of the New Testament books, so that I find the more traditional dating of this book at between A.D. 90–95 less probable than an even earlier dating just prior to or at the time of the fall of Jerusalem at about A.D. 69–72. This places the book, then, as having been written during the reign of Nero or Vespasian.

We are now ready to consider the text of the Book of Revelation.

NOTES

1. J. M. Ford identifies 400 such allusions in chapters 4 through 22, *Revelation, Anchor Bible* (New York: Doubleday).

2. See B. W. Bacon, *The Making of the New Testament.*

3. Hans Lilje, *The Last Book of the Bible* (Muhlenberg Press, 1957).

4. L. Morris has an excellent survey of this whole linguistic discussion in *The Revelation* (Grand Rapids: Eerdmans, 1969), pp. 27–32.

5. Jacques Ellul, *Apocalypse* (New York: Seabury Press, 1977), p. 18.

6. See the commentary on John's Gospel, *The Intimate Gospel* by Earl F. Palmer (Waco, Tex.: Word Books, 1980), for arguments in favor of the apostolic authorship of the Gospel of John.

T'HE BOOK OF REVELATION: AN OVERVIEW

The book as a whole begins with a Prologue (1:1–3), which is immediately followed by a First Vision (1:4–20). Chapters 2 and 3 contain Seven Letters to Seven Churches, which are located in cities scattered on the eastern side of the Mediterranean Sea. Chapter 4 contains a Song to God the Creator, and chapter 5 a Song to God the Redeemer. These two Great Chorales stand at the theological heart of the book. Following chapter 5, there begins what I call the Symphonic Part of Revelation, which in my view consists of Four Great Movements, and a final Epilogue or coda. I divide the four movements as follows:

I	6:1—11:19	*The Great Boundary*
II	12:1—16:21	*The Cosmic Baffle*
III	17:1—20:15	*The Triumph of God*
IV	21:1—22:5	*A New Heaven and a New Earth*
	22:6–21	*The Epilogue*

If I were a composer, I would compose a four-movement symphonic-choral work to express the inner drama and suspense of these texts encompassing chapters 6 through 22. There are on these pages the mixtures of sheer terror and of surprising peace; of dangers too perilous to contemplate. Then, at just the last moment, the Lion, to whom we belong, appears in our behalf. The cadences are swift, with sudden titanic jolts, and yet there is a steady, surepaced movement of sovereign intent. Such texts deserve to be stated musically by a Beethoven or Tchaikovsky or Bruckner. This book has had the attention of many artists; for example, the sixteenth-century artist Dürer carefully and in elaborate detail sketched in his own conception of the visual impact of the great visions of Revelation.

What I am now suggesting is that the Revelation needs to be heard as much as watched in terms of its sounds and rhythms. The profound and moving chorales that draw together each of the four movements should be sung. The awesome battle scenes and the jagged, awkward in-between parts might be experienced symphonically, because it is with symphonic intensity that they really emerge when the texts unfold to the reader of Revelation. The sounds confront us with such totality that descriptive words fail us.

Let me suggest one rule for biblical interpretation that I believe is valid for the study of any Old Testament or New Testament text; this rule is especially urgent for the study of this book. The rule may be stated as follows: *lean is better than luxurious.* We should beware of interpretations that import into the text itself premises or conclusions which the interpreter has already determined ahead of time. When it comes to biblical study, if we were to err, it would be better to err on the side of interpretive restraint than on the side of interpretive excess. Our goal as Christian interpreters must be first of all to let the text speak for itself, and in its own terms.

Let me give two illustrations of the importance of the principle to show what I mean in practical terms.

On one occasion, when I was teaching the Gospel of John, a student spoke to me to ask my opinion of his interpretation of certain events that are recorded by John in connection with the arrest of Jesus Christ in the garden (John 18). This person had become intrigued by one sentence in John's narrative of that incident: "When Jesus said, 'I am He,' they drew back and fell to the ground" (John 18:6). He said to me, "Do you not feel that this text gives to us an example of people swooning because of the power of the Holy Spirit over their lives?" My reply to this individual and this special interpretation of the text was that such an interpretation was luxurious in that John's narrative does not invite such an interpretation. Therefore, I cautioned him not to impose such a demand upon the garden incident. If we were to develop a theology of swooning on the basis of this incident, we would have imposed a doctrine upon the text.

The lean interpretation, which refuses to shape the incident into a previously determined doctrinal requirement, is admittedly not as fascinating at first glance, but it is still more honest to the actual text and in the end, I believe, results in the deeper interpretation of the text. Notice how a "swoon theology" grid system that is superimposed upon this narrative has the net effect of drawing the reader's attention away from the actual scene in John's account toward the highly original and imaginative doctrine of the interpreter. Our eyes are no longer upon the Lord Jesus Christ and His lonely hour but rather upon the swoon thesis of a particularized theology of the Holy

Spirit. It is my observation that luxurious interpretations of biblical texts slow and always diminish the real force and intensity of the text itself. It is a clear case where addition results in subtraction.

I believe that we must always be alert to the dangers of luxurious interpretational schemes when it comes to the Bible. Let me share one more example of the danger I am describing. I was shown a book recently that proposes the theory that the Bible is authenticated to us as God's faithful Word because of the very mathematical inner structure of the Old and New Testament vocabulary. The book advances the theory that when each letter in the Hebrew and Greek alphabets is granted a numerical weight, the result provides a basis for "proof" of the validity of the biblical witness. For example, this theory argues that the numerical weight of the Hebrew word *Elohim* is the same as the Greek word for Jesus and, therefore, this fact "proves" that the Bible teaches that Jesus is God.

Here is another example of an alien criterion that is being imposed upon the texts of the Bible. Those who impose this alien criterion do so as friends of the Bible, but the result is not friendly or helpful to the Bible. Nowhere within the Bible are we encouraged to seek our assurance of the trustworthiness of God's Word by such an elaborate and highly contrived means; rather, we are urged to hear the Word and trust God. The result of such an apologetic is to divert the attention of those who become fascinated with the argument away from hearing the meaning of the text and toward an artificial and novel theory about trustworthiness that has no basis within the text.

There are many such examples of the dangers of sometimes skillful and sometimes awkward interpretive models or grid systems that continually face us as serious readers of the Bible. I believe it is a testimony to the truth and inner integrity of the Bible as God's faithful, holy Word that, in spite of the thousands of schemes that have assaulted the Bible through the ages, the text nevertheless stands and holds its own for *what* it says and because of the One toward whom it points. The Bible makes sense to those who read it. The Holy Spirit is the convincer and convicter of the human heart and mind; therefore, we should read the text as simply as we can with as much inductive integrity as we can bring to the text. Let the words speak for themselves.

Our task then is to attempt to understand what is taught in the text and then to relate its message to our own generation and time, so that our discipleship may be obedient to the message of the Word of God. Christian faith is biblical faith; therefore, we need to be cautious in the face of all grid systems and those luxurious interpretive schemes that filter the text through a fully formed set of doctrinal expectations. We must first of all take the Book of Revelation as it is, and listen closely to what John tells us about his vision. Then we must try to understand what it means in its own setting, and for our lives today.

For me, as I write this commentary, this means that my goal in this commentary will be to understand the text of Revelation as we find it in the Bible and to then make a theological and discipleship commentary upon that text. What does the text say within its own setting, and what does it mean for our lives and our time today?

An Outline of Revelation

I. The Vision: 1:1–20
   A. The Radical Breakthrough: 1:1–3
   B. Portrait of the King: 1:4–8
   C. Lord of the Seven Lampstands: 1:9–20
II. Seven Letters to Seven Churches: 2:1—3:22
   A. The First Love: 2:1–7
   B. The Church under the Sign of Death: 2:8–11
   C. The Tempted Church: 2:12–17
   D. In the Marketplace: 2:18–29
   E. Like a Thief: 3:1–6
   F. The Open Door: 3:7–13
   G. The Best Promise: 3:14–22
III. The First Chorale: 4:1–11
   A. The Throne of God: 4:1–7
   B. The Chorale to God the Creator: 4:8–11
IV. The Second Chorale: 5:1–14
   A. A Great Scroll: 5:1–8
   B. The New Song: 5:9–14
V. The Great Symphony: 6:1—22:5
   A. Movement I: The Great Boundary: 6:1—11:19
   B. Movement II: The Cosmic Battle: 12:1—16:21
   C. Movement III: The Triumph of God: 17:1—20:15
   D. Movement IV: A New Heaven and a New Earth: 21:1—22:5
VI. Epilogue: 22:6–21
   A. Holy Colony: 22:6–11
   B. Come, Lord Jesus: 22:12–16
   C. All Who Are Thirsty: 22:17–21

Scripture Outline
> The Radical Breakthrough (1:1–3)
> Portrait of the King (1:4–8)
> Lord of the Seven Lampstands (1:9–20)

THE RADICAL BREAKTHROUGH

1:1 The Revelation of Jesus Christ, which God gave Him to show His servants—things which must shortly take place. And He sent and signified it by His angel to His servant John, **2** who bore witness to the word of God, and to the testimony of Jesus Christ, to all things that he saw. **3** Blessed is he who reads and those who hear the words of this prophecy, and keep those things which are written in it; for the time is near.
> —*Revelation 1:1–3*

We have already commented upon the two decisive words that appear in this prologue, Revelation: *apokalupsis,* "apocalypse," and *prophēteia,* "prophecy." In the case of both words, the theological emphasis in John's text is upon the divine origin of what is said. The prophet speaks on behalf of the Lord. "Thus saith the Lord" is the key phrase of Old Testament prophets, and the word *apokalupsis* means the radical uncovering or breakthrough of what was previously hidden. We are told in Revelation 1:1 that this surprising and radical breakthrough comes from Jesus Christ.

John then identifies himself as the author and by name! In the Gospel of John, the autograph of authorship was quite different; in that Gospel his autograph was the deliberate avoidance of the name John, and in that case the very fact of avoidance gives to the reader the clue to John's identity. What this means is that now, in the later period of his life, the autograph changes appropriately since the phrase used in the Gospel of John, "the one whom Jesus loved," was one that drew particular attention to the youthfulness of John during the events of the life and ministry of Jesus. Perhaps he was the youngest of the apostles. Now in his later years, that phrase is replaced by the author for a direct identification of himself. He further identifies himself as the one who *"bore witness to the word of God, and to the testimony of Jesus Christ, to all things that he saw"* (v. 2). These expressions are similar in style and vocabulary to the prologue of 1 John.

This self-description is very important from a deeper standpoint; it gives us a valuable clue to the nature of the New Testament books. John tells us that they surround the center, who is Jesus Christ, and bear witness to what Jesus said and what He did. John *heard* and *saw* the living Word of Cod.

The theological and practical importance of this is significant in that we have here, therefore, a criterion for the testing of every doctrine; the criterion is the biblical text itself as it surrounds the living center—Jesus Christ.

John's perception of himself and his writings might be seen in terms of a line model as follows:

John's witness is like a circle that surrounds and points to Jesus Christ; the witness is dependent upon the true center for its authority.

Note that by his own statement, his witness—his uncovering of the mystery—gains its authority in borrowed fashion from the center, Jesus Christ. We in our century live a step further out and must therefore test all of our doctrines on the basis of the biblical witness that surrounds Jesus Christ—the Old Testament in anticipation of that true center and the New Testament in fulfillment.

When the early church recognized John's Book of Revelation as a rightful part of the canon of the New Testament, it thereby included the Book of Revelation into that authoritative circle. When we today speak of biblical authority, what we mean is that all of our doctrines and our very lives are to be tested by that biblical witness to the living center, Jesus Christ, who, as John says here, is the Word of God.

John tells his readers that we are *"blessed"* if we hear and keep the message we are to hear from him. Seven times in the

Revelation the word *"blessed"* appears (1:3, 14:13, 16:15, 19:9, 20:6, 22:7, and 22:14). "Blessed" in Greek means simply "happy," but the Hebrew word from the Old Testament which lies behind this word in John's mind is probably the word *ashar,* and its meaning is very interesting. In Old Testament usage, the two words for "bless" are *bârak* which means kneel or bow down before, and the second is *ashar,* which means to find the right pathway in the face of false pathways. It has to do with the discovery of meaning in the face of chaos. This is the principal intent of the word "blessed" in the Proverbs. Note Proverbs 3:13 RSV: "Happy [blessed] is the man who finds wisdom, and the man who gets understanding." This is true also in the Psalms. Note Psalm 1, "Blessed is the man who walks not in the counsel of the ungodly . . . but his delight is in the law of the LORD."

John has made a profoundly Hebraic promise to us; the first of seven similar promises in Revelation. We shall be on the right pathway when we derive the meaning of our life and the pattern of our living from the character of God, from His holy will.

John has brought into focus early in his book a question that will be central: What is it that grants meaning to my life? What is it that blesses me with the true pathway in the face of tempting and false pathways? What is it that blesses me with hope in the face of dreadful dangers? John's answer to that question is that the Word of God, as it has broken in upon the world in Jesus Christ, is that "blessed" pathway that makes sense and brings the wholeness of *ashar.* According to John and his book we are in the deepest sense blessed when we have discovered that meaningful path. The times may be dangerous and awesome, as in fact John signals to us by the phrase "the time is at hand," but neither the circumstances nor a timetable about potential circumstances are themselves the pathway. Our worth, and the meaning of our life, come from God's decision about us, and not the dangers we face or the times of our history.

Dietrich Bonhoeffer expressed this same prophetic immediacy that we discover in the Book of Revelation in this way: "We live each day as if it were our last, and each day as if there was a great future because of Jesus Christ."[1] Our pathway in the present we dare to live from the decision of the eternal Father because Jesus Christ is Lord of history and we are blessed because of that fact. All of the other facts of our lives and our history are important, but not final. They affect us, but they do not define us. This is the Bible's definition of success.

C. S. Lewis has captured this sense of the biblical meaning of blessed in his novel *The Horse and His Boy*. Shasta is the name of the boy, and his journey has been a very hard one because of the task given to him to warn King Lune of the impending attack by the armies of Tash. In one scary scene, Shasta is a lone rider upon a mountain pass in the darkness; he rides an unfamiliar horse that won't obey his commands. Then Shasta is suddenly aware of a large presence alongside him. That presence is Aslan. Finally Shasta speaks out in fear, "Who are you?" The great Lion, still at this point only known as a large presence to Shasta, says to the boy, "Tell me your sorrows." Then it is that Shasta complains to the large voice of his dangerous journey, his frightening experience with lions, his unhappy childhood, and now the fact that he is hungry and thirsty and cold. The answer of Aslan is a big surprise to Shasta: "I do not call you unfortunate . . ." In other words, Shasta is blessed; he is on the right road. Then in successive waves of surprise, Shasta learns many things about his own life and journey, and the path where even now he has a task to do. The danger is still real, Shasta is still tired and hungry, but he has been blessed and he now knows that where he is, dangerous as it really is, is still where he should be, and even where he wants to be. But best of all, he has met the great Lion himself, Aslan.

When we understand the word "blessed" in this biblical context, we are not so likely to use the word as casually as we have in the past. The word is a tough word in the Bible. It does not express superficial sentiment but instead the rugged and tested assurance that it is a good thing to be walking in the pathway of God's will. We are now able to understand the provocative and strong usage of this word at the opening of our Lord's Sermon on the Mount: "Blessed are the poor in spirit. . . ."

PORTRAIT OF THE KING

4 John, to the seven churches which are in Asia:

Grace to you and peace from Him who is and who was and who is to come, and from the seven Spirits who are before His throne, 5 and from Jesus Christ, the faithful witness, the firstborn from the dead, and the ruler over the kings of the earth.

To Him who loved us and washed us from our sins in His own blood, 6 and has made us kings and priests to His God and Father, to Him be glory and dominion forever and ever. Amen.

7 Behold, He is coming with clouds, and every eye will see Him, even they who pierced Him. And all the tribes of the earth will mourn because of Him. Even so, Amen.

8 "I am the Alpha and the Omega, the Beginning and the End," says the Lord, "who is and who was and who is to come, the Almighty."

—*Revelation 1:4–8*

This text begins with the identification of seven churches *"in Asia,"* referring to the first-century Roman province of Asia, the land area on the northeastern Mediterranean in what is modern Turkey.

John uses the same phrase "grace and peace" that we find in the letters of Paul and also in the letter of 2 John. John makes the vital connection that both *"grace"*—the surprise gift—and *"peace"*—wholeness and health—come from God. By means of stiff grammatical usage, John constructs a threefold reference to God as the One who *"is now"* and who *"was"* and who *"is to come."* This deliberate enforcement of the grammar of the "to be" verb has unmistakable Jewish overtones as an allusion to the holy name of God, *Yahweh,* which in the grammar of the Hebrew language is the third-person singular of the "to be" verb. God first identified Himself to Moses by this name: "I am what I am," or "I will be what I will be" (Ex. 3:14). The Hebrew word Yahweh is the expression of this first identification that God made of Himself to Moses—literally, "He is."

The second part of the portrait given to us by John is unlike any other New Testament description of the character of God, *"And from the seven Spirits who are before His throne."* It is my understanding of this text that by this different way of expression John identifies for his readers the Holy Spirit. Later on in this chapter, and also in chapter 5, the same manner of identifying the Holy Spirit will again appear. Seven is a fulfillment number in Jewish tradition. The word seven in Hebrew means literally "Sabbath, cease, rest." Therefore, it is not so strange that it is here used first of all, not so much in a numerical sense as in fulfillment or wholeness sense. Also, there are seven churches that are to receive this letter, and I find it impressive that the Holy Spirit, who is the Creator of the church and the Sustainer of the church, should be identified in a way that highlights His ministry alongside and within the seven struggling churches of Asia Minor.

The third description is of Jesus Christ, about whom a series of statements are made. Note the different descriptions that John now makes of Jesus Christ: He, like the Father and Holy Spirit, is (1) the author of grace and peace. He is (2) the faithful witness. He is (3) first-born of the dead. He is (4) ruler of kings on earth (RSV).

Following these great noun phrases, Jesus Christ is described by means of several verbs as the One who (5) loves us;[2] who (6) has set us free from our sins by His blood (RSV). The word "blood" means His "life given" by the event of the Cross, in which Jesus Christ has once and for all identified with us and has taken our place. I believe that this is the intent of John's word "blood."[3] John continues: Jesus Christ has (7) made us a kingdom, priests, to His God and Father (RSV). (8) To Him be glory and dominion forever. (9) He is coming again. This is the ninth description that John gives of Jesus Christ.

Finally, John draws together the total portrait with the words: "'I am the Alpha and Omega, the Beginning and the End,' says the Lord, . . . 'the Almighty.'" The first letter of the Greek alphabet is alpha, and the last is omega. Notice that the affirmation that all of history, its beginning and its ending, is bounded by the decision of God is stated at both the opening and the close of this portrait.

What has been presented to us in this prophetic announcement is a dramatic theological statement of triune Christian faith. God the Father is described as Yahweh, the One who ultimately is, and who makes Himself known, the One who is author of grace and peace. The Holy Spirit is described as being in fellowship with the Father and Son (v. 4) and who from that presence also sends grace and peace to the churches. Jesus Christ is described in the most detail because as the living Word in Jesus Christ, God is speaking for Himself, the very radical breakthrough of God in history. Jesus Christ is God making Himself known as Lord, Savior, Victor over death, as the One who loves and sets free by the event of His own suffering on our behalf, the One who is now our living Lord and who will come again.

This portrait of God's character also uncovers two secondary portraits. The one has to do with the Christians in Asia, and the other has to do with the meaning of history itself. First of all, notice the features of John's portrait of the churches: (1) They are the gatherings (the word "church" is literally the Greek word for gathering), real people in real places. They exist in seven actual cities in a Roman province. (2) They are people to whom God the Father, Son, and Holy Spirit sends grace and peace. Therefore, at the outset we are reminded of the love of God for people. (3) Note that John includes himself with the churches, and claims that we are the ones whom Jesus Christ *loves* here and now, present tense, not only by a sacrificial moment in the past, but in the living present. (4) John also affirms that we have been *set free* from our sins by the costly grace of Jesus; and this gift of freedom is a very dynamic daily experience and obligation for those who receive it. That sense of dynamic ongoing significance of freedom is preserved here by the way the sentence continues. (5) *We are made a kingdom* (RSV). John gives us here a fascinating insight into the kingdom theology of the New Testament. The kingdom of God is not seen in the New Testament in territorial terms, but rather in relationship terms. "It is the Kingly Reign of Jesus Christ" (Bonhoeffer). Ordinary and garden-variety people who receive the love and freedom from Christ are the ones who, as we are willing to become Christ's servants (1:1), thereby become His very kingdom in the world. (6) Immediately in this context we are all described as priests, that is, as those who have the task of reconciliation granted to us. Consider the way we are described: servants, in 1:1; blessed, in 1:3; beloved, 1:4–5; set free, 1:5; and, 1:6, now commissioned to represent the kingship of God in the world as His priests and as citizens of His kingly reign. (7) John's final comment in this passage about the kingdom people is that with all of the human family we will *witness the mighty return of the High King,* Jesus Christ.

At this point in our study, let me suggest that a creative way to study any New Testament book is to track the development within the book of the major themes about which the author is writing. For example, in John's Gospel, it is helpful to track throughout the Gospel the unfolding portrait of who Jesus Christ is and what He is like. John invites his readers to do just that in his comment in John 20:30–31. Let me suggest that you will also benefit as you track themes throughout this book. We have in this part of the text tracked the unfolding portrayal and disclosure of God the Father, Son, and Holy Spirit. Continue to track this theme throughout the whole of the Book of Revelation.

In addition to the portrayal of God's character, so we who read the book in a fascinating and parallel fashion are introduced to ourselves, and we learn of our own worth, the meaning of our lives, and the task of our living in the world. We also gain a perspective from these opening verses as to the meaning of history itself, which becomes one of the central themes in this book. These themes, too, should be tracked.

We have discovered to this point in the book that this letter is addressed to people within the time and space frame of the real history of the first century. The existence of earthly kings is acknowledged, and the names and places of first-century cities are to play a major part in the book. Moreover, the book is not only about the church, but it is also about the age within which the church exists.

This portrait concludes, as it begins, with the affirmation that all of history is bounded by the decision of God. The word "amen" which appears in the text in two decisive points is the literal Hebrew word *amen*. Within the Old Testament, *amen* means faithful when it refers to God, and it means having faith when it refers to human beings. This means that faith in the Old Testament understanding of *amen* contains the sense of trusting in the faithfulness of God. "Even so God is faithful." That is the intent of John's statement in the text.

Let me make a final reflection upon this passage. Notice that in the New Testament world of thought we make discoveries about who *we* are while we are pondering the revelation of who *God* is. We discover our own belovedness when we perceive the love of God. When we catch a vision of God's love for all the earth, we then catch a clear and awesome vision of our task toward the creation as His priests. When we discover that all of history is bounded by the decision of God, we are set free from the need to panic about our own generation; instead, we are challenged to take hold of our time as disciples of Jesus Christ. What we do and say has lasting significance because of Jesus Christ.

THE LORD OF THE SEVEN LAMPSTANDS

⁹ I, John, both your brother and companion in the tribulation and kingdom and patience of Jesus Christ, was on the island that is called Patmos for the word of God and for the testimony of Jesus Christ. ¹⁰ I was in the Spirit on the Lord's Day, and I heard behind me a loud voice, as of a trumpet, ¹¹ saying, "I am the Alpha and the Omega, the First and the Last," and, "What you see, write in a book and send it to the seven churches which are in Asia: to Ephesus, to Smyrna, to Pergamos, to Thyatira, to Sardis, to Philadelphia, and to Laodicea."

¹² Then I turned to see the voice that spoke with me. And having turned I saw seven golden lampstands, ¹³ and in the midst of the seven lampstands One like the Son of Man,

clothed with a garment down to the feet and girded about the chest with a golden band. [14] His head and hair were white like wool, as white as snow, and His eyes like a flame of fire; [15] His feet were like fine brass, as if refined in a furnace, and His voice as the sound of many waters; [16] He had in His right hand seven stars, out of His mouth went a sharp two-edged sword, and His countenance was like the sun shining in its strength. [17] And when I saw Him, I fell at His feet as dead. But He laid His right hand on me, saying to me, "Do not be afraid; I am the First and the Last. [18] I am He who lives, and was dead, and behold, I am alive forevermore. Amen. And I have the keys of Hades and of Death. [19] Write the things which you have seen, and the things which are, and the things which will take place after this. [20] The mystery of the seven stars which you saw in My right hand, and the seven golden lampstands: The seven stars are the angels of the seven churches, and the seven lampstands which you saw are the seven churches.

—Revelation 1:9–20

John identifies himself as a brother to the Christians who are to receive this letter. He wants them to know that because of his witness to Jesus Christ he is imprisoned on the island of Patmos. This small, 8 x 4-mile island is one of the Dodecanese islands off the coast of Turkey. Scholars of the first-century period have found evidences that the Roman government maintained rock quarries on Patmos to which prisoners and banished troublemakers were sent to live out their lives. I want to make the linguistic observation at this point that the use of hidden and cryptic language by the writer of this book may be due at least in part to the realities of that banishment, and the need for caution, especially with reference to the seven letters to the seven city churches nearby.

John tells his readers he was *"in the Spirit"* (v. 10). This phrase would not be an uncommon way of expressing worship to an early Christian reader. Our Lord tells the Samaritan woman that God seeks those who will worship Him "in Spirit" and in truth (John 4:24). Paul uses the exact phrase "in the Spirit" in 1 Corinthians 14:2. However, the expression *"the Lord's Day"* is new, and does not appear at any other place in the New Testament. We assume John means by this phrase the first day of the week, because that is the sense in which the early Christians would later make use of this expression. There is evidence that

New Testament Christians met together on the first day of the week, as we note in Acts 20:7 and 1 Corinthians 16:2, but it is in the Revelation that a title is given that will, from that time onward, describe the day for the Christian church: *the Lord's Day,* the day in which we remember the victory of Christ over death.

John tells his readers that he heard a voice "like" a trumpet. Notice that a distinction is made by the author which shows that he will be endeavoring to express by words, inadequate as they are, the vision he has experienced. He does not say he heard a trumpet, but rather that the loud voice he heard could best be described as sounding like the sound of a trumpet. John, the poet, is here setting forth for us, his readers, the linguistic ground rules for his book. Throughout this book, he will describe the flood of visions that are too immense for the limited possibilities of language. It is very important that interpreters of John's visions remain faithful to John's ground rules; otherwise, the theological heart of the book could easily become blurred and even distorted by a fascination with the remarkable vocabulary of the book. The linguistic signposts, as we discover here, should be closely observed by the reader, since it is the theological discipleship pathway that is the goal of the book.

What are the ground rules for interpretation that we who read the Book of Revelation should therefore observe? I will suggest three basic guidelines that I feel are essential for the interpretation of the vision portions of the book, as indeed for any other book in the Old or New Testament.

1. First we shall endeavor to understand each passage within its own immediate textual setting. In other words, how does the text define and explain itself? Our very first goal will be to understand each image or vision description in that way.

2. In the case of vision imagery within this book, the next step will be to seek clues to the possible intent or meaning of an image or word choice for parallel descriptions in the Old Testament or in other parts of the New Testament. In some instances, intertestamental books will also give us interpretive assistance.

3. We will stand back in reverence and restraint when a particular sentence or image or choice is not clear. This is the application of the "lean-is-better-than-luxurious" interpretive guideline. At several places within this remarkable book, there will be times when we as readers of the book will be most loyal to the text by restraining our natural desire to immediately develop a theory of interpretation. We who read of the fascinating vision of John

must not miss the discipleship teaching of Revelation because we become entangled in the designs that adorned the signposts.

You will note that at this point in the text (1:11), our New King James Version repeats the sentence stated earlier in our text (1:8): *"I am the Alpha and the Omega, the First and the Last."* This sentence does not appear in the most ancient Greek manuscripts in verse 11.

When John turns to look toward the voice, he sees seven golden lampstands, and one like a Son of Man.[4] We are then granted a profoundly moving description of Jesus Christ standing in the midst of the seven lampstands. John's vision brings to mind many Old Testament messianic phrases and images: *"Son of Man"* is a messianic phrase from Daniel (7:13); the white wool is found in Daniel 7:9 and the flame of fire in Daniel 10:6; the sound of water is from Ezekiel 43:2 and the sword from Isaiah 49:2. Though the name of our Lord does not appear in this description, it is clear that Jesus is the One whom John has seen. "I died, and behold I am alive forevermore" (Rev. 1:18 RSV). In the vision, John is assured of the reign of Jesus Christ, even over death and the place of death (Hades). At the close of the vision, the seven lampstands and the stars are explained to John. The stars are the messengers *("angel"* is literally the word "messenger") of the churches, and the lampstands are identified as the seven churches in Asia Minor. Most of the vision images we will later read in this book will not be so fully interpreted for us, but these images are interpreted and, therefore, we are encouraged to reflect with more boldness upon their meaning.

This is a vision of Jesus Christ that is both awesome and comforting. The feelings I have in this vision are like the feelings that Peter seemed to have in the fishing incident of Luke 5. He finally *discovered* Jesus so that now he understands the majesty of who Jesus Christ really is, and in the presence of that discovery he can only say, "Depart from me, for I am a sinful man . . ." (Luke 5:8). But the words that Peter then hears from his Lord are the same words that John hears: "Fear not." We must be careful to keep the two feelings together in the interpretation of this experience of John. The vision is frightening, but not devastating. He is struck down by its impact, and then quickly lifted up. He discovers both the sovereign, divine otherness of Jesus Christ, so vast that words fail to describe the wonder, and also the kindness and sensitivity of Jesus. Jesus is not a ghost, a vapor from the realm of death, and this is the first great fact John is told. "Fear not, I am . . . the living One" (v. 18, RSV).

The result for John, as it was for Peter at Galilee, is not despair, but joy. The Lord who *found* John and the disciples on that first day of the week after Good Friday has again found His friend at the rock quarry of Patmos on the first day of the week. What a reunion! I think it is just this kind of breakthrough that G. K. Chesterton was describing in his marvelous sentence, "The serious business of heaven is joy."

John makes no secret of the fact that he himself and the churches to which he writes are in danger. Note these words to be found in verse 9 of the RSV: "tribulation . . . kingdom . . . patient endurance. . . ." What is a surprise, however, is that he places the word *kingdom* in the middle of these expressions! This realism mixed with hope is a mark of the New Testament throughout. There is no escapism in the New Testament. The New Testament people are set within a real world; it is within that twenty-four-hour-a-day world that the gospel works! The kingdom is squarely planted within the turbulent line of history, and on that turbulent line it has been granted a strategy for not only its survival but also its mission.

But John makes another discovery, and that discovery is the unfolding of the mystery about the seven churches, called *"lamp-stands."* Jesus Christ is in their midst, and the messengers of the churches are in His hand. We cannot be certain what the reference to the messengers may fully imply, but it is clear that the churches are very important to the living Lord, and He has not abandoned them. They are of priceless value (gold); they give light (much like the image of a city set on a hill given by Jesus in the Sermon on the Mount in Matt. 5). These seven churches will learn even more in the seven letters that follow concerning the vision and its meaning.

Theologically, this portrayal of the Christian church is of very decisive importance for the formation of healthy church doctrine for us today. Notice that the churches are not only addressed in their uniqueness, and indeed each one will receive a specific letter, but they are also addressed in their connectedness to each other. But also notice that this connectedness, about which modern ecclesiologists are often preoccupied, is not a connectedness of government or polity, but of the common center and the common source of life. It is Jesus Christ who unites the seven lamp-stands by the reality of His presence in their midst. This is the only source of living for the church: it is more fundamental than the order of the apostolic succession of bishops, or of a common experience of the gifts of the Holy Spirit. It is the unity of the common Savior-Lord. It is the living Word and the gospel that surrounds that Word which give order and unity to the church through the confirming ministry of the Holy Spirit.

Therefore, we have theologically come full circle back to the centrality of Jesus Christ. His authority makes the church possible in the first place, and as we shall see in the seven messages to the seven churches, our obedience to Jesus Christ as the true center will be the criterion by which the seven churches are judged.

NOTES

1. Dietrich Bonhoeffer, *Letters and Papers from Prison* (New York: Macmillan), p. 15.

2. The King James text is incorrect in its rendering of the verb "love" in past tense in this verse. In the Greek, it is the present tense that is used by John.

3. Once again, the King James translation has incorrectly translated the verb, with the word "washed." The Greek word is *lusanti,* which means "loosed."

4. "A son of man" is the correct translation, since the definite article "the" does not appear in the Greek.

CHAPTER TWO—SEVEN LETTERS TO SEVEN CHURCHES
REVELATION 2:1—3:22

Scripture Outline

    The First Love (2:1–7)

    The Church under the Sign of Death (2:8–11)

    The Tempted Church (2:12–17)

    In the Marketplace (2:18–29)

    Like a Thief (3:1–6)

    The Open Door (3:7–13)

    The Best Promise (3:14–22)

THE FIRST LOVE

2:1 "To the angel of the church of Ephesus write,

'These things says He who holds the seven stars in His right hand, who walks in the midst of the seven golden lampstands: **2** "I know your works, your labor, your patience, and that you cannot bear those who are evil. And you have tested those who say they are apostles and are not, and have found them liars; **3** and you have persevered and have patience, and have labored for My name's sake and have not become weary. **4** Nevertheless I have this against you, that you have left your first love. **5** Remember therefore from where you have fallen; repent and do the first works, or else I will come to you quickly and remove your lampstand from its place—unless you repent. **6** But this you have, that you hate the deeds of the Nicolaitans, which I also hate.

7 "He who has an ear, let him hear what the Spirit says to the churches. To him who overcomes I will give to eat from the tree of life, which is in the midst of the Paradise of God."

—Revelation 2:1-7

The first letter is written to the church of Ephesus. This city, though not the capital of the province of Asia, is the most well-known city in the province. The trade route from the Euphrates civilizations terminated at Ephesus. It was a beautiful city with great temples, the most notable being the temple to Artemis, which was one of the seven wonders of the ancient world. The famous amphitheater which could seat 45,000 people was also a grand monument in the city. The city was well known for its Greek-Roman mystery cult religions, and in fact "Ephesus charms" were sold widely as ensurers of good luck. Paul had been in this city, as had been Timothy, Priscilla, Aquila, and Apollos. According to the tradition of the early church, the apostle John himself also lived in Ephesus in his old age.

To this city comes the first word from the Lord of the seven lampstands. Notice that the words to each of the seven churches are similar in form, though each letter is unique. All the letters contain references to the imagery of John's vision in chapter 1. In each case, the messenger *("angel")* of the church is addressed. In each case, the people are told that Jesus Christ *knows* (discerns) who they are and where they are. In each case, there are three parts to the message: a statement about the church, an exhortation, and a promise. Toward the close of each letter, the word *overcome* is used, e.g., *"To him who overcomes . . ."* (2:7). In the context of the letters the word "overcome" becomes a strong expression for "repent."

The Ephesian Christians are described as brave, as hardworking, and as people who are devoted to the truth over/against falsehood. They hold to the central truth about God with courage and perseverance. The only clue we have in this first of the letters as to the nature of the falsehood which the Ephesian Christians have resisted is the one-sentence reference toward the close of the letter *you hate the deeds of the Nicolaitans, which I also hate"* (2:6). What are the false doctrines and works of the Nicolaitans? This is not an easy question to answer. We have no other reference in the New Testament to this movement. There is no reason to relate what John calls the Nicolaitans to the disciple called Nicolaus of Acts 6:5. The question then is, who are they? What do they teach? The early church father Hippolytus (Haereses 7:24) identifies the Nicolaitans as an early protognostic group who practiced immorality. We are strongly influenced toward this view by the second reference to this group in the letter to the Church of Pergamos where the Nicolaitans are identified as those who are immoral, who worship idols and hold to the teachings of Balaam. This is a very fascinating connection, because in Philo's writings (a first-century Jewish writer), Balaam is called a great sorcerer. He is also described as a false prophet in Jude 11. Balaam's role in the life of early Israel (Num. 22–25) is a complex and murky story to trace, but when the result of his life is summed up in Numbers 31:16, the evaluation is negative: "Behold, these caused the people of Israel, by the counsel of Balaam, to act treacherously against the Lord" (RSV). Thus Balaam, as a sorcerer and as an opportunistic false prophet, becomes the hidden symbol in Revelation of such false teaching.

But the Ephesian Christians have a serious problem in spite of their doctrinal purity and their resistance to the false teachers. There is tremendous impact in the very word order of the Greek sentence of verse 4 which announces their crisis. The sentence in the literal order of the Greek sentence would read as follows: "But I have against you this the love (agapē is the word used here), you the first (and now at the end of the sentence comes the all-important verb) you abandoned." This is the problem of the brothers and sisters at Ephesus. Somehow they have left behind the very best and the most important of all their discoveries.

The way the text is written resists any sort of limitation upon the extent of the Ephesian problem. The crisis at Ephesus is total. They had left behind the first love. This totality means that there was a theological, spiritual, psychological, and an ethical crisis at Ephesus. We can only wonder how this happened. Had the Ephesian Christians outgrown in their own thinking their need for God's grace? Perhaps in their view they had gone on beyond such a primitive bedrock fact as the agapē love of God, and in their "progress" they had moved on toward "deeper" theological truth.

In this way the love of God had become for the Ephesians a theoretical starting fact, one of the sentences on the menu, but not the very daily bread by which they were even alive in the first place and through which they would continue to stay alive. This was a spiritual illness that haunted Ephesus, and until this letter arrived, it was an illness of which they were probably unaware. It was not only a spiritual but also a theological crisis for Ephesus, because if they had left the agapē love behind, it meant that some other fact or doctrinal truth for them would then have been integrating and motivating their theological existence. But there was no other integrating center apart from the first love, which theologically could only refer to the redeeming love of Jesus Christ.

The battle against idolatry in which the Ephesians heroically shone was always a secondary and never a primary concern for Christian discipleship and theology. What was and is primary is the first love, and in fact without that center all of the secondary Christian concerns become corrosive, because apart from their true center they inevitably move toward theological specialization and self-righteousness.

The Ephesian Church was in crisis psychologically as well. The first love starting point of biblical Christianity embraces an anthropology that is realistic about human personality. The search for psychological meaning is resolved in the revelation of God's character in Jesus Christ, and from that center there is the basis for a healthy understanding of the human being that faces up squarely to who we are, to the complexity of personality, to the reality of sinfulness. It is the only source for the resolution of sinfulness and that is because of God's love. Then and only then are we able to *celebrate* who we are. Therefore, from the first love comes a healthy way of looking at the self. Take away or sidetrack that healthy source, and psychologically the Ephesians were (and we are) uprooted from the nourishment that human personality needs to stay whole.

The first love is also a fundamental first principle that ethics must begin at the beginning. We have a gospel ethic that starts and exists in and from the love of Christ for the world; it is an ethic that moves out toward that world through us as we ourselves discover and obey that first love. In New Testament ethics, it is not so much that we are commanded to love as that in the gospel we experience the love that commands. The Barmen Declaration of 1934, written by the German confessing Christians, was correct in its ordering of the mandates of Christianity. At the very beginning they affirmed the first love, and then secondly they grappled with the false gods of twentieth-century Europe. Article I of the Barmen Declaration begins, "Jesus Christ is the one word we have to hear and obey both in life and in death." All healthy theology, ethics, and also Christian psychology begin with this discovery of the first love which is revealed in Jesus Christ. "In this is love, not that we loved God, but that He loved us and sent His Son" (1 John 4:10).

How could it happen? Did the Ephesians intellectually outgrow their most exciting idea? Did the dangers of the battle against false teaching harden them so that they failed to trust the power of God's love? Did they resent the childlike dependence that their first-love discovery invited from them? Did they resent the maturity and freedom demanded by God's love, since to know that one is beloved sets a person free from the games and deceptions we use to hide behind when we really feel unloved?

The "Ephesus problem" happens quietly and by gradual, imperceptible shifts of focus. Let me sketch in a contemporary scenario that may explain this devastating shift of focus. What happens is that a man or woman is first united with the Christian church because of having discovered and believed in Jesus Christ and His love. After a few years of being a Christian, that person becomes a leader in the church with very heavy responsibilities for the fellowship. But something happens along the way. That person who, because of giftedness and hard work may now stand at the vortex of church politics and decision-making, experiences a subtle shift in style of life. That person is adrift as a disciple and finds himself or herself motivated and nourished by the organization or by the controversy or by ambition to hold power. The first love has been replaced while perhaps no one was aware of the replacement. The first love has been abandoned and in its place is the starchy, high cholesterol diet of activity and church work that will never nourish the human soul.

The irony of this latter condition of the "Ephesus syndrome" is that the Christian becomes totally preoccupied, fascinated by themes and goals which would have never won him or her in the first place to have joined the church: arguments over fine doctrinal points, distinctives of polity, esoteric giftedness, etc. How can it happen to us? It happens to marriages; it happens to human friendships; it happens to the life of discipleship.

This stern and good letter to the Christians at Ephesus is a letter to all persons who have drifted into the loss of first love. There is no easy solution for Ephesus. They must vigorously repent and rediscover the true center. When such wanderlust takes over our lives, what we need to hear is the sharp prophetic command of a loving adversary—Stop! What we need to experience is the kind of cold water in our faces that God's people heard from the Lord's Prophet:

> When you come to appear before me, who requires of you this trampling of my courts? Bring no more vain offerings; incense is an abomination to me. New moon and sabbath and the calling of assemblies—I cannot endure iniquity and solemn assembly. Your new moons and your appointed feasts my soul hates; they have

become a burden to me, I am weary of bearing them. When you spread forth your hands, I will hide my eyes from you; even though you make many prayers, I will not listen; your hands are full of blood. Wash yourselves; make yourselves clean; remove the evil of your doings from before my eyes; cease to do evil, learn to do good; seek justice, correct oppression; defend the fatherless, plead for the widow. Come now, let us reason together, says the LORD: though your sins are like scarlet, they shall be as white as snow; though they are red like crimson, they shall become like wool. If you are willing and obedient, you shall eat the good of the land; but if you refuse and rebel, you shall be devoured by the sword; for the mouth of the LORD has spoken (Is. 1:12–20, RSV).

This letter to the Christians at Ephesus is in the same tradition as the Isaiah confrontation. This letter does not explain the downward slide; instead it abruptly shouts out the warning to the church at Ephesus about the devastating result. There is an overwhelming forcefulness in the warning, and yet the gracious word of hope is spoken to those who repent. I interpret the word "overcome" that appears at the close of each letter as another term for repentance; it is a term that emphasizes the totality and the life-changing power of repentance. When we turn in genuine repentance toward the Lord who speaks these words, the result is full-scale victory. This is how powerful the first love really is, and the Ephesians need to realize the nature of that true and awesome source of power.

The promise contains a reference to the *"tree of life"* which may possibly refer to Genesis 2:9. It is also an interesting sign to the Ephesians in another way. Ephesian coins of this period contain engravings of a sacred tree used in the nature worship of first-century Ephesus. The Christians at Ephesus are assured of a source of life that originates from a deeper reality than that which the cultic nature goddess images of their city coins are able to confer. This letter has found the Ephesians where they are, and has called them to return to the source of their life, to the good beginning where they started.

THE CHURCH UNDER THE SIGN OF DEATH
Letter 2

8 "And to the angel of the church in Smyrna write,
'These things says the First and the Last, who was dead,
and came to life: 9 "I know your works, tribulation, and

poverty (but you are rich); and I know the blasphemy of those who say they are Jews and are not, but are a synagogue of Satan. [10] Do not fear any of those things which you are about to suffer. Indeed, the devil is about to throw some of you into prison, that you may be tested, and you will have tribulation ten days. Be faithful until death, and I will give you the crown of life.

[11] "He who has an ear, let him hear what the Spirit says to the churches. He who overcomes shall not be hurt by the second death." '

—Revelation 2:8–11

Smyrna is a coastal city of great wealth, some forty miles north of Ephesus. It is an old city that was founded about 1200 B.C. There is evidence that first-century Jewish settlements in Asia Minor had compromised their pure monotheism and in certain of the synagogues of these Greek-Roman cities had imported into their worship the worship of Zeus.[1] In addition, Smyrna was noted as a strong center of emperor worship. In 195 B.C. a temple to the Goddess of Rome was constructed, and in A.D. 26 a temple to Tiberius was also constructed. These and other temples were built upon an acropolis which produced a very dramatic visual effect and was popularly described by the phrase "the Crown of Smyrna."

The Christian church in this city is a suffering church. The very strong word "tribulation" (Gk., *thlipsis),* which denotes crushing pressure, is used to describe the experiences of these Christians. They live in a wealthy city, but they are poor. Poverty is always a harder burden to bear in the centers of wealth, not only because of the inflationary economic pressure within a prosperous city, but because of the oppressive contrast between rich and poor. But their gravest suffering has to do evidently with the persecution that overshadows the future. This persecution may be coming because of slander from those syncretistic members of the synagogue who worship Zeus, or from those citizens of Smyrna who worship the emperor of Rome and who are now persecuting the church in Smyrna.

But the Christians are challenged by the Christ who died and lives not to fear this coming threat to them. They are told that the devil is the power that orchestrates their coming peril, but that his authority is limited. This is the most obvious interpretation of the term *"ten days"* in verse 10. The devil has power, but there are limits to that power. Even if Christians at Smyrna were to perish in the coming trials, they are promised that death itself is bounded by the decision of God. The term *"second death"* (v. 11) appears here in this context. This phrase is not used in any other New Testament book, but does appear in the Revelation in four places (Rev. 2:11, 20:6, 20:14, 21:8). Whatever the term means, it pictures for the Christians at Smyrna the larger context into which their life and their death are placed. The power of evil is not the final power.

This is the first place in the Revelation where the existence of the devil has been mentioned. Two words for the devil are used in this paragraph: (1) *"Satan,"* which in English is a direct transliteration of the Greek word *Satan,* literally "adversary," and (2) the word translated *"devil,"* which is the Greek *diabolas,* literally "slanderer."

From this passage, and other places in the Bible, we are confronted with the biblical recognition of the existence of the devil. The portrayal of the devil throughout the Bible is that of personal will against the will of God at the cosmic level of the created order. It is clear in this passage that the devil has both freedom and power. God in His sovereign wisdom has granted freedom not only in the human realm of the created order, but at the cosmic level as well, so that the devil is possible only because of that sovereign decision made by God. Now in this text we learn of the devil's will against God's will, and against God's people, but we also have learned that the power of the devil is not ultimate or final. There is a limit upon his reign of terror.

Note that in each letter the plural is used at the close of the letters: *". . . hear what the Spirit says to the churches"* (2:7, 11, 17, 29; 3:6, 13, 22). This means that all of the churches, not alone the congregation at Smyrna, are challenged in this letter to join with the suffering Christians at Smyrna in not fearing the devil.

The Book of Revelation is realistic about the existence of evil in the world. There is harm which must be squarely faced for what it is. No attempt is made to explain away the reality of evil in its many forms. It is neither true nor helpful for the Christian to interpret all crisis events in the story of human existence as "according to God's will."

There are many events that happen in our lives that are *against God's will.* The speeding car that crashes because its driver was under the influence of alcohol or drugs is not an event that happened according to God's will. Murder, suicide, adultery, racism, white-collar crime—these acts of violence are against the will of God. They are the result of the bad use of freedom which sours into chaos and menace. The mystery of the real freedom that God designed into our human journey has made human evil possible just as that same mystery of design has made faith and hope and love possible, too.

But evil has a larger dimension than simply the bad choices that we make as human beings. There is the cosmic dimension which this letter to the church at Smyrna puts into sharp focus. The bad choice against the will of God at the cosmic level of creation produces its own kind of chaos. The clear affirmation of this letter is that cosmic evil as well as human evil are bounded by the greater boundary of Almighty God. The evil and its damage are a real danger, but that damage is not ultimate; the last word, both of judgment and of hope, belongs to God.

How does this work in practical terms? It means that as a Christian I am able to face up to tragedy as tragedy and not artificially to assume the stance that it has somehow not really happened. It means that there are bad experiences and events that happen to us and because of us. These events are negative and harmful. They are like jagged rocks that scar the landscape of our life's journey. But the discovery we make in the gospel of Jesus Christ is that the very landscape upon which these angry outcroppings stand is surrounded by a larger grace and will so that life can go on. The field will grow seed and bear healthy crops because the power of God's gift of life is greater than the deadening effects of either human sin or cosmic evil. This is the reason we do not lose hope; this is also the reason we are enabled to call a jagged rock a jagged rock. *"I will give you the crown of life."*

This letter is a strong rebuke to the cultisms of fear that have thrived in unusual numbers within the past century. The major temptation of the cultisms of fear is their claim that because of the immensity of the needs and dangers of this age, demonic and otherwise, the gospel of Jesus Christ of itself is no match for such dangers. Therefore, they argue that we who would survive in such perilous times will need the special aid that only this or that cultic movement has to offer. It may be machine guns, or it may be special spiritual strategies known uniquely and especially to the leader of the movement. The only way that this temptation is able to undermine our faith in Jesus Christ, and His sufficiency, is if the power of the devil can be inflated beyond its actual size. The letter to the church at Smyrna is an antidote to such cultism. The resources we have in Jesus Christ are fully adequate. They are the resources we need—the *only* resources we need.

This second letter ends with a very personal assurance to the Christians who live in the shadow of Smyrna's acropolis: *"I will give you the crown—not of Smyrna—but of life"* (v. 10). What an exciting and deeply personal greeting to these people. Their Lord knows their city as well as He knows them. That helps too.

THE TEMPTED CHURCH
Letter 3

12 "And to the angel of the church in Pergamos write, 'These things says He who has the sharp two-edged sword: 13 "I know your works, and where you dwell, where Satan's throne is. And you hold fast to My name, and did not deny My faith even in the days in which Antipas was My faithful martyr, who was killed among you, where Satan dwells. 14 But I have a few things against you, because you have there those who hold the doctrine of Balaam, who taught Balak to put a stumbling block before the children of Israel, to eat things sacrificed to idols, and to commit sexual immorality. 15 Thus you also have those who hold the doctrine of the Nicolaitans, which thing I hate. 16 Repent, or else I will come to you quickly and will fight against them with the sword of My mouth.

17 "He who has an ear, let him hear what the Spirit says to the churches. To him who overcomes I will give some of the hidden manna to eat. And I will give him a white stone, and on the stone a new name written which no one knows except him who receives it."'

—Revelation 2:12–1 7

In the year 133 B.C., Pergamum (Pergamos, NKJV) became the capital of the Roman province of Asia. This city is forty-five miles north of Smyrna, and is built upon a high rock outcropping, a natural fortress. It had become, by the time of the first century, the center of emperor worship in the Roman world. There are many impressive temples in Pergamum—to Zeus, Athena, Nikephoids, Dionysus—but the city was most famous for its temples to Asklepios.

Two references in this letter point in an indirect way to the fact that Pergamum is the capital city of Asia: one is the reference to the "throne of Satan" (v. 13) and the other is the twofold reference to the sword: the words of him *"who has the sharp two-edged sword"* (v. 12) and *"the sword of My mouth"* (v. 16). The Romans expressed the authority of governors of provinces in terms of the "right of the sword." Thus there is a direct play on words within the text as the Christians at Pergamum are reminded that it is Jesus Christ who reigns and who holds the two-edged sword of ultimate authority. The letter tells of a disciple named Antipas who was slain for his faith. We have no other New Testament witness to Antipas apart from this moving tribute to his faithfulness.

The church is challenged to repent of the Balaam-Nicolaitan error. In other words, some of these Christians have been tempted by Nicolaitan false teaching which has lured them toward the sins of idolatry and interpersonal immorality.[2] The Christians are called to repent, and they are warned that the Lord will war against His own people if they fail to repent of these grave sins. Notice that this warning language is in the same prophetic style as that which is found in the prophetic passages of the Old Testament. It will be instructive for us to note an example of this prophetic style.

Listen to Jeremiah's prophecy of judgment upon the people of God: ". . . All your lovers have forgotten you; they care nothing for you; for I have dealt you the blow of an enemy, the punishment of a merciless foe, because your guilt is great" (Jer. 30:14, RSV). But this letter in Revelation, as also the Jeremiah prophecy, calls the reader to faith and repentance, and with repentance there is healing. The portrayal of that healing in this letter is subtle and far-reaching. The implications are as psychologically important as they are theologically important.

1. *"He who has an ear, let him hear."* This sentence is not original with the Book of Revelation. Our Lord makes use of the sentence in His teaching in Luke 14:35 and Matthew 13:43, and there is a special use of a similar phrase in Matthew 13:16–17.

This sentence is at the close of each of the seven letters. In each case it is addressed to a wider audience than the particular church being addressed. The sentence is a freedom sentence that reinforces the call to repentance. The sentence proves that the Christians are *called* to decide in favor of God's truth, but they are not *forced* to decide in favor of God's truth.

The sovereign decision by which God provided for the possibility of cosmic evil to will against His will—hence the devil—has a counterpart reality within the created order of our human history. God has provided for our real freedom, and therefore words like repentance and faith have meaning. God is secure enough within His own character that He is able to allow freedom around Him. *"He who has an ear to hear"* teaches that regardless of the truth of a great fact it cannot become our truth until we are able and willing to hear it.

There is a time for truth, as far as a human being is concerned, and even so great a truth as these wondrous themes in the seven letters to the seven churches must wait for their time to become relevant to a human being. The mighty will of God does not force our obedience even from the people who trust His grace. Seven times in this book that fact is repeated.

We must be careful in our discussion of the doctrine of the Holy Spirit and the doctrine of the sovereignty of God to preserve this theological perspective. The Holy Spirit's ministry of *convicting* and *assuring* the believer must not be confused with the *eros* love in Greek thought with its sweep and overwhelming compulsion of the will. The persuasion of the Holy Spirit of God is the persuasion that has freedom at the heart of it, and therefore the Holy Spirit's persuasive love that convinces us is the love with freedom at its center—*agapē*.[3] The healing needs our act of freedom-repentance before it makes us well.

2. Following the call to repentance two promises from the Spirit of the Lord are made to the readers: "I will give to you a mysterious food (the manna), and I will give to you the white stone with the new name upon it" (2:17). The first image is an Old Testament one, and the second image is a first-century Roman one. Both images promise a psychological-spiritual healing ministry at work in these believers who have become tempted by the idolatries and immoralities of a swift-moving, highly charged city. Both images in a very subtle way reveal to us an insight into some of the initial reasons that first caused the people to drift toward the false gods at Pergamum.

First of all, notice that idolatry and interpersonal immorality are combined in an earlier part of the passage. This means that at the heart of interpersonal hurtfulness and broken relationships is a basic confusion of primary loyalty. When a person worships something other than the true God, the result is that a confusion sets in; there is a breakdown of personal identity because the "no gods" we choose to worship other than the true God always robs us of our own identity first of all; then what follows is an inevitable hurtfulness toward the persons of our lives.

We can think of these same dynamics with another set of metaphors. When a person is hungry for food and cannot find health-giving food, that person may be tempted to satisfy hunger with junk foods high in refined sugars, salt, and chemical additives. The result of such a diet is insidious. There are bursts of sudden caloric power, but the strength supplied by junk food is a deceptive strength, and in the case of certain finely tuned persons, the resulting nutritional confusion may produce the emotional side effects of depression and sometimes even psychotic behavior.

Both of these images are employed within this letter to the Christians at Pergamum. First they are promised wholesome food. This is what people most need. Those who have been malnourished on the falsehoods of hatred, fear, selfishness, sexual narcissism, self-indulgence, etc., need not only to repent of the falsehood, but they need the protein, minerals, and body-building vitamins of God's love, truth, faith, hope, peace. It does little good to scorn the falsehoods. It is the good food that people really need, and this is why the long-term strategies that seek to share the substantial and health-giving gospel with people, young and old, are those that best express the biblical intent.

The second image that this letter presents is an identity image. The white stone was a symbol in the Roman world used in legal trials, academic grading systems, and at athletic games. The stone with the Roman letters *SP* imprinted upon it was given in Roman games as an award for valor. Also it was first-century practice that after a serious illness a patient who recovered would often take a new name to signify his or her complete recovery. The point is dramatically symbolized for the Christians at Pergamum. Their drift into sinfulness does not need to be the last word for either themselves or for others. In spite of the harm that has happened, there can be healing—a new identity to fulfill the identity distorted by sin; healthy food from God who knows of the human need to be fed and healed, and made whole.

The good news of the healthy, healing lordship of Jesus Christ still echoes from the New Testament to the Pergamum of our generation, too. I have discovered as a pastor in a university city that those persons who most often are entrapped by cultic movements are individuals who were programmed for the entrapment in pre-cultic homes. Perhaps they grew up in a family where the mood at every meal was pessimistic and cynical. The result for such an individual and for the family was the gradual development of low-grade paranoia, adriftness, a feeling of helplessness, a conviction that all people are basically hypocritical, all systems bad or hopeless. Such a person grows up starved for warm relationships and a sense of hope because a human being cannot live on cynicism and pessimism. If such a person does not find true food, then false foods will find a welcome in his or her life.

Another pre-cultic scenario is the person who grows up in a highly communicative, rich-menu family. But in this case the food is false.

The value system is selfish and twisted. The problem is not one of adriftness or pessimism; it is rather the problem of value confusion. Both settings are pre-cultic, because both drive the person in upon himself or herself without a foundation large enough and good enough to build upon. The result finally is loneliness and intense vulnerability which the cultic movements are able to exploit.

But what is the cure? C. S. Lewis gives some very good advice: "The best safeguard against bad literature is a full experience of good; just as a real and affectionate acquaintance with honest people gives a better protection against rogues than a habitual distrust of everyone."[4]

IN THE MARKETPLACE
Letter 4

[18] "And to the angel of the church in Thyatira write,

'These things says the Son of God, who has eyes like a flame of fire, and His feet like fine brass: [19] "I know your works, love, service, faith, and your patience; and as for your works, the last are more than the first. [20] Nevertheless I have a few things against you, because you allow that woman Jezebel, who calls herself a prophetess, to teach and seduce My servants to commit sexual immorality and eat things sacrificed to idols. [21] And I gave her time to repent of her sexual immorality, and she did not repent. [22] Indeed I will cast her into a sickbed, and those who commit adultery with her into great tribulation, unless they repent of their deeds. [23] I will kill her children with death, and all the churches shall know that I am He who searches the minds and hearts. And I will give to each one of you according to your works.

[24] "Now to you I say, and to the rest in Thyatira, as many as do not have this doctrine, who have not known the depths of Satan, as they say, I will put on you no other burden. [25] But hold fast what you have till I come. [26] And he who overcomes, and keeps My works until the end, to him I will give power over the nations—

[27] 'He shall *rule them with a rod of iron;*

They shall be dashed to pieces like the potter's vessels'—

as I also have received from My Father; [28] and I will give him the morning star.

[29] "He who has an ear, let him hear what the Spirit says to the churches."

—*Revelation 2:18–29*

134

Thyatira is some thirty miles inland from Pergamum, and boasts of no high-fortress land formations and, therefore, is not suitable as a major city. It was originally a military outpost town maintained to protect the road from Pergamum to Sardis. The trade guilds play an important religious role in this city, which at the time of the first century was primarily a commercial center of weavers, leather-workers, potters, and bronze-workers. Sir William Ramsey observes, "More trade guilds are known in Thyatira than in any other Asian city."[5] The Christians who are members of these commercial trades would have a difficult time holding to a noncompromised faith in view of the pressure from the guilds to worship at the various city temples, and attend the guild feasts, most of which have religious connotations. In this letter the speaker to the church is identified as *"the Son of God"* (2:18). This title for our Lord appears in only this single place in the Book of Revelation.

The church is honored for its love, faith, service, courage, and the fact that it is growing in good works. The crisis at Thyatira has to do with a person or perhaps a movement which or who is described by the name of *"Jezebel."* We assume that in this case, as in the case of the earlier reference to Balaam, the name is used symbolically, and yet likely refers to a real person and a specific situation within the Thyatira church. From the name we also would assume that this person is a woman who calls herself a prophet. The earliest Old Testament introduction to Jezebel as the wife of Ahab appears in 1 Kings 16:31. She is described as the one who worshiped the Canaanite god Baal. She was a murderess and was finally overthrown during the time of Elijah. In 1 Kings 21:25 a final comment is made about Jezebel and her husband King Ahab: "There was none who sold himself to do what was evil in the sight of the Lord like Ahab, whom Jezebel his wife incited" (RSV).

The Christian church at Thyatira has perhaps been deceived by a woman who evidently claims to be a prophetess, and who, like the Jezebel of Ahab's time, is tempting the people toward immorality, and also to eat foods offered to idols. (The apostle Paul was also compelled to grapple with the problem of meats sold in the market after prior use in temple worship. See 1 Cor. 10:19–30.)

It is important to note first of all that the issue in this text is not the correctness of women as prophets in the first-century church. The New Testament does not oppose women as prophets, and indeed the messianic prophecy that is especially announced by Peter at the birth of the church on the Day of Pentecost is from the prophet Joel: "Your sons and your daughters shall prophesy. . ." (Joel 2:28–32; Acts 2:17). There are women prophets in the early church (note 1 Cor. 11:5), but here at Thyatira the problem is a false prophet. Her sex is not the basis for the judgment in this text, but solely her false teaching and her false way of life.

The warning to the Christians who have followed this teacher is stern, and yet there is preserved in the warning the word of hope for those who are willing to repent. The Lord also warns about the drastic results in their lives of the way of sin. The portrayal of these results takes on an intense, overwhelming quality: *"I will cast her into a sickbed, and those who commit adultery with her into great tribulation"* (v. 22).

This realism about the ravages that occur in human life as the result of interpersonal sinfulness and idolatry may appear heavy-handed at first glance, but that heavy-handedness is necessary to keep the record straight. It is something like what would happen if a youthful offender, who had broken the law but because of the circumstances of age was not sentenced by the court to an adult prison. Instead, imagine if that youthful offender were taken into a state prison like the California State Penitentiary at San Quentin and left in that environment for a few days to observe for himself the terrifying loneliness, constant physical danger, and brutalization that really takes over the human soul in a maximum-security prison. He is shocked by the caustic and destructive end that awaits a life of crime. Though such a warning is heavy-handed and harsh, the goal is to produce a shock reaction for his benefit and in his best interests.

In the same way this letter to Thyatira shocks its readers in a few short sentences with the portrayal of the terrifying results of human sinfulness. The theological principle that underpins this passage is that the created order of God is moral, and the violation of that moral order does not go unpunished. Interpersonal immorality has always been destructive to human relationships, because such sins, just as the sins of false gods, pride, selfishness, etc., go crossgrain to the grand design built by God into the very fabric of life.

But it is very important to notice that within the judgment descriptions of these sentences the good news of forgiveness is also present. The three words *"unless they repent"* are the good-news words planted firmly within the judgment. It is not too late for Thyatira to reach out to the Lord of the grand design. Nevertheless, one warning remains true. Because of God's love, the grand plan for human life must judge sternly the injustice of sexual exploitation of human beings, the sins of pride, greed, anger, and every other transgression.

It is because of God's love that Jezebel is condemned for her treachery toward the farmer Naboth (1 Kin. 21:1–24). She wanted his vineyard, and she arranged for his death—he was brutally stoned as if he had cursed God and king. But Naboth was innocent; his only guilt was that he had what Jezebel wanted. Because of God's love, sins like the treachery of Jezebel must not go unpunished. But because of God's love, there is also the possibility of the forgiveness of human sins. That forgiveness is not a "cheap grace which justifies the sin, but the costly grace that justifies the repentant sinner" (D. Bonhoeffer, *Cost of Discipleship).*

In the final part of this letter, the Christians are assured of their relationship to God, and are encouraged to ignore what the false teacher has evidently described as *"the depths of Satan"* (RSV has "deep things"). They need not fear the magic and spells of the devil himself. We are not informed as to what these "deep things" include, but we are assured that they are no match for the authority of Jesus Christ who is the very Son of God.

The reference to *"the morning star"* (v. 28) is an Old Testament image of hope, an allusion from Old Testament messianic yearning for the morning, as in the references in Jeremiah 33:15 and 23:5, in which the word "branch" or "shoot" of Jesse can be translated "morning." These "morning" yearnings are combined in Revelation with the word "star," as in Revelation 22:16 in which Jesus Christ is called the "bright and morning star."

This becomes one more attestation to these Christians at Thyatira that they are God's people and, therefore, they shall reign with Him in His kingdom. These Christians have a responsibility, a mandate toward the nations. What we must understand in this letter to the church at Thyatira is the fact that the temptations which these Christians faced in this city were interwoven into trade skills, the success in business and the economic survival of the Christians. If they were leather-workers or bronze-workers and their families were supported by these skills and jobs, then what they were up against was not only the problem of false teaching at a church meeting or social pressures in their neighborhoods, but they were contending with temptation within the places where they worked. If they stood against temptation in their very jobs, the real option they had to face was economic suffering as well as spiritual suffering.

It is this thread in the Thyatira letter that makes it an especially meaningful letter for today's readers of the book. The most subtle challenge to faith does not usually originate in public amphitheaters but in the daily places where we earn the money we need to live. The question is then—how are we to survive such tests and even turn them toward a new and redemptive direction?

The approach of this letter is to place the daily lives of the Christians upon a larger stage and within a larger context. I must see my task, my daily deployment, as a part of the larger goal of my life. This is the only way that I can correctly size up the demands of any job so that on the one hand I am a good and hard worker and yet on the other I keep faith with my integrity and my greater loyalties. The letter quotes Psalm 2 to assure these Christians there is a greater management to which we belong. I believe that as I see my daily economic life within this larger context it makes me a better worker! It is a fact that a job that is worshiped is a job badly done. This is because we ask too much from the job we are doing—from the company, from the union, from the success of financial achievement. What the trades need, what professions need, what all deployments of our lives need is not our soul but our skill, not our worship but our hard work. When we once learn this vital alignment of values, we will do better in our work, and have fewer ulcers too. Idolatries, whether of the dramatic amphitheater type or the low-grace office type, always make us sick.

I am convinced that what the marketplaces at Thyatira or Los Angeles need is a worker who knows this and shares his health-giving perspective not in anger or fear but with style.

LIKE A THIEF
Letter 5

3:1 "And to the angel of the church in Sardis write,
'These things says He who has the seven Spirits of God and the seven stars: "I know your works, that you have a name that you are alive, but you are dead. ² Be watchful, and strengthen the things which remain, that are ready to die, for I have not found your works perfect before God. ³ Remember therefore how you have received and heard; hold fast and repent. Therefore if you will not watch, I will come upon you as a thief, and you will not know what hour I will come upon you. ⁴ You have a few names even in Sardis who have not defiled their garments; and they shall walk with Me in white, for they are worthy. ⁵ He who overcomes shall be clothed in

white garments, and I will not blot out his name from the Book of Life; but I will confess his name before My Father and before His angels.

6 "He who has an ear, let him hear what the Spirit says to the churches." '

—Revelation 3:1–6

Sardis is thirty miles to the east of Thyatira. This city, which occupies a proud acropolis commanding the intersection of five highways, is an ancient city with a famous past, but by the midpoint of the first century, a declining future. It was once the capital of the Lydian kingdom, which had boasted the fabulously rich King Croesus. But Sardis has had an odd history. Twice it was totally surprised and humiliated by military defeat. The city that seemed militarily impregnable had been defeated by Cyrus (549 B.C.) and Antiochus (218 B.C.), and on both occasions the city was taken by surprise in a nighttime attack by soldiers who quietly scaled her steep fortress walls. The earthquake of A.D. 17 destroyed the city, but through the kindness of Tiberius Caesar, the city had been rebuilt. Now, in the second half of the first century, Sardis was once again prosperous, primarily because of its trade and its wool-dyeing industry. Modern archeologists have found very significant ruins at Sardis, including the remains of a second/third-century Jewish synagogue, as well as evidences of early Christian and also gnostic symbols. These include a picture of the evangelist John.[6]

The words to this church are exceedingly stern. The people look alive, and yet are dead. The word *"dead"* (3:1) is used here in a special way, which becomes clear in the next sentence in which people are called to repentance and are challenged to *wake up.* All is not lost, even though the overwhelming word "death" has been used to describe the Christian church at Sardis. The disquieting news in this letter is that Jesus Christ is the restless judge of His church. The judgment of these passages is not directed against the wealthy and corrupt city of Sardis, but against the Lord's colony within Sardis. The history of the earlier surprise attacks by earthquake, Antiochus, and Cyrus lingered in the memory of the citizens of that city, and the Lord of the church warns that like a thief who scales the walls of the citadel He will judge His church when His people least expect it. We do not have the rights of first refusal, nor do we have time to prepare for an orderly, scheduled audit of our books; rather those rights belong to Jesus Christ Himself.

A disquieting theological element in this warning has to do with the question of the security of believers in their relationship with God. The unrepentant person is under threat of having his name "blotted out of the book." The image of the book and the names first appears in the warning made by the Lord to Moses: "But the Lord said to Moses, 'Whoever has sinned against me, him will I blot out of my book" (Ex. 32:33, RSV). That very sentence is now used in this letter to the Christians at Sardis. What is clear in this text is that God's gift of salvation is received and heard, and it is kept by the faith of repentance (3:3). It is, therefore, theologically irresponsible to theorize about a doctrine of grace that keeps our names in the great Book of Life against our will. This text is a freedom text. The letter to Sardis in no way diminishes the authority and saving power of Jesus Christ on one side, nor on the other side will this text allow the self-serving "easy-street" doctrines of general grace to reduce redemption into a general truth like the physical law of gravity. We simply must keep in biblical tension the all-sufficiency of Christ's forgiveness and the vital importance of our repentance.

That repentance must be a present reality. It is not a transaction that we are able occasionally to acknowledge as we would the illustrious victories and achievements of our ancestors. Our salvation is a daily, living, dynamic relationship. At the same moment, there is a garden-variety commonness about it too. This may, in part, be the importance of *"white robes"* (3:5) as the image for the repentant Christians. White is the color for purity, but also it is the color a slave would wear who could not afford the luxurious and colorful dyed woolens of Sardis. To a city famous for its colors, how common and peasantlike is this promise that the mark of the disciples of Christ is the clothing and color of the poorest, not the gorgeous shades of the rich.

The letter to Sardis has taught the doctrine of C. S. Lewis's *Mere Christianity*. The Christian never moves or advances beyond the need for forgiveness and, in fact, the vigilance that this letter demands is precisely that vigilance of remembering that every Christian man or woman must live a life of daily relationship and of daily forgiveness and of daily joy. Then we may welcome the Holy thief.

What we see in the letter to the church at Sardis is a bold portrayal of the theology of surprise. The surprise does not negate the faithfulness. The God who surprises is the faithful God, the One who is Alpha and Omega, the Foundation of all that is durable.

Science and faith both make their wager upon the dependability of God's creation and providence. But at the heart of this dependability is the grand surprise. Creation itself is a surprise; redemption is a surprise, and judgment is a surprise, too.

This brief letter to the Christians at Sardis makes the point dramatically. The Lord of the church does not belong to the church "as its possession but as its possessor" (D. T. Niles). God is the One who preserves our freedom, and He preserves His own freedom as well. He cannot be brought under the control of the church. This means that we as Christians have a restraint, a good and healthy boundary within which our theological task is mandated. We are restrained from making threats about future judgment, since both the hope and the awesome measuring of the future belong to God.

Our best promises are the promises that claim the love and justice that has been revealed in Jesus Christ. Our task is to trust on a day-to-day basis in His faithfulness and to rejoice gratefully in His surprise of our expectations. The world is a volatile, even fragile order of energy and mass, of light and darkness, of good and evil, of dangerous freedom and wonderful possibility. Jesus Christ is the surprise who steadies everything.

THE OPEN DOOR

Letter 6

7 "And to the angel of the church in Philadelphia write,
'These things says He who is holy, He who is true, "He who has the key of David, He who opens and no one shuts, and shuts and no one opens": 8 "I know your works. See, I have set before you an open door, and no one can shut it; for you have a little strength, have kept My word, and have not denied My name. 9 Indeed I will make those of the synagogue of Satan, who say they are Jews and are not, but lie— indeed I will make them come and worship before your feet, and to know that I have loved you. 10 Because you have kept My command to persevere, I also will keep you from the hour of trial which shall come upon the whole world, to test those who dwell on the earth. 11 Behold, I am coming quickly! Hold fast what you have, that no one may take your crown. 12 He who overcomes, I will make him a pillar in the temple of My God, and he shall go out no more. I will write on him the name of My God and the name of the city of My

God, the New Jerusalem, which comes down out of heaven from My God. And I will write on him My new name.
13 "He who has an ear, let him hear what the Spirit says to the churches."'

—*Revelation 3:7–13*

Philadelphia is a very young city some twenty-eight miles southeast of Sardis. It had been first founded by Attalus II (Philadephus) about 150 B.C. Like Sardis, it suffered destruction during the earthquake of A.D. 17, and it also was rebuilt though not on the same grand scale as Sardis. At that time the name of the city was changed in honor of Tiberius to the name Neocaesarea. During the reign of Nero, A.D. 54–68, the original name of the city—Philadelphia—was restored. During the reign of Vespasian, 70–79, the city was again renamed, this time with the name Flavia.

The history of the names of this city offers an impressive argument in favor of the dating of the Book of Revelation at or near the time of Nero. It would seem logical to assume that the writer of Revelation, who has shown such accurate knowledge of the geography and idiosyncrasies of each city to which he writes, would certainly address the church in this city with its current and official name. But in Revelation there is no hint of an awareness either directly or indirectly of the name Flavia. The reason, in my judgment, is that this remarkable book by John was written prior to the renaming of the town. He knows it as Philadelphia. The town is an outpost settlement at the doorway of the land routes to the east, and the city was thought of in those terms from its earliest formation.

In this letter the speaker identifies himself as holy, true, and as holder of the *"key of David"* (v. 7). Isaiah 22:22 (RSV) gives an Old Testament clue to this fascinating image: "And I will place on his shoulder the key of the house of David; he shall open, and none shall shut; and he shall shut, and none shall open." The house of David is probably best interpreted as Jerusalem which is David's city. Later in Revelation these important images of the key, and also of David's city Jerusalem, will once again play significant roles (Rev. 9:1; 20:1; 21:2).

This letter first honors and then challenges the Christians at Philadelphia. They are honored for their works and their loyalty to the Word and name of Christ. But beyond that they are promised that they will experience amazing breakthroughs within their own city, because people who now worship the false gods in the synagogues of Satan will turn toward the gospel. The challenge to the Christians at Philadelphia is to faithfully point to the Word and name of Christ.

One of the important doctrinal features of this sixth letter is found in its very basic and forthright theology of evangelism. Notice the main features of that theology. It is Jesus Christ who opens and shuts. He holds the decisive key in His hand. It is this same Lord who has set the Christians in this outpost city before an open door which no one is able to shut.

What is important to notice at this point is that which the Christian church is responsible for and that for which it is not responsible. In the logic of this letter, the Christians have a four-fold task: (1) first to remain loyal disciples of their Lord; (2) then to affirm to the people around them of their own loyalty and trust in the Word and name of Jesus Christ; (3) to live in the realm of His love; and (4) to welcome the people who will surprise them by responding to this witness.

The reason that the people who had formerly worshiped false gods will come to their own place of faith is because Jesus Christ Himself has opened up the doorway. He has authenticated the witness of His disciples at Philadelphia.

It seems very significant to me that the turning point of that validation of the truth of the Word and the name of Christ occurs when the inquirers at Philadelphia discover the love that is at work in the lives of the Christians. That turning point is vital: they will "learn that I love you" (v. 9).

This first-century doctrinal portrayal of the missionary task of the Christian church is as relevant and strategic today as it was then. The task given to the church is neither too easy—"*I know you have but little power*" (v. 8, RSV)—nor is it too hard. We Christians are not asked to open the heavy doors, but to walk through doors that the Lord opens. The task is too hard unless the Lord of this mission empowers His people. On the other hand, the Christians are granted a realistic, down-to-earth strategy, with four sensible and workable parts:

1. This strategy begins at the beginning. There is nothing to share if there is nothing to have. This strategy begins with the living relationship already true in the lives of the Christians.

2. This strategy calls upon the Christians to find a way to proclaim the gospel source of their identity. This is the direct implication of the open-doorway imagery. The Christian faith has always been an evangelical faith which seeks to share the *name* of

Jesus Christ, and also to share the *Word* of Jesus Christ. In the Greek world of thought, the word "word" *(logos)* has to do with the *meaning* of it all. In the Hebrew world of thought, "word," *dabar,* and the evocation of the name of God both have to do with the *authority* of the One who creates by His Word. In both ways, the preaching task of the church is to share with the world the meaning and the lordship of the person, Jesus Christ.

3. These Christians are to live the love of Christ, because that love at work in and between them and toward their neighbors will be the identifying mark of the Christian. It will be the fragrance which their neighbors at Philadelphia will notice and respect. That mark of love stirs up within those neighbors a curiosity to discover the living Source behind that love.

4. The Christians are instructed to welcome the people who will come to the people of God as a result of this combined divine and human evangelical strategy. Once again, a major thesis about the Christian church is hereby established. It is God who invited people into His church, and very often those who are invited are an unexpected surprise for the church itself. We who are in the church are usually unprepared for the response of people to Jesus Christ. It is all to the good; therefore, our only task in this regard is to welcome these who are called, and then begin again the fourfold cycle with those who have been added to the fellowship by the Lord of the church.

Two things are very impressive about this Philadelphia strategy. First, I am impressed by the naturalness and basic realism of this strategy of evangelism. It does not idealize the Christian missionary task; it does not call for "super Christians," but rather for garden-variety Christians who are experiencing the miracle of the love of Jesus Christ in their own lives and fellowship.

Second, the power of love is strongly stated in this letter. The persuasive cutting edge of the Christian fellowship is the fact of belovedness. When we know and trust this belovedness, we have the basis for our ethics as well as our evangelism. When the world observes this love alive and growing within the Christian fellowship, the doors swing wide because the world is starved for this love.

This letter closes with another reference to the triumphant return of Jesus Christ as Lord. He who stands at the beginning and center of history is the One who stands at its end as well. We see in this letter the same prophetic shortening of time which can be noted throughout all New Testament eschatological teaching (cf. 1 Thess. 5:1–11).

THE BEST PROMISE
Letter 7

[14] "And to the angel of the church of the Laodiceans write,

'These things says the Amen, the Faithful and True Witness, the Beginning of the creation of God: [15] "I know your works, that you are neither cold nor hot. I could wish you were cold or hot. [16] So then, because you are lukewarm, and neither cold nor hot, I will vomit you out of My mouth.
[17] Because you say, 'I am rich, have become wealthy, and have need of nothing'—and do not know that you are wretched, miserable, poor, blind, and naked— [18] I counsel you to buy from Me gold refined in the fire, that you may be rich; and white garments, that you may be clothed, that the shame of your nakedness may not be revealed; and anoint your eyes with eye salve, that you may see. [19] As many as I love, I rebuke and chasten. Therefore be zealous and repent. [20] Behold, I stand at the door and knock. If anyone hears My voice and opens the door, I will come in to him and dine with him, and he with Me. [21] To him who overcomes I will grant to sit with Me on My throne, as I also overcame and sat down with My Father on His throne.
[22] "He who has an ear, let him hear what the Spirit says to the churches."'"

—Revelation 3:14–22

Laodicea is almost 100 miles inland from Ephesus on the south bank of the River Lycus. The city had been founded as a major urban center around 250 B.C. by Antiochus II (Seleucid) and named for his wife, Laodice. The city at the time of the mid-first century was prosperous as a commercial center, noted for its black wool and carpets. It also had a medical school and was well known for the eye salve called Phrygian ointment. We gain some insight into the wealth and independent spirit of Laodicea from the Roman historian Tacitus *(Annals* 14:27) who notes that Laodicea refused government aid from Rome after the earthquake damage of A.D. 60. Another interesting feature about this city is the fact that Laodicea, which had no local water supply, had developed a stone aqueduct system to bring water from the hot springs of Hierapolis some six miles away. By the time this water reached Laodicea, however, it was tepid and distasteful. The

Jewish population in Laodicea was large and wealthy. According to William Ramsey, Flaccus collected more than twenty-two and a half pounds of gold from the 7,500 Jewish males who lived in Laodicea for an offering to the temple of Jerusalem in 62 B.C.

We know something of the Christian church in Laodicea from Paul's Letter to the Colossians. The church at Laodicea is mentioned four times (Col. 2:1; 4:13, 15, 16), and many interpreters speculate that Epaphras was the founder of the Christian church in Laodicea and that the Christians in the three cities of Colossae, Hierapolis, and Laodicea were yoked in special friendship.

As we now consider the last of the seven letters, we must propose some explanations of the purpose of the seven letters and their relationship to the total book. I believe the most obvious conclusion is also the most helpful both theologically and devotionally. The letters were written by John to seven congregations of real people in real places. He knew the people and their cities very well, as our study of the letters has made clear. Like the prophets of the Old Testament, who were wise and shrewd observers of their own historical setting, so in the same way John spoke the Word of God as he had seen in his vision to the people and their cities. The accuracy and inside knowledge about the special character of each city is impressive, and adds greatly to our historical appreciation of the book.

I cannot accept the hypothesis that these letters are part of a Christian preface and postscript (Rev. 22:6–21) to an otherwise Jewish apocalyptic book. We can demonstrate within the seven letters that the vocabulary and themes are in a basic theological harmony with the later chapters 4 through 22. The Jewish flavor is as much a part of these seven letters as it is of chapters 4 through 22. Likewise, the Christian imagery in chapters 4 through 22 is in harmony with the imagery of these first three chapters.

I also caution students of Revelation to practice restraint in the imposition of prophetic schemes upon the meaning of the letters to the seven churches. One schematic overview teaches that these seven letters represent "an exact foreview of the spiritual history of the Church," of seven stages of the growth of the Christian church throughout history.[7]

There is no encouragement within the texts themselves toward such an interpretation. I believe we must avoid all luxurious interpretations of the seven letters. These seven letters of the Book of Revelation make better sense and are more spiritually and theologically helpful when they are seen in the same light as the other letters of the New Testament. They teach the gospel and its implications for life.

This letter begins with a description of Christ that is founded upon the Hebrew word *amen,* which in the Old Testament means literally "foundation" and, therefore, "faithful, trustworthy." This dramatic Old Testament allusion makes good sense in view of the longstanding Jewish presence in this city.

This opening statement is followed by the philosophically significant Greek word *archē,* translated in the English "beginning." This word reminds the reader both of 1 John 1 and John 1. Both of these passages contain the decisive use of this same word, John 1:1–3, "In the *beginning* was the Word. . . . All things were made through Him." Note also 1 John 1:1, "that which was from the beginning . . ." Later in Revelation this same word will be used again (Rev. 21:6 and 22:13).

John does not teach that Jesus Christ is the first part of creation. Rather the theological reference point in all of these passages is to the Book of Genesis 1:1: "In the beginning God created. . ." Jesus Christ is prior to the creation, and in the mystery of the holy fellowship of the triune God, the created order has come into being because of Jesus Christ. He is the very *Word,* the very decision of God by which the created order has come into existence.

This greeting for the letter to the church of Laodicea would be very meaningful to them on two counts: (1) because of the rich Old Testament allusions in *amen* and *beginning;* (2) it is very probable also that John is aware of the letter of Paul to the Colossian church, and that letter contains a broad and sweeping statement of the same theology. Paul teaches in that letter that Jesus Christ ". . . is the image of the invisible God, the first-born of all creation;. . . and in him all things hold together" (Col. 1:15–17 RSV).

Therefore, this letter to the church at Laodicea has gathered together themes and convictions that the Christians at Laodicea would especially know and understand.

Suddenly and without warning a heavy charge against the church in Laodicea is now spoken. They are accused of being like their water supply, and they hear the language of judgment: *"I will vomit you out of my mouth."* The image of lukewarmness is powerful and contemporary, because they know from experience the reputation they have for their nauseating water. Now it is they, the people of the Lord, who are accused of the same distasteful condition.

These words are very similar to the prophetic judgment passages of the Old Testament, both in the emotional power of the imagery as well as the apparent sense of hopelessness in the result. The painful fact is that *as they now are, they are unacceptable to God.* There are reasons that explain this lukewarmness, and they are written to the church in Hebrew poetic parallelism: "You say, *I am rich, I have prospered, and I need nothing*" (3:17, RSV). This forms one side of the poetic balance, and on the other side are opposed virtually the same number of words "not knowing that you are *wretched, pitiable, poor, blind, and naked.*" In the Greek, because of the similar endings upon most of the words of the second half of the parallelism, there is an intensifying poetic force in this accusation.

What is their problem at Laodicea? The prophetic accusation against this church possesses a bittersweet irony. These Christians have become lukewarm because they perceived virtues within themselves, and because of that confident self-understanding they were blinded to the steady deterioration that had already turned them into hollow shells reaching out to hollow shells. Here is the tragedy of a person who has gone soft and indolent by overestimating his or her wealth for too long. It is the person who has always intended to get started and was certain that time was on his side. It is the tragedy of King Theoden who has been steadily deceived by his traitorous advisor Wormtounge as to the real status of his crumbling empire (J. R. R. Tolkien, *Two Towers*). What we have in this poetic description is the raw material of human decadence and the tragedy of adriftness. It is like the inner deception of the chemical assault on the brain, so that by imperceptible inches a man or woman is robbed of a clear mind and vigorous imagination, while all the time self-assured that cocaine, or marijuana, or alcohol was enhancing perception, feeling, and well-being.

But now the Stormcrow Gandolf has thrown open King Theoden's castle windows; the fresh air rushes in, and the old king has his vision cleared. It has been a shocking and painful experience, but the result is thrilling.

Lukewarmness as a spiritual, emotional disorder is so insidious and so self-deceptive that it takes the kind of vigorous shock we witness in this letter to clear the air. Lukewarmness, when it becomes a way of life, so completely blurs and dulls the colors that it becomes almost impossible to tell differences when they occur. Lukewarmness is low-grade paranoia, low-grade cynicism, low-grade immorality. The result is always fatigue, and finally despair.

But low-grade or not, it is still despair. It is what T. S. Eliot's J. Alfred Prufrock is left with: "Like a patient etherized upon a table . . . who measured out his life with coffee spoons."

But Jesus Christ is the Stormcrow for Laodicea, and He judges them because He loves them. He offers to that church in the town of eye salves and wools and wealth the very gifts that they thought they already owned. *"Gold refined . . . white garments . . . salve to anoint your eyes"* (v. 18).

This letter is both the sternest of the letters, and the most tender. Jesus Christ assures this church of their belovedness. He is not scolding them; He is fighting with them, throwing water in their faces, challenging His beloved children because they mean so much to Him He cannot simply stand by and watch their downward spiral. This love is true to its own ground rules and, therefore, it does not *compel* the Christians at Laodicea to repent, but rather *calls* them to repent. They, and they alone, must open the door that their own lukewarmness has closed. Jesus Christ knocks, and the freedom of the one who lives within the house is preserved. Only the one in the house may open such a door.

In Jewish and Greek daily life there is a special significance to the meal taken together. It has the deeper significance of interpersonal commitment and joyous fellowship. That note of joy is the final gospel sound of the seven letters. Now we are ready to hear the two great chorales and the four symphonic movements.

NOTES

1. J. M. Ford has examined this phenomenon in detail in *Revelation (Anchor Bible)*, pp. 392–96.

2. See discussion of 2:1–7.

3. See E. F. Palmer, *Love Has Its Reasons* (Waco, Tex.: Word Books, 1977).

4. C. S. Lewis, *An Experiment in Criticism* (London: Cambridge, 1961), p. 94.

5. William Ramsey, *Letters to Seven Churches* (1904), pp. 32–48.

6. See *Bulletin of the American Schools for Oriental Research*, 1958, 1959, 1966, and also J. M. Ford's discussion of these finds, p. 410.

7. C. I. Scofield, *Holy Bible, Scofield Reference Edition*, n. 3., p. 1331.

CHAPTER THREE—THE FIRST CHORALE
REVELATION 4:1–11

Scripture Outline

The Throne of God (4:1–7)

The Chorale to God the Creator (4:8–11)

THE THRONE OF GOD

4:1 After these things I looked, and behold, a door standing open in heaven. And the first voice which I heard was like a trumpet speaking with me, saying, "Come up here, and I will show you things which must take place after this."

² Immediately I was in the Spirit; and behold, a throne set in heaven, and One sat on the throne. ³ And He who sat there was like a jasper and a sardius stone in appearance; and there was a rainbow around the throne, in appearance like an emerald. ⁴ Around the throne were twenty-four thrones, and on the thrones I saw twenty-four elders sitting, clothed in white robes; and they had crowns of gold on their heads. ⁵ And from the throne proceeded lightnings, thunderings, and voices. Seven lamps of fire were burning before the throne, which are the seven Spirits of God.

⁶ Before the throne there was a sea of glass, like crystal. And in the midst of the throne, and around the throne, were four living creatures full of eyes in front and in back. ⁷ The first living creature was like a lion, the second living creature like a calf, the third living creature had a face like a man, and the fourth living creature *was* like a flying eagle.

—Revelation 4:1–7

The Book of Revelation begins with the dramatic vision John experiences at Patmos: *"Then I turned to see . . ."* (1:12). Now the second unfolding of John's vision begins in chapter 4 with what amounts to that same phrase repeated again, *"After these things I looked. . . ."* As we listen to this next part of John's experience, we have the advantage of already having had explained to us certain key elements in the imagery from the earlier part of the book. Moreover, we will notice in this vision in chapter 4 that John's careful allusion to Old Testament writings which we noted in chapters 1 through 3 continues and increases. Nevertheless, even with these two valuable textual guides to interpretation, there are parts of the descriptions in this chapter as well as the remainder of Revelation that we shall simply observe and then stand back in reverence. We watch and hear but do not fully understand; we must wonder at what it all may fully mean.

"A door standing open in heaven . . ." The open-door image is not strange to us, because of the letter to the church of Philadelphia. We also remember the Isaiah prophecy that God's Messiah would open David's door (Is. 22:22). *"Heaven"* is used in at least three ways in the Book of Revelation: (1) as the place of God's dwelling, as in 3:12; (2) as the description of the cosmic order of creation, a place of conflict, as in 12:7; and (3) as a common description of the sky, as in 6:13. The word, usually in the plural, appears fifty-two times in this book.

"Like a trumpet." Because of this repetition of the trumpet image, which in the first chapter referred to Christ's voice, we interpret this passage in that direction. Jesus Christ calls out to John and invites him to see "what will happen next."

John then has a vision of the One who is seated upon the throne. This vision is filled with movement and sounds and color. The vision is a flood of Old Testament symbols and experiences from Old Testament prophetic and apocalyptic visions. There are similarities to the vision of Isaiah in the year that King Uzziah died (Is. 6:1–5). There are even more similarities to the vision of Ezekiel (Ezek. 1). The green jasper (jade) and red sardius (cornelian) remind us of the breastplate stones of the High Priest (Ex. 28:17–21). The rainbow, or as J. B. Phillips translates it, "A halo like an emerald rainbow," reminds us of both Noah's rainbow (Gen. 9:16) and Ezekiel's bow (Ezek. 1:28). The twenty-four elders may refer to the twenty-four priestly divisions who conducted the worship of Israel according to the tradition of the Levites. The elders in the vision seem to represent the saints of God in their act of worship, just as the Levitical priests represented Israel in the worship of the temple.

The vision is splendid. It is also unsettling and strange with the sight of the four living creatures *"full of eyes in front and in back."*

These creatures may represent the whole of living creation as symbolized by the lion, ox, man, bird. There is a Jewish rabbinic saying that offers support to this view. The saying in its present form dates to A.D. 300 but is probably much older than that date: "The mightiest among the birds is the eagle, the mightiest among the domestic animals is the bull, the mightiest among the wild beasts is the lion, and the mightiest among all is man." The same four faces are also noted in the creatures of the vision in Ezekiel.

What is important for those who read this text is to sense and feel the color, movement, and wonder of the total scene. Individual parts in themselves are baffling, but the large scene is what we must try to see. Then we must listen closely to the words of the chorale that follows in verses 8–11. It is the great song that brings together the central message of the vision. The same principle of interpretation will hold true throughout the Book of Revelation. The splendor of the vision has the effect of shocking our senses much like the pageantry of the grand entrance of Her Majesty, the Queen, into the House of Lords on the opening day of Parliament. The excitement and splendor are secondary to the words of her message to Parliament; they are the most important part of the event as she speaks on behalf of the Prime Minister and the government.

THE CHORALE TO GOD THE CREATOR

[8] The four living creatures, each having six wings, were full of eyes around and within. And they do not rest day or night, saying:

"Holy, holy, holy,
Lord God Almighty,
Who was and is and is to come!"
[9] Whenever the living creatures give glory and honor and thanks to Him who sits on the throne, who lives forever and ever, [10] the twenty-four elders fall down before Him who sits on the throne and worship Him who lives forever and ever, and cast their crowns before the throne, saying:
[11] "You are worthy, O Lord,
To receive glory and honor and power;
For You created all things,
And by Your will they exist and were created."
—*Revelation 4:8–11*

There are two parts to the chorale.

> "Holy, holy, holy,
> Lord God Almighty,
> Who was and is and is to come!"

This song combines an equal mixture of the great *Sanctus* passage of Isaiah 6:3 and the *Alpha-and-Omega* affirmation of Revelation 1:8. This song affirms God's holiness. Holiness in the Bible expresses the oneness of the *presence* and the *wholly otherness* of God. The song then, in its third line, affirms God's mighty name as Yahweh, "I am who I am; I will be who I will be." This, in my view, is the force of the sentence in the Revelation *"who was and is and is to come."*

The second part of the chorale is sung following this heavenly salute of honor to God by the living creatures and the elders.

> "You are worthy, O Lord,
> To receive glory and honor and power;
> For You created all things,
> And by Your will they exist and were
>   created!"

This song is more than an adaptation of an Old Testament song. It is the song of praise to the gospel of Genesis 1 and the gospel of John 1. It is the chorale of praise to God the Creator.

This first chorale makes a very important affirmation about God which validates the theology of creation of the Old and New Testaments and sets the Book of Revelation squarely upon a collision course with the Greek world of thought about origins and meaning. This song of Revelation 4 teaches that the God of Jesus Christ is the God of creation. The song teaches that everything that exists in heaven and earth exists because of the decision of God. The Jews have always believed this, and they have rejoiced in its implications. This is why Jewish piety is not at home in the spiritualism of the heart or theological flights of intellectual escapism. Old Testament ethics are practical, definite, and earthy because it is fundamental to the world-view that God made the earth by His good decision. Therefore, piety has a practical earthy implication. The Law tells about harvests and work schedules, as it should, because the God of creation cares about the earth He made.

But the Greeks are not so sure! There is an essential difference in the way of looking at the earth between the Jewish Old Testament world-view on the one side and on the other side the Greek world-view that has been permanently influenced by the perspectives of Plato. This difference will become a very sharp and open cleavage by the time of the first and second centuries when the Christian churches must decide whether Jesus Christ was a real man who really suffered and died, or was a phantom man—a spirit man who only appeared to be physically human, who only appeared to suffer the humiliation of death. The Greek world of thought will prefer its highest deities to live above creation; above the concrete, sweaty reality of the daily twenty-four-hour cycle within which we humans live out our physical existence. That Greek affection for the spiritual sought to capture the Jesus Christ of the Christian gospel and to transform Jesus Christ into a spiritualized Christ of pure idea. The movement that grew up in the later first century around this spiritualization effort has been called gnosticism.

When John writes his epistle (1 John), he is not able to counter all of the doctrines that will finally emerge in the gnostic church, but he has recognized one of the central false teachings and he sternly challenges that false doctrine by his warning: "Little children, it is the last hour; and as you have heard that the Antichrist is coming" (1 John 2:18). "Beloved, do not believe every spirit, but test the spirits, whether they are of God; because many false prophets have gone out into the world. By this you know the Spirit of God: Every spirit that confesses that Jesus Christ has come in the flesh is of God" (1 John 4:1–2).

The gnostic understanding of salvation is the ideology of grand spiritualization—the elevation of the spiritual flame within man/woman to the fullness of its potential breakthrough. For them redemption meant for the enlightened man/woman to gain the ability to escape the entrapment of the earth with its physical captivity and its evil. In such a system Christ is the aid or one of the aids toward this spiritual discovery process. Basic to this understanding of redemption is a rejection of the earth and even of our bodies since they are part of the earth's concreteness. It is the spiritual that is loved—not the concrete. We now know as a result of the discovery of the gnostic library at Nag Hammadi, Egypt, that this gnostic world-view went on to develop a complete system of cosmology to contradict the biblical world-view of the Old and New Testaments. Gnostic documents at Nag Hammadi teach that the world was created by the corrupt subdeity called Jaljabaoth.[2] This bad origin of the earth then explains, in terms of gnostic cosmology, the problem of evil and pain. Redemption happens when the "believer" discovers the true secret and knowledge *(gnōsis)* that will make possible an escape from this meaningless physical prison house to the higher spirit-world pavilions of enlightenment. Gnosticism yearns for the *"civitas platonica,"* what one Greek philosopher called the "cloud cuckooland." It regrets the earth, and, therefore, all relationship to the earth is of very little real meaning. But that is not the vision that now confronts John. The Gnostics who would read his vision of chapter 4 will be profoundly disappointed. Their whole system is under direct assault.

John's vision is the vision of the goodness of creation because of its good origin. It is by God's decision that the world was created, and, though the world is in crisis, as indeed this Book of Revelation will confirm, nevertheless, the good decision of God stands immovable. John's vision honors God for the whole created order with the salute of "Well done!" John means that however tragic the world and its particular parts may be, the prior fact is this: each part of the whole is in no sense an accident of playful gods or the bad joke of cynical deities. The creation of the world is the good act of the one holy God.

What does this amazing song mean for us today? We have been confronted in Revelation 4 by a fresh vision of our origins; therefore, we can never take the creation lightly nor despise it because of its brokenness. Here we have the biblical doctrine of creation restated in the last book of the Bible just as it was stated at the beginning in the first book of the Bible.

The Book of Revelation is, therefore, at sharp crossgrain to the incipient gnosticism which already in a primitive form was tempting the churches at Pergamum, Ephesus, and Thyatira.

As a result of this first chorale, we know that the Christian's faith in the God who has will for creation will produce an ethics that must care deeply about the earth, about harvests, about labor-management relationships, about the care of animals, about the meaning of our sexual nature, about ecology, about prisoners, about widows, unborn children, neglected children, about all of the details of being truly human. As a result of the first chorale, we know that redemption when it happens to us by the grace of God will not remove us out of the twenty-four-hour cycle within which we live our lives, but will forgive, enable, and offer compassion to us in the midst of the days and months and years that exist by the will of God. God's will, His awesome decision, is the beginning point for every other fact about life or living.

NOTES

1. See L. Morris's discussion, *The Revelation,* p. 91.

2. See W. C. Van Unnik, *Newly Discovered Gnostic Writings,* Sum. 1960, p. 75.

Chapter Four—The Second Chorale

Scripture Outline

A Great Scroll (5:1–8)

The New Song (5:9–14)

A GREAT SCROLL

5:1 And I saw in the right hand of Him who sat on the throne a scroll written inside and on the back, sealed with seven seals. [2] Then I saw a strong angel proclaiming with a loud voice, "Who is worthy to open the scroll and to loose its seals?" [3] And no one in heaven or on the earth or under the earth was able to open the scroll, or to look at it.

[4] So I wept much, because no one was found worthy to open and read the scroll, or to look at it. [5] But one of the elders said to me, "Do not weep. Behold, the Lion of the tribe of Judah, the Root of David, has prevailed to open the scroll and to loose its seven seals."

[6] And I looked, and behold, in the midst of the throne and of the four living creatures, and in the midst of the elders, stood a Lamb as though it had been slain, having seven horns and seven eyes, which are the seven Spirits of God sent out into all the earth. [7] Then He came and took the scroll out of the right hand of Him who sat on the throne.

[8] Now when He had taken the scroll, the four living creatures and the twenty-four elders fell down before the Lamb, each having a harp, and golden bowls full of incense, which are the prayers of the saints.

—Revelation 5:1–8

"In the right hand . . . a scroll . . . with seven seals." It was first-century tradition to validate and secure books and scrolls with a clay or wax seal imprinted with the special mark of the sender. The seal then had to be removed or broken in order to read the

document. In some cases, more than one seal was placed upon a document. The seal was considered the personal property of the sender.

This chapter begins with a great question that echoes throughout the whole created order of *"heaven, . . . earth, or under the earth."* The phrase "under the earth" would be understood by a first-century listener as the realm of death and even possibly the realm of punishment, Hades or Gehenna. That profound question is this: *"Who is worthy* [able] *. . . to open . . . the seals?"* The scroll is not defined in this vision in the same way as were the seven lampstands in chapter 1; therefore, we must endeavor to understand the vision's meaning from the context of the two chorales and the symphonic visions that follow. In view of that larger context, I believe the image of *"scroll written inside and on the back"* is a symbolic expression of the whole sweeping history of the creation. The words from the song of chapter 4 are still ringing in our ears, *"By Your will they exist and were created!"* It is now reasonable to see this amazing scroll with its seven seals as the narratives and meanings of that whole created order. No one in the whole of creation from heaven to hell is able to open the seals. The one who must open them cannot be found within creation. John tells us that he wept loudly because no one was found to take authoritative hold of the scroll to claim its seals as their rightful owner. The dramatic tension in this vision of chapter 5 is both emotionally and physically expressed by John.

John weeps because he senses the profound significance of the scroll and of the great question. This is a question that has haunted mankind from the opening of the story of life. It is the philosopher's question, and it is the child's question: "What is the meaning of my life, my name, my past, my present, my future? What is the meaning of the world?" That form of the question asks about the great nouns. The question has also been asked even more urgently about the verbs: "Why do I want to live? Where am I going?" When John hears that the scroll that contains these ancient and new questions cannot be opened and known, he breaks down and cries in the same way that men and women before and since John have cried in the face of the question of meaning.

John is comforted by an elder who speaks to him. "Don't cry. The Lion of the tribe of Judah . . . is able." The lion is the most often named animal in the Bible, yet only in this place in the Old and New Testament documents is the lion given unmistakable messianic meaning. Judah is called the whelp of a lion in Genesis 49:9, and is the one other text that comes the closest. However, in the intertestamental book of 2 Esdras 12:31, a messianic identification appears that has strong similarities to this phrase: "And as for the Lion whom you saw rousing up out of the forest and roaring and speaking to the eagle and reproving him for his unrighteousness and as for all his words that you have heard, this is the Messiah whom the Most High has kept until the end of day, who will arise from the posterity of David. . . ." The elder continues to speak to John and further identifies this lion as the "root of David he has conquered." Here we find another expression that is not found in this precise form in the Old Testament, although there are messianic references to the root of Jesse who was David's father (Is. 11:1, 10). Once again, it is an intertestamental book, *Sirach* 47:22, that has a reading closest to this phrase: "But the Lord will never give up His mercy . . . so He gave a remnant to Jacob, and to David a root of His stock."

Following this description of the kingly Lion, John looks toward the throne and he sees a *"Lamb, standing, as though it had been slain"* (RSV). This Greek word for lamb—*arnion*—will appear twenty-nine times in Revelation; strictly translated, *arnion* should be given as "little lamb" because the Greek here is in the diminutive. The only other place where this diminutive word for lamb appears in the New Testament is in John 21:15 where our Lord asks Peter to "feed My lambs." The word used in other places in the New Testament is the Greek word *amnos*—adult lamb—as in John 1:29, 36, Acts 8:32, 1 Peter 1:19. Therefore, there is a surprise for the reader of Revelation. It is the modesty of this word. John sees a *little lamb,* but the remarkable language of the text tells that this Lamb is alive though He was dead! He bears the marks of death, but He has triumphed over death. This Lamb is able to see all seven of His churches and the whole world through the Holy Spirit who proceeds from Him. This is John's interpretation of the seven eyes.

This Lamb, who is Jesus Christ, is the One who now takes the scroll.

The theological importance of John's dramatic vision for us today cannot be overemphasized. It is the conviction of every New Testament writer that the whole of human history finds its meaning, its convergence point, in this Lion-Lamb who is Jesus Christ. He is the critical center from which all of the parts make sense and toward which all of the parts converge. C. S. Lewis expresses this theological center by means of a literary analogy:

Let us suppose we possess parts of a novel or a symphony. Someone now brings us a newly discovered piece of manuscript and says, "This is the missing part of the work. This is the chapter on which the whole plot of the novel really turned. This is the main theme of the symphony." Our business would be to see whether the new passage, if admitted to the central place which the discoverer claimed for it, did actually illuminate all the parts we had already seen and "pull them together." Nor would we be likely to go very far wrong. The new passage, if spurious, however attractive it looked at first glance, would become harder and harder to reconcile with the rest of the work the longer we considered the matter. But if it were genuine, then at every fresh hearing of the music or every fresh reading of the book, we should find it settling down, making itself more at home, and eliciting significance from all sorts of details in the whole work which we had hitherto neglected. Even though the new central chapter or main theme contained great difficulties in itself, we should still think it genuine, provided that it continually removed difficulties elsewhere. Something like this we must do with the doctrine of the Incarnation. Here, instead of a symphony or a novel, we have the whole mass of our knowledge. The credibility will depend on the extent to which the doctrine, if accepted, can illuminate and integrate that whole mass. It is much less important that the doctrine itself should be fully comprehensible. We believe that the sun is in the sky at midday in summer not because we can clearly see the sun (in fact, we cannot) but because we can see everything else.[1]

Karl Barth shows the theological, philosophical, political, and ethical implications of Jesus Christ as the true convergence point in his commentary on the Apostle's Creed.

This is why Article II, why Christology, is the touchstone of all knowledge of God in the Christian sense, the touchstone of all theology. "Tell me how it stands with your Christology, and I shall tell you who you are." This is the point at which ways diverge, and the point at which is fixed the relation between theology and philosophy, and the relation between knowledge of God and knowledge of men, the relation between revelation and reason, the relation between Gospel and Law, the relation between God's truth and man's truth, the relation between outer and inner, the relation between theology and politics. At this point everything becomes clear or unclear, bright or dark. For here we are standing at the centre. And however high and mysterious and difficult everything we want to know might seem to us, yet we may also say that this is just where everything becomes quite simple, quite straightforward, quite childlike. Right here in this centre, in which as a Professor of Systematic Theology I must call to you, "Look! This is the point now! Either knowledge, or the greatest folly!"—here I am in front of you, like a teacher in Sunday School facing his kiddies, who has something to say which a mere four-year-old can really understand. "The world was lost, but Christ was born, rejoice, O Christendom!"[2]

The convergence theology of John's vision of the Christ and the scroll is affirmed throughout the New Testament church. Paul expressed this convergence theology in his letter to the Ephesians: "For he [God] has made known to us in all wisdom and insight the mystery of his will, according to his purpose which he set forth in Christ as a plan for the fullness of time, to unite all things in him, things in heaven and things in earth" (Eph. 1:9–10, RSV). John the Baptist, the forerunner prophet of Christ, has the vision of a grand convergence in the Lamb which he proclaimed in stern words as recorded by Luke: "I baptize you with water; but he who is mightier than I is coming, the thong of whose sandals I am not worthy to untie; he will baptize you with the Holy Spirit and with fire" (Luke 3:16, RSV).

The unknown writer to the Hebrews proclaims the same convergence in the prologue to his book: "In many and various ways God spoke of old to our fathers by the prophets; but in these last days he has spoken to us by a Son, whom he appointed the heir of all things, through whom also He created the world" (Heb. 1:1–2, RSV).

The Christology of 1 Peter has a strong Hebraic feel. Listen to his words: "You know that you were ransomed . . . with the precious blood of Christ, like that of a lamb without a blemish or spot. He was destined before the foundation of the world but was made manifest at the end of the times for your sake" (1 Pet. 1:18–20, RSV).

Right at this moment, we who read and study the Book of Revelation are at the theological center of the book. This little Lamb has the scroll! Not the devil, not the emperor, not even a scheme of history—none of these make sense of the scroll of Creation. It is Jesus Christ who holds history in His hand and, therefore, whatever fears John or his readers have in their hearts about life or death must be radically refocused. The one to fear is the Lamb, as John the Baptist had rightly announced. Paul's song in Romans 8 has made the same discovery, "Who is to judge (that is, who has the right to say the last word)? Is it Jesus Christ?" Paul answers this question, "Yes, it is Christ who says the last word, and it is this Jesus Christ who has died for us and now lives to be our advocate" (Rom. 8:31–39).

THE NEW SONG

9 And they sang a new song, saying:
"You are worthy to take the scroll,
And to open its seals;
For You were slain,
And have redeemed us to God by Your blood
Out of every tribe and tongue and people and nation,
10 And have made us kings and priests to our God;
And we shall reign on the earth."
11 Then I looked, and I heard the voice of many angels around the throne, the living creatures, and the elders; and the number of them was ten thousand times ten thousand, and thousands of thousands, 12 saying with a loud voice:
"Worthy is the Lamb who was slain
To receive power and riches and wisdom,
And strength and honor and glory and blessing!"
13 And every creature which is in heaven and on the earth and under the earth and such as are in the sea, and all that are in them, I heard saying:
"Blessing and honor and glory and power
Be to Him who sits on the throne,
And to the Lamb, forever and ever!"
14 Then the four living creatures said, "Amen!" And the twenty-four elders fell down and worshiped Him who lives forever and ever.

—Revelation 5:9–14

Now the second chorale is sung for John as all of heaven rejoices. Thousands of thousands, myriads of myriads sing this chorus of praise. The numerical description in the Greek text is constructed in a way to discourage any precise numbering of the great company. The sense of the word usage is of a number beyond counting. John has his eyes on the Lamb, not on the crowd. But what they sing to the Lamb is very important. The song is titled *"a new song."* The phrase *"new song"* has deep roots in the Old Testament messianic psalms. David sings these words in Psalm 144, "I will sing a new song to thee, O God; upon a ten-stringed harp I will play to thee, who givest victory to kings, who rescuest David thy servant" (Ps. 144:9, RSV). Also, in Psalm 96: "O sing to the Lord a new song . . . tell of His salvation from day to day . . ." (Ps. 96:1–2, RSV).

The "new" then has the connotation of the surprising gift of life and hope in the face of danger. The word "new" also becomes part of the fulfillment language of Revelation. The yearnings of David and the psalmists are now fulfilled. This new song of Revelation 5, first of all, praises God that the Lamb is worthy to hold history and to open up history's meaning.

The chorale gives thanks because redemption has been won by the life of Jesus Christ given. The RSV uses the word "ransom" in this text. This word implies the purchase of a slave out of bondage.

The song identifies those who have been ransomed as people coming from every *"tribe and tongue and people and nation"* (v. 9). This universal relevance of Christ's salvation is nowhere in the New Testament more dramatically announced. Christ has made this worldwide fellowship a "kingdom and priests" (v. 10, RSV). These two words were earlier used to describe God's people in chapter 1 of Revelation (1:6).

The final chorus is an exalted affirmation of the worth and authority of Jesus Christ the Lamb. The song ends with the whole of creation joining in praise. The last sound is a wondrous *Amen:* "Thou art the rock, Thou art trustworthy."

I know of no single musical work as compelling and grand as G. F. Handel's *"Worthy Is the Lamb"* at the end of his *Messiah*. It seems to me he has caught the surprise and joy of this vision: the exciting incongruity of it all—the mighty Lion who is the little Lamb; that Lamb, despised and rejected, broken at Mt. Calvary, now alive and rightly honored. God is so sure of Himself that He came in humility; He came alongside our lives to find us. "Proud man would have died had not a lowly God found him," St. Augustine put it. How right and good it is that we now praise this Lamb.

In the light of this vision of chapters 4 and 5, history is not as ominous and frightful as it seemed before. Whatever may come, we have met the One who gives it meaning and hope. And we must not forget this chorale in the journey ahead as the seven seals are opened. The Lamb has won in the battle against death. We grow old but "God is younger than we are" (G. K. Chesterton).

NOTES

1. C. S. Lewis, *Miracles* (New York: Macmillan, 1947), pp. 132–33.

2. Karl Barth, *Dogmatics in Outline*, p. 66.

CHAPTER 5—THE GREAT SYMPHONY

REVELATION 6:1—22:5

It is my conviction that the theological center of the Book of Revelation is found in chapters 4 and 5. Those chapters record for us the sights and the sounds of John's vision of the throne of God. The two chorales recorded in chapters 4 and 5 contain the central affirmation of the Book of Revelation. The remaining part of the Apocalypse I divide into two parts: The first part is 6:1—22:5 which consists of four symphonic movements. The second part, 22:6–21, is the postlude or epilogue of the Apocalypse.

Now let us look in more detail at the great symphony. It has four parts.

Scripture Outline

Movement I: The Great Boundary (6:1—11:19)

Movement II: The Cosmic Battle (12:1—16:21)

Movement III: The Triumph of God (17:1—20:15)

Movement IV: A New Heaven and a New Earth (21:1—22:5)

Chapters 6 through 22 form what might be described as a choral-symphonic variation upon the implications of the songs of chapters 4 and 5. Most of the rich imagery which now follows will not be explained by John for the reader, as was the case in the seven-lampstands imagery of chapter 1. It is important that we who read this book today should read these passages with reverent restraint and respect for the sense of hiddenness that envelops these visions. What is clear, however, throughout the symphonic part of this book is that Jesus Christ's reign is sure and faithful. The terrors are real, but the victory of Christ is greater and stronger.

The thematic design that unites the first two movements is the mixture of intensifying danger and terror which builds in frightfulness in each of the groups of seven. But then at a surprising moment in each of the separate visions there is a cease (Sabbath), an abrupt halt, and following that cease, a sign is revealed of the sovereign authority of the Lamb. The theme that unites the second two movements is the demonstration of the authority of Jesus Christ, as shown by the decisive acts of the sovereign Lamb in judgment and in redemption.

Movement I: The Great Boundary

Revelation 6:1—11:19

THE HORSEMEN AND THEIR FURY

6:1 Now I saw when the Lamb opened one of the seals; and I heard one of the four living creatures saying with a voice like thunder, "Come and see." ² And I looked, and behold, a white horse. He who sat on it had a bow; and a crown was given to him, and he went out conquering and to conquer.

³ When He opened the second seal, I heard the second living creature saying, "Come and see." ⁴ Another horse, fiery red, went out. And it was granted to the one who sat on it to take peace from the earth, and that people should kill one another; and there was given to him a great sword.

⁵ When He opened the third seal, I heard the third living creature say, "Come and see." So I looked, and behold, a black horse, and he who sat on it had a pair of scales in his hand. ⁶ And I heard a voice in the midst of the four living creatures saying, "A quart of wheat for a denarius, and three quarts of barley for a denarius; and do not harm the oil and the wine."

⁷ When He opened the fourth seal, I heard the voice of the fourth living creature saying, "Come and see." ⁸ So I looked, and behold, a pale horse. And the name of him who sat on it was Death, and Hades followed with him. And power was given to them over a fourth of the earth, to kill with sword, with hunger, with death, and by the beasts of the earth.

—Revelation 6:1–8

We remember how the Book of Revelation opened: "I John . . . who share with you in Jesus the tribulation . . ." (1:9, RSV). The great symphony begins with the specter of the intense pressure of tribulation. Four horses and riders are revealed as the first four seals are opened. Of the four horsemen, only the fourth is fully explained by John, but the fact that this one is defined aids in the interpretation of the first three. I would interpret the four horsemen and their horses in the following way. The first is a white horse; its rider has a bow and a crown. This is the specter of tyranny and the conquering threat of power. The second is a red horse; its rider has a great sword. This is the specter of the slaughter of war. The word that is translated in the New King James Version as *"kill"* and the Revised

Standard Version as "slay" is a stronger word in Greek. It should be literally translated "slaughter."

The third horse is black; its rider holds a balance. The third horse is the specter of famine. The saying, *"a quart of wheat for a denarius* [a day's work]," implies overwhelming poverty and hardship—the runaway inflation of an economy in ruins. The fourth horse is pale; its rider is named Death. This is the specter of death, and the place of death is *"Hades."*

Certain interpreters have held that the first rider represents Jesus Christ and/or the gospel advancing into the world. This is held because of the later vision of Christ upon a white horse in Revelation 19:11 which clearly is a portrayal of Jesus Christ. I do not feel that such an interpretation is warranted for this first horse and its rider in Revelation 6. Such an interpretation reads back to this sixth chapter the vision of chapter 19 and completely subverts the most obvious context that is present here in this text. Rather, in that second encounter in 19:1, when we meet the second great white horse and his rider, there is the genuine shock that John experiences when he sees the second white horse. This time (19:1) it is not the first of four dreadful horses of tragedy but the one horse of the triumph of the *power* of Jesus Christ over evil. The impact of the horse of chapter 19 is heightened by the fact that in the first encounter with a white horse in chapter 6, that horse with its rider is the servant of tyranny and the power of evil.

The four horses of the Apocalypse bring horror and death and famine. There is probably no picture of terror as frightening as these four horses of the Apocalypse and their riders. The relentless approach of power, of war, of famine, of death—each is an enemy of humanity and is seen as such in John's vision of the opening of the first four seals. Each dread is both ancient and contemporary. We today face the real dangers of these four foes in modern civilization just as first-century men and women faced the same terrors in the era of Roman civilization. They are timeless specters, though the means of their power have changed from generation to generation. The archer who hunted down his victim in the first century employs intercontinental ballistics missiles in this century. The rider of war chariots menaces our final third of the twentieth century with high-speed tanks, helicopters, and surprise terrorist assaults on city streets. Only famine and death stay the same. A starving child in the agrarian first century looks the same as a starving child in the industrialized twentieth century. Death is the same at all ages. It is pale as life gives way to the stillness without color.

But what we must be sure to notice in this terrible vision is that the terror of the four horsemen is bounded. The power of evil is permitted by God's decision. Notice the limitation upon the third and fourth horsemen: the horror of famine is real but not total, ". . . *do not harm the oil and the wine"* (v. 6). The power of the fourth horseman is also restrained ". . . *over a fourth of the earth"* (v. 8).

This restraint theme shall become a very vital and important ingredient in the remaining chapters of the Book of Revelation. The boundaries are a sign of hope that stands like a signpost within the whirlwind dust storm of terror.

I believe these eight verses of chapter 6 stand today as a text of hope for our generation as well as for the seven churches of the Roman province of Asia in the first century. We need to know these enemies of humanity; conquering, runaway, persecuting power is our enemy and always has been. It is our enemy when we are the ones who are pursued by it, and it is our enemy even more when we possess and use it. Power must be subject to the larger authority of God's will as revealed in the Law and the gospel; otherwise, it becomes the first horseman of the Apocalypse. War has always been the foe of humanity. Its dehumanizing and hot edge of hate has deeply scarred the story of our own century.

And what of famine, of death? Each of these is our foe *but* each of these is restrained within a larger boundary. And when we know that fact we are not as frightened as we once were, nor are we reduced to fatalistic panic by the conclusion that nothing can be done in the face of these four terrors.

Watch the text closely as John's book unfolds. We shall yet win over these horses and their riders. Therefore, we must begin right now to fashion the strategy of the gospel against these four enemies. The seven letters to the seven churches have already provided us with the strategy of hope and now we see what we are up against, but "greater is he who is for us than he that is against us" (Rom. 8). When we dare to share with other people and live out in our own lives the implications of the authority of Jesus Christ and of His gospel, we have begun the battle against death and famine and war and persecuting power.

THE FIFTH SEAL OPENED

[9] When He opened the fifth seal, I saw under the altar the souls of those who had been slain for the word of God and for the testimony which they held. [10] And they cried with a loud voice, saying, "How long, O Lord, holy and true, until You

judge and avenge our blood on those who dwell on the earth?" [11] Then a white robe was given to each of them; and it was said to them that they should rest a little while longer, until both the number of their fellow servants and their brethren, who would be killed as they were, was completed.
—*Revelation 6:9–11*

The opening of the fifth seal reveals the tragedy of the suffering and death of those who had been slain *"for the word of God."* This seal recognizes the reality of a suffering church set in the midst of the world. These servants of the Lord cry out in complaint. Their cry is very much like the cry of the prophets in the Old Testament who lament the apparent slowness of holy judgment upon evil.

> Righteous art Thou, O Lord, when I complain to thee; yet I would plead my case before thee. Why does the way of the wicked prosper? Why do all who are treacherous thrive? Thou plantest them, and they take root; they grow and bring forth fruit; thou art near in their mouth and far from their heart. But thou, O Lord, knowest me; thou seest me, and triest my mind toward thee. Pull them out like sheep for the slaughter, and set them apart for the day of slaughter. How long will the land mourn, and the grass of every field wither? For the wickedness of those who dwell in it, the beasts and birds are swept away, because men said, "He will not see our latter end" (Jer. 12:1–4, RSV).

In the Revelation, these suffering saints are not comforted by a spoken answer, but each is given a white robe and then told to wait.

THE SIXTH SEAL

[12] I looked when He opened the sixth seal, and behold, there was a great earthquake; and the sun became black as sackcloth of hair, and the moon became like blood. [13] And the stars of heaven fell to the earth, as a fig tree drops its late figs when it is shaken by a mighty wind. [14] Then the sky receded as a scroll when it is rolled up, and every mountain and island was moved out of its place. [15] And the kings of the earth, the great men, the rich men, the commanders, the mighty men,

every slave and every free man, hid themselves in the caves and in the rocks of the mountains, [16] and said to the mountains and rocks, "Fall on us and hide us from the face of Him who sits on the throne and from the wrath of the Lamb! [17] For the great day of His wrath has come, and who is able to stand?"

—*Revelation 6:12–17*

The sixth seal startles us with the vision of the earth itself in shattering upheaval. The vision is geologic and astronomic; now it is the whole physical creation that is suffering. When we come to this point in the dreadful opening of the seals, we wonder how anyone will be able to survive such wholescale upheaval. Then comes a surprise. It is in the form of a dramatic cease, a halt just at the very last moment—and none too soon.

RESTRAIN THE WIND

7:1 After these things I saw four angels standing at the four corners of the earth, holding the four winds of the earth, that the wind should not blow on the earth, on the sea, or on any tree. [2] Then I saw another angel ascending from the east, having the seal of the living God. And he cried with a loud voice to the four angels to whom it was granted to harm the earth and the sea, [3] saying, "Do not harm the earth, the sea, or the trees till we have sealed the servants of our God on their foreheads." [4] And I heard the number of those who were sealed. One hundred *and* forty-four thousand of all the tribes of the children of Israel *were* sealed:
[5] of the tribe of Judah twelve thousand *were* sealed;
of the tribe of Reuben twelve thousand *were* sealed;
of the tribe of Gad twelve thousand *were* sealed;
[6] of the tribe of Asher twelve thousand *were* sealed;
of the tribe of Naphtali twelve thousand *were* sealed;
of the tribe of Manasseh twelve thousand *were* sealed;
[7] of the tribe of Simeon twelve thousand *were* sealed;
of the tribe of Levi twelve thousand *were* sealed;
of the tribe of Issachar twelve thousand *were* sealed;
[8] of the tribe of Zebulun twelve thousand *were* sealed;
of the tribe of Joseph twelve thousand *were* sealed;
of the tribe of Benjamin twelve thousand *were* sealed.

—*Revelation 7:1–8*

Angels are commanded not to harm the earth until the servants of God have been "sealed." A holy restraint is placed upon the terrors of the four horsemen. This passage contains an interesting mixture of metaphors. It is usually a scroll or book that is sealed, as we observed in the vision of the scrolls in chapter 5. The seal denotes the ownership of the scroll. But this seal is now seen as a mark upon the foreheads of the servants of the Lord. Ezekiel 9:3–8 contains an almost identical vision. "And the Lord said to him, 'Go through the city, through Jerusalem, and put a mark upon the foreheads . . .'" (Ezek. 9:4, RSV).

John's vision now goes on to identify those who are marked, and he gives the number 144,000, which is the multiple of the square of twelve and the square of ten. It is impossible to fasten down interpretively the symbolic significance of this large number designation. The number certainly represents a completeness, as each number is multiplied by its own kind. This text preserves the mystery of God's intention for His original people founded in Abraham and Abraham's children. The next part of this vision envelops this large number into an even larger fulfillment number, and so Israel is itself fulfilled in the universal church of Jesus Christ.

SALVATION BELONGS TO GOD

9 After these things I looked, and behold, a great multitude which no one could number, of all nations, tribes, peoples, and tongues, standing before the throne and before the Lamb, clothed with white robes, with palm branches in their hands, 10 and crying out with a loud voice, saying, "Salvation belongs to our God who sits on the throne, and to the Lamb!" 11 All the angels stood around the throne and the elders and the four living creatures, and fell on their faces before the throne and worshiped God, 12 saying:

"Amen! Blessing and glory and wisdom,
Thanksgiving and honor and power and might,
Be to our God forever and ever.
Amen."

—Revelation 7:9–12

The cease occurs at the very razor's edge between the sixth seal and the seventh. As we have noted earlier, in the Hebrew language, the number seven is literally the word "Sabbath," meaning cease, rest. By surprise we are told of a vast number—*"a great multitude which no one could number"*—of people from all of the earth who are drawn together to stand before the Lamb. These are clothed in white robes, and this great company now honors the Lamb with palm branches. It is John's Gospel that tells of the palm branches the people held on the Sunday of Holy Week (John 12:13). Palm branches are significant for Israel; beginning during the time of Judas Maccabaeus they were the sign in Jewish feasts of kingly expectation. They were especially used in the feast of tabernacles and the feast of dedication as signs of victory.

This great company sings out a song of praise: *"Salvation to our God who sits on the throne, and to the Lamb!"* The word "salvation" in Greek means to be made safe, to be salvaged, and therefore carries the connotation of wholeness, healing. It is the New Testament word that expresses the rich meaning of the Old Testament word *Shalom.*

THE LAMB WHO IS THE SHEPHERD

13 Then one of the elders answered, saying to me, "Who are these arrayed in white robes, and where did they come from?"

14 And I said to him, "Sir, you know."

So he said to me, "These are the ones who come out of the great tribulation, and washed their robes and made them white in the blood of the Lamb. 15 Therefore they are before the throne of God, and serve Him day and night in His temple. And He who sits on the throne will dwell among them.
16 They shall neither hunger anymore nor thirst anymore; the sun shall not strike them, nor any heat; 17 for the Lamb who is in the midst of the throne will shepherd them and lead them to living fountains of waters. And God will wipe away every tear from their eyes."

—Revelation 7:13–17

The final song is sung to John by one of the twenty-four elders, who tells him that these who now praise the Lamb have *"come out of the great tribulation."* The tribulation of Patmos and Smyrna are not the end of the story, because the Lamb has not forgotten His people. They shall enjoy His presence, and He *"will wipe away every tear from their eyes."*

This book is written to people who are suffering, and it is in places like this great event of the seventh seal that we are helped to discover the purpose of this book in God's pastoral ministry to His people. "The consolation which *Revelation* proclaims is not based on the fact that it extols human heroism, but that it proclaims the future victory of God."[1]

This song comes at the very edge between the sixth and seventh seals. There has been a growing intensity and buildup of almost unbearable pressure throughout the opening of each of the seals, but now there comes into view a sovereign gathering in at the very border of the seventh seal. A vast choir sings to the Lord and for John the song of thanksgiving. The thrilling affirmation of this chorale is that Jesus Christ the Lamb is the One who has the might to bring salvation and wholeness. The Lamb has done it! John hears this song of praise to God that God's people who have suffered the pressure and turbulence of history have not suffered in vain. They trusted in God's promises, and God has been worthy of their trust.

The question we, as readers of this great text in Revelation, must ask is this: What is the significance, theologically and for discipleship, of this song, both to the first-century reader and to the twenty-first-century reader? I believe the implications of this hymn of praise are very important for us in our generation, just as they were important to the Christians who received this letter in the first-century Mediterranean world. Whoever we are and wherever we are in the journey of our lives, we need to know this assurance of the cease at the boundary of the sixth and seventh seals. We need to know that God's faithfulness stretches beyond the times and seasons of our own measurable existence here on earth. God's promises extend beyond these time-space dimensions that we watch so closely. John is privileged to hear a great song that bears crystal-clear witness to this fact. He hears the triumphant shout of thanks to God for the salvation that has crossed over the barrier of death. This song gives us a glimpse beyond death into the mystery of vindication.

But we must still ask: What are the effects upon a person's life and perspectives that result from such assurances that come to us from this song? What kinds of influences and motivations does such a hope have upon our daily lives here and now? I believe it is clear from the witness of the New Testament Church and throughout a study of Christian history that the influence of this song of vindication is dynamic and positive, both ethically and personally.

Just as an honest person is encouraged to pursue honesty when he or she is convinced of the triumph of justice over the long run, so this vision in the Revelation has the same effect personally and ethically. The best and most long-lasting motivational influence comes from the assurance that the Lord of my daily walk of faith today is the same Lord I shall meet at the end of my journey. The song is the song of relationship; the future hope is portrayed in relationship language. It is not a stranger who stands at the boundary of all human history but the same Lord Jesus Christ who stood at Galilee and Jordan and at the harsh hill near Jerusalem. This makes all the difference. The believer who lives in the harsh streets of a twentieth-century city or in the suffocating atmosphere of first-century Smyrna has a source of hope here and now that originates in the fact that Jesus Christ reigns at the end boundary just as He reigns at the beginning and at the middle. We live our lives in the present because of this living hope from the past, the present, and the future. It is not ideology that sustains the Christian with the kind of hope that produces relevant ethical and interpersonal action in the present and real world of our daily twenty-four-hour cycle. "Ideology, like mythology, always goes stale in the afternoon" (G. K. Chesterton). It is the living Jesus Christ who motivates us from the past as we remember His costly grace; from the present as He companions us by the Holy Spirit; and from the future as we look toward the vindication of truth, justice, love, and faith. This is the ethics of hope, and it has staying power that ideology and mysticism have never known.

THE SILENCE AND THE SOUND

8:1 When He opened the seventh seal, there was silence in heaven for about half an hour. 2 And I saw the seven angels who stand before God, and to them were given seven trumpets. 3 Then another angel, having a golden censer, came and stood at the altar. He was given much incense, that he should offer it with the prayers of all the saints upon the golden altar which was before the throne. 4 And the smoke of the incense, with the prayers of the saints, ascended before God from the angel's hand. 5 Then the angel took the censer, filled it with fire from the altar, and threw it to the earth. And there were noises, thunderings, lightnings, and an earthquake.

—*Revelation 8:1–5*

"But the Lord is in his holy temple; let all the earth keep silence before him" (Hab. 2:20, RSV). At the opening of the seventh seal, John tells us there is a stillness in heaven for about half an hour. This quietness has as much dramatic impact as the sounds and colors that have dominated the vision up to this point—perhaps even more. It is not the silence of emptiness, of the yawn of boredom, but it is the silence of mystery and intense waiting. But most important of all, it is the silence of sovereignty. There is communicated in a very dramatic way in this quietness the full and awesome authority of God. Everything must wait for His kingly move. Once again, the vision of John has taught the gospel to us. This time it is taught by the enigmatic silence which waits for the Lamb and His Father to give the trumpet to the angel. History is not a jumble of chances. There is in this interlude the portrayal of holy restraint. The sabbath of stillness proves God's might.

With verse 5 the vision moves from this intensity of stillness to the intensity of sound: ". . . there were peals of thunder, voices, flashes of lightning and an earthquake" (RSV).

THE TRUMPETS

6 So the seven angels who had the seven trumpets prepared themselves to sound.

7 The first angel sounded: And hail and fire followed, mingled with blood, and they were thrown to the earth. And a third of the trees were burned up, and all green grass was burned up.

8 Then the second angel sounded: And something like a great mountain burning with fire was thrown into the sea, and a third of the sea became blood. 9 And a third of the living creatures in the sea died, and a third of the ships were destroyed.

10 Then the third angel sounded: And a great star fell from heaven, burning like a torch, and it fell on a third of the rivers and on the springs of water. 11 The name of the star is Wormwood. A third of the waters became wormwood, and many men died from the water, because it was made bitter.

12 Then the fourth angel sounded: And a third of the sun was struck, a third of the moon, and a third of the stars, so that a third of them were darkened. A third of the day did not shine, and likewise the night.

13 And I looked, and I heard an angel flying through the midst of heaven, saying with a loud voice, "Woe, woe, woe to the inhabitants of the earth, because of the remaining blasts of the trumpet of the three angels who are about to sound!"

—*Revelation 8:6–13*

Now the trumpets blow. The first four trumpets sound and there follows geologic, astronomic devastation—*"a third of the earth . . . a third of the trees. . . ."* Note that the tragedy is extensive but not total. The bitter wormwood does harm, but not total harm.

There is an interruption prior to the final three trumpets, and an eagle (RSV) cries in a loud voice, *"Woe, woe, woe . . ."* The text in Greek reads, *"one eagle."* The eagle is an omen of danger in other places in the Bible. Jesus makes reference to the eagle as a sign of danger in Matthew 24:28: "Wherever the body is, there the eagles will be gathered together." The eagle is a bird of prey, and for a traveler upon the desert the sight of an eagle is a sign of danger. The implication of this sign is that the cry of the eagle signals even worse dangers ahead.

APOLLYON

9:1 Then the fifth angel sounded: And I saw a star fallen from heaven to the earth. To him was given the key to the bottomless pit. [2] And he opened the bottomless pit, and smoke arose out of the pit like the smoke of a great furnace. So the sun and the air were darkened because of the smoke of the pit. [3] Then out of the smoke locusts came upon the earth. And to them was given power, as the scorpions of the earth have power. [4] They were commanded not to harm the grass of the earth, or any green thing, or any tree, but only those men who do not have the seal of God on their foreheads. [5] And they were not given authority to kill them, but to torment them for five months. Their torment was like the torment of a scorpion when it strikes a man. [6] In those days men will seek death and will not find it; they will desire to die, and death will flee from them. [7] The shape of the locusts was like horses prepared for battle. On their heads were crowns of something like gold, and their faces were like the faces of men. [8] They had hair like women's hair, and their teeth were like lions' teeth. [9] And they had breastplates like breastplates of iron, and the sound of their wings was like the sound of chariots with many horses running into battle. [10] They had tails like scorpions, and there were stings in their tails. Their power was to hurt men five months. [11] And they had as king over them the angel of the bottomless pit, whose name in Hebrew is Abaddon, but in Greek he has the name Apollyon.

—Revelation 9:1–11

The fifth trumpet blows and John watches a strange thing happen, "a star fallen" opens the shaft of the bottomless pit so that warriors which are described as locust-horse-scorpion-human hybrids are loosed upon the earth. They have power, but once again as before, their power is restrained. They cannot do final harm. Their king is named by John as *Abaddon* (Hebrew), *Apollyon* (Greek).

The word *Abaddon* in Hebrew has the meaning of destruction, as in Psalm 88:11, "Shall your lovingkindness be declared in the grave? Or your faithfulness in [Abaddon] the place of destruction?" The word also appears in Job 26:6; in that text it is used as a parallel word for Sheol, which means literally "the place of death." The Greek word *Apollyon* means destroyer. Here then we have another term presented to us in Hebrew and in Greek that is used to describe the devil. He is the destroyer, and yet it is important to note that he does not, in fact, have the power to destroy. There is a sovereign restraint upon his authority and the powers of his soldiers. They *look* more powerful than they really are.

It is very important that the power of cosmic evil, the devil, not be overrated. Evil always weighs less than it looks. It always masquerades with threats and promises that it cannot keep. This is the very essence of temptation by the devil. When we overrate the devil's power to harm us, we have fallen for his temptation just as we have when we trust in his luxurious promises to help us. Both are false, and both temptations have one goal—to lure us away from confidence in God's faithfulness and God's love toward the world He created.

THE SIXTH TRUMPET

12 One woe is past. Behold, still two more woes are coming after these things.

13 Then the sixth angel sounded: And I heard a voice from the four horns of the golden altar which is before God, 14 saying to the sixth angel who had the trumpet, "Release the four angels who are bound at the great river Euphrates." 15 So the four angels, who had been prepared for the hour and day and month and year, were released to kill a third of mankind. 16 Now the number of the army of the horsemen was two hundred million; I heard the number of them. 17 And thus I saw the horses in the vision: those who sat on them had breastplates of fiery red, hyacinth blue, and sulfur yellow; and the heads of the horses were like the heads of lions; and out of their mouths came fire,

smoke, and brimstone. [18] By these three plagues a third of mankind was killed—by the fire and the smoke and the brimstone which came out of their mouths. [19] For their power is in their mouth and in their tails; for their tails are like serpents, having heads; and with them they do harm.

[20] But the rest of mankind, who were not killed by these plagues, did not repent of the works of their hands, that they should not worship demons, and idols of gold, silver, brass, stone, and wood, which can neither see nor hear nor walk. [21] And they did not repent of their murders or their sorceries or their sexual immorality or their thefts.

—*Revelation 9:12–21*

The next danger does not come from the king of the locust army but from God Himself, *"The golden altar before God."* This time a terrible judgment sweeps across the earth. The first-century Mediterranean world would have especially understood the Euphrates cavalry image. The Roman world feared the crack cavalry forces of the Parthians who came from the region of the Euphrates River in much the same way as the twenty-first-century world would fear the "smart bombs" of the United States. This cavalry force is made up of thousands of strange horselike warriors; yet it is still under the restraint of the Lamb's authority. Even their destructive power is not total, though they march by the command of God's angels.

John laments the fact that the human family which he observes in this vision is still unrepentant even in the face of such woe. Human beings continue to worship false gods and to carry on in the way of unrepentant sinfulness.

A BITTER AND SWEET BOOK

10:1 I saw still another mighty angel coming down from heaven, clothed with a cloud. And a rainbow *was* on his head, his face *was* like the sun, and his feet like pillars of fire. [2] He had a little book open in his hand. And he set his right foot on the sea and *his* left *foot* on the land, [3] and cried with a loud voice, as *when* a lion roars. When he cried out, seven thunders uttered their voices. [4] Now when the seven thunders uttered their voices, I was about to write; but I heard a voice from heaven saying to me, "Seal up the things which the seven thunders uttered, and do not write them."

5 The angel whom I saw standing on the sea and on the land raised up his hand to heaven 6 and swore by Him who lives forever and ever, who created heaven and the things that are in it, the earth and the things that are in it, and the sea and the things that are in it, that there should be delay no longer, 7 but in the days of the sounding of the seventh angel, when he is about to sound, the mystery of God would be finished, as He declared to His servants the prophets.

8 Then the voice which I heard from heaven spoke to me again and said, "Go, take the little book which is open in the hand of the angel who stands on the sea and on the earth."

9 So I went to the angel and said to him, "Give me the little book."

And he said to me, "Take and eat it; and it will make your stomach bitter, but it will be as sweet as honey in your mouth."

10 Then I took the little book out of the angel's hand and ate it, and it was as sweet as honey in my mouth. But when I had eaten it, my stomach became bitter. 11 And he said to me, "You must prophesy again about many peoples, nations, tongues, and kings."

—Revelation 10:1–11

The first symphonic movement has been building toward a devastating crescendo. John is bewildered at the vision. At this point, near to the boundary of the sixth and seventh trumpet, there is yet another interlude. John is called by a voice from heaven to eat a little scroll which a mighty angel holds. He is told, "It will be bitter to your stomach, but sweet as honey in your mouth" (10:9, RSV).

What is this little book? Ezekiel had been told to eat a scroll from the Lord and then to go to his people and speak God's Word to them. Ezekiel tells of his experience which, except in one detail, is identical to the experience of John: "Then I ate it; and it was in my mouth as sweet as honey" (Ezek. 3:36, RSV). But the little book of the Apocalypse was bitter in John's stomach.

The most obvious interpretation of this image of the little book is that John was given the Word of God to eat just as Ezekiel had been given God's Word, and John, like Ezekiel, is now commissioned to proclaim that Word from God. It has universal implications that are both bitter and sweet. The hope and the judgment are bound together.

The message of judgment and the message of hope have always been united together in the prophetic teaching of the Old and New Testaments. Jeremiah sees a vast boiling cauldron which is an omen of judgment; yet within the same vision Jeremiah sees an almond branch which is the sign of hope in the midst of winter (Jer. 1). The stern John the Baptist proclaims a bitter message that is also profoundly sweet. He challenges sin and he points to the Savior.

It was Luther who described our Christian message as "the message of Law and Gospel." "In fact, we cannot hear the last word until we have heard the next to the last word" (Bonhoeffer). Even in the message of forgiveness is the implication of guilt and judgment. What is important to note is that John is commissioned to tell the whole world the twofold message, the whole truth—it is bitter and sweet.

A MEASURING ROD

11:1 Then I was given a reed like a measuring rod. And the angel stood, saying, "Rise and measure the temple of God, the altar, and those who worship there. ² But leave out the court which is outside the temple, and do not measure it, for it has been given to the Gentiles. And they will tread the holy city underfoot for forty-two months. ³ And I will give power to my two witnesses, and they will prophesy one thousand two hundred and sixty days, clothed in sackcloth."

⁴ These are the two olive trees and the two lampstands standing before the God of the earth. ⁵ And if anyone wants to harm them, fire proceeds from their mouth and devours their enemies. And if anyone wants to harm them, he must be killed in this manner. ⁶ These have power to shut heaven, so that no rain falls in the days of their prophecy; and they have power over waters to turn them to blood, and to strike the earth with all plagues, as often as they desire.

⁷ When they finish their testimony, the beast that ascends out of the bottomless pit will make war against them, overcome them, and kill them. ⁸ And their dead bodies will lie in the street of the great city which spiritually is called Sodom and Egypt, where also our Lord was crucified. ⁹ Then those from the peoples, tribes, tongues, and nations will see their dead bodies three-and-a-half days, and not allow their dead bodies to be put into graves. ¹⁰ And those who dwell on the earth will rejoice over them, make merry, and send gifts to one

another, because these two prophets tormented those who dwell on the earth.

11 Now after the three-and-a-half days the breath of life from God entered them, and they stood on their feet, and great fear fell on those who saw them. 12 And they heard a loud voice from heaven saying to them, "Come up here." And they ascended to heaven in a cloud, and their enemies saw them. 13 In the same hour there was a great earthquake, and a tenth of the city fell. In the earthquake seven thousand people were killed, and the rest were afraid and gave glory to the God of heaven.

14 The second woe is past. Behold, the third woe is coming quickly.

—Revelation 11:1–14

Up to chapter 10 in the Book of Revelation, John has been an observer. Now he has been told to eat the small book so that he might proclaim the Word of God *"about many peoples, nations, tongues, and kings"* (10:11). Following this commission by the voice from heaven, John is commissioned with yet another task. He is given a measuring rod ("reed" is the word in Greek). The New King James text reads at this point, *"And the angel stood, saying . . ."* (11:1). The most ancient manuscripts do not include this reference to the angel. The sense of the context is that he receives the measuring rod from the same angel that he received the little book. Whatever else is taught in these very complicated sentences, it is clear that a measuring is under way. It appears to be a judgment of the earth since the final descriptions at the close of the tenth chapter had implied the inclusive, sweeping language of *"peoples, nations, tongues, and kings."*

The imagery that explains this measurement commission contains some of the most obscure and difficult imagery to be found in the Revelation. Because of that very hiddenness, we must exercise caution in attempting to interpret the imagery. The "lean-is-better-than-luxurious" rule for interpretation is the most faithful.

John's vision contains many Old Testament themes and images. The problem is to unite them into an interpretive totality.

Temple imagery is used and an allusion is made to the inner court (Jewish male precincts of the temple) and the outer court of the temple (the Gentile precincts of the temple). Two witnesses will have power to prophesy for 1,260 days. Note that even the prophetic task of the Lord's witnesses is restrained and limited by

God's authority. Their work, though it is in God's behalf, is itself not final or total. The Lord preserves the completion of every judgment for Himself.

The witnesses are described as *"two olive trees"* and *"the two lampstands."* We know from earlier references in this book that the lampstand image has referred to the Christian churches. Now what is added to that lampstand symbol for the church is the olive tree symbol, placed in poetic parallelism to it. Paul in Romans 11 also makes use of the olive tree as an image of the people of God. These witnesses have authority, but even this authority is limited as all other authority has been limited in this first symphonic movement, "no rain may fall during the days of their prophesying. . ." (11:6, RSV).

The vision continues with the news of the persecution of these witnesses in the very city where their Lord was crucified. This city is Jerusalem, even though in the hidden language of chapter 11 the city is redefined. John says it is spiritually called Sodom and Egypt.

These witnesses are slain in the persecution by the devil's beast that comes up from the bottomless pit. But now we are confronted with another surprise. Their defeat is not final. The death lasts for three and a half days, so that in John's vision even death itself is within the sovereign boundary of the Lord and these witnesses are raised up by God's *"breath of life."*

Now we stand at the edge of the sixth trumpet. The visions have been dramatic and awesome. At the midpoint in this first movement and after the sixth seal, a clear affirmation was made of the reign of Jesus Christ and of His love for His people. At that midpoint, we saw Jesus Christ as the Lamb who is the shepherd and who guides His people to springs of living water (Rev. 7:17). Then following that midpoint as an echo of the first six seals comes the even more terrifying portrayal of the six blasts of the trumpet. The battle is more far reaching than before.

As we have noted before, the one thematic unity throughout the first movement is the restraint upon every terror, whether from heaven or hell; the restraint extends upon the witnesses of the Lord as much as upon the troops of the devil. That restraint is the major theological theme of the first symphonic movement.

I believe that if we in the twenty-first-century were to understand fully this theology of Revelation 6–11, we would be protected from one of the principal temptations of twenty-first-century cultism. All cultic movements tempt the believer in Christ to abandon the central part of the gospel in order to embrace a special theme which is held as the exclusive possession of the particular cultic movement. The cultisms of fear frighten the Christian by the claim that simple faith in the gospel of Christ is not an adequate resource in the battle against evil.

These cultisms of fear are not new. First-century Christians faced the cultism of fear, too. First-century Christians faced in their own world the intensity of real danger and real terror that gave these false movements their leverage. The reality of that danger is one of the reasons that this Book of Revelation is written with cryptic, hidden vocabulary. If the documents were to be intercepted by those who wanted to harm the Christians, they would thus be unable to find in the document an outward basis to accuse the Christian congregations. But the Christians were versed in the Old Testament and intertestamental literature, and they were also fully aware of the events of the life and ministry of Jesus Christ. These Christians were able, therefore, to understand enough to hear the central message.

The big question for us in our century is this: What is the central message? Listen for it in the seven letters. Listen for it in the chorales, and watch for it in the visions. Certainly in this first movement the central message is: regardless of how frightful and dangerous the suffering in the world is, the last word, the all-important word, belongs to the Lamb. Everything else, whether the judgments of heaven or the threats from hell, is bounded by the lordship of Jesus Christ. Jesus Christ stands at the boundary— not an inky abyss or the locust dragons but He who is the Lamb. He is the One who stands there. The first movement draws to a close with the surprise interruption of the seventh trumpet.

THE KINGDOM OF THE WORLD HAS BECOME THE KINGDOM OF OUR LORD

15 Then the seventh angel sounded: And there were loud voices in heaven, saying, "The kingdoms of this world have become the kingdoms of our Lord and of His Christ, and He shall reign forever and ever!" 16 And the twenty-four elders who sat before God on their thrones fell on their faces and worshiped God, 17 saying:

"We give You thanks, O Lord God Almighty,
The One who is and who was and who is to come,
Because You have taken Your great power and reigned.
18 The nations were angry, and Your wrath has come,
And the time of the dead, that they should be judged,

And that You should reward Your servants the prophets
and the saints,
And those who fear Your name, small and great,
And should destroy those who destroy the earth."
^{19} Then the temple of God was opened in heaven, and
the ark of His covenant was seen in His temple. And there
were lightnings, noises, thunderings, an earthquake, and great
hail.

—*Revelation 11:15–19*

We are expecting to hear a third woe at the blast of the seventh
trumpet and, instead, this first movement ends with a surprise. Loud
voices in heaven sing another incredibly beautiful song of praise to
God the Father and to His Son. The term *"our Lord"* is used in this
text as a reference to God the Father. The singular noun, "kingdom,"
as the RSV has it, is the correct word, not the plural *"kingdoms."*

Now it is that we hear the central teaching of the first movement. All of the world order belongs to its true King and that King
shall reign forever and ever. The song makes clear that the Lord of
heaven is fully aware of the fury of the nations. That rebellion is
acknowledged within the song! The time (in Greek *kairos,* literally
"critical moment") has come now for God's measurement. The
song closes with an important clue to what will become the theme
of the second symphonic movement, and that theme is presented
in the final line of the chorale (vv. 17, 18): "The kairos is now for
the measurement of all and reward for God's servants and the
destruction of the destroyers of the earth."

The temple of God is opened for John to see. The ark is standing there, in the Old Testament the symbol of the presence of
God. The ark in this passage is described as the ark of His
covenant. "Covenant" is the word more than any other Old
Testament word that reminds Israel of the permanent and trustworthy promise of God. Jeremiah speaks of the hope for messianic
salvation in covenant language, "I will make with them an everlasting covenant . . ." (Jer. 32:40, RSV). Now this treasured word is
recalled and restated again.

Following the song there is an overwhelming shower of fire-
works and sound. Notice that this display of sheer power does not
come at first as if to intimidate the senses and destroy thought.
The words of the chorale are first; then there is the celebration of
sound. The content of the gospel message comes prior to the exu-
berance of worship. This order is observed in heavenly worship,

and it should be observed in the worship of God's people here on earth.

The music and sounds of celebration are the major ingredients in the Old Testament Psalms, and indeed many of the Psalms contain instructions to the instrumentalists. The Book of Revelation is the musical book of the New Testament, and very large parts of chapters 4 through 22 are pure celebration. But, as with the Psalms, the celebration in the Revelation is the result of the people's discovery of God's grace and justice. Celebration in this biblical sense is not a superficial or contrived production; it is the acceleration of joy. It seems to me that the imitation of this wondrous celebrative experience is a very dangerous thing. It is then something like the pasted-on smile of a celebrity who is suddenly aware of a news photographer. But when the gospel is present and when the people have discovered the reality of belovedness, it is very hard to keep quiet.

In my mind, the melody Handel puts with these words in his *Messiah* irresistibly accompanies them: "The kingdom of this world shall become. . . ." John is caught up by the vision of the ark, the very presence of Almighty God, and then the sights and sounds that are beyond imagination: "flashes of lightning, voices, peals of thunder, an earthquake, and heavy hail" (11:19b, RSV).

The end of the first movement . . . .

NOTES

1. Hans Lilje, *The Last Book of the Bible* (Philadelphia: Muhlenberg Press, 1957), p. 286.

MOVEMENT II: THE COSMIC BATTLE

REVELATION 12:1—16:21

A GREAT SIGN

1   Now a great sign appeared in heaven: . . .

Revelation 12:1a

The word translated here as "sign" or "portent" (RSV) is the Greek word *sēmeion*. This word is used frequently in the fourth Gospel, as for example the following: "And truly Jesus did many other signs . . ." (John 20:30). Note also, after the miracle at Cana, John's comment, "This the first of his signs, Jesus did at Cana in Galilee, and manifested his glory . . ." (John 2:11, RSV). This choice of vocabulary is another important argument in favor of the same authorship for both documents.

The second movement will consist of two major parts: The first part, Revelation 12:1—14:20, is the portrayal of a great cosmic battle in which Satan is defeated. There are seven distinct parts of this first section. The second part of the movement, Revelation 15:1—16:21, consists of a preface in the verses 1–8 of chapter 15, and that preface is followed by seven plagues against the devil and the devil's followers.

The central theme of this second symphonic movement is quite clear, but many details of the vision are more difficult to interpret precisely. Leon Morris wisely commented regarding this part of the Revelation: "While we may speak with some confidence of the main thrust of the visions, the significance of many of the details eludes us."[1]

In biblical interpretation, there is a natural instinct in an interpreter to want to fasten down as many of the details within a text as is possible. The Book of Revelation is a book that defies that instinct. In fact, this book has its richest impact in the life of the Christian and the church when the great broad strokes of the book are allowed to make their mark without being artificially interpreted or overread. We must again emphasize that too much interpretation can be as dangerous as too little. An important principle for the interpretation of all documents, this is as true interpersonally as it is in the study of the books. Some people ask too many questions in an interpersonal relationship, with the result not that more of the person is communicated but very often just the opposite: a jumble of dismantled parts.

The same is true in biblical criticism. In my view, one of the subtle dangers in the method of biblical criticism known as *form criticism,* as it has been practiced by certain New Testament scholars, is that an artificial list of situational and contextual questions are asked of the background of the Gospels with the result that the texts are not allowed simply to speak as they are actually written. It seems to me that Dorothy Sayers has described the dangers inherent in such scholarly trivialization with both wit and accuracy in her chapter, "The Bible and the Modern Reader" in *Christian Letters to a Post-Christian World.*[2]

Another kind of overreading has happened with the Book of Revelation by certain of the nineteenth, twentieth, and twenty-first-century Christian prophetic movements. Prophetic interpreters have searched so earnestly for predictive guideposts in the Book of Revelation that they sometimes steer a course of interpretation of the texts that results in highly speculative and artificial interpretations of this vision literature. Let us look for what is most clearly and plainly taught in each text and be thoughtfully cautious about the interpretation of the rest.

Now we are ready to seek to understand this opening of the second movement.

THE WOMAN AND HER SON

12:1b . . .a woman clothed with the sun, with the moon under her feet, and on her head a garland of twelve stars.
[2] Then being with child, she cried out in labor and in pain to give birth.
[3] And another sign appeared in heaven: behold, a great, fiery red dragon having seven heads and ten horns, and seven diadems on his heads. [4] His tail drew a third of the stars of heaven and threw them to the earth. And the dragon stood before the woman who was ready to give birth, to devour her Child as soon as it was born. [5] She bore a male Child who was to rule all nations with a rod of iron. And her Child was caught up to God and His throne. [6] Then the woman fled into the wilderness, where she has a place prepared by God, that

they should feed her there one thousand two hundred and sixty days.

—Revelation 12:1b–6

The first great sign is of a woman in the anguish of childbirth and in a place of grave danger. Who is this woman? Is the woman Mary the mother of our Lord now symbolically portrayed in an awesome flashback? Is the woman the symbol of Israel from whose lineage the Savior is born? The most obvious interpretation of this sign is that this is a dramatic flashback vision of the event of the birth of our Lord which shows in a dramatic fashion that the birth of Jesus in Bethlehem was a moment of cosmic significance. Herod's attempt to destroy the infant Jesus was an historical event that is overshadowed by a greater search and the intention of a more ominous foe than Herod the Great. That opponent is introduced as the second sign. It is the red dragon who seeks to devour the woman and her son. But the dragon fails in his attempt.

Once again, the *restraint, cease* theology that dominated the first movement of the symphony is already a major thematic thread in this part of the symphony as well. All of the powers that we have encountered thus far in the Book of Revelation are under restraint. Nothing has free reign apart from God the Father, Son, and Holy Spirit. God alone has what might be called total authority. All other authority we meet in this book is under the restraint of the great cease—the Sabbath of God.

In this opening of the portents, the dragon is portrayed in majestic scale with his seven heads (something like one of the hydra monsters of Greek mythology and therefore difficult to destroy). The horns symbolize power, as do the diadems. His tail sweeps down a third of the stars. This last sign of cosmic strength is terrible; however, it is still less than total. Even though parts of the heavenly creation have submitted to his false reign, a remnant still endures his rage.

WAR IN HEAVEN

[7] And war broke out in heaven: Michael and his angels fought with the dragon; and the dragon and his angels fought, [8] but they did not prevail, nor was a place found for them in heaven any longer. [9] So the great dragon was cast out, that serpent of old, called the Devil and Satan, who deceives the whole world; he was cast to the earth, and his angels were cast out with him.

10 Then I heard a loud voice saying in heaven, "Now salvation, and strength, and the kingdom of our God, and the power of His Christ have come, for the accuser of our brethren, who accused them before our God day and night, has been cast down. 11 And they overcame him by the blood of the Lamb and by the word of their testimony, and they did not love their lives to the death. 12 Therefore rejoice, O heavens, and you who dwell in them! Woe to the inhabitants of the earth and the sea! For the devil has come down to you, having great wrath, because he knows that he has a short time."

13 Now when the dragon saw that he had been cast to the earth, he persecuted the woman who gave birth to the male Child. 14 But the woman was given two wings of a great eagle, that she might fly into the wilderness to her place, where she is nourished for a time and times and half a time, from the presence of the serpent. 15 So the serpent spewed water out of his mouth like a flood after the woman, that he might cause her to be carried away by the flood. 16 But the earth helped the woman, and the earth opened its mouth and swallowed up the flood which the dragon had spewed out of his mouth. 17 And the dragon was enraged with the woman, and he went to make war with the rest of her offspring, who keep the commandments of God and have the testimony of Jesus Christ.

—*Revelation 12:7–17*

The angel Michael fights against the dragon and the dragon's angels. Michael is noted elsewhere in the Old and New Testament. In Jude 9 he is identified as the archangel who contends with the devil. In Daniel, there is a mysterious appearance of a great prince called Michael (Dan. 10:13, 21, and 12:1), who is a helper for Daniel.

In this battle the red dragon is defeated and thrown down. At this point in the vision, the dragon is identified to us as *"that serpent of old, called the Devil and Satan, who deceives the whole world . . ."* (v. 9). *"Serpent of old"* reminds us of the Genesis 3 temptations narrative. The name Devil, *Diabolis* in Greek, means "slanderer." The name *Satan* is the transliteration of the Hebrew word *Satan* and in Hebrew means "adversary." In the Old Testament this word is used in the sense of adversary in 1 Samuel 29:4 in connection with the battle between the Philistines and the Israelites: ". . . do not let him go down with us to battle, lest in the battle he become our adversary." In the Old Testament when this word *Satan* ("adversary") is used as a spiritual adversary against mankind, it takes on this special cosmic spiritual sense as in the description of Satan in Job 1:6. Here Satan the accuser stands over against the will of God and against the good of humanity.

The downward fall of Satan happens because Jesus Christ is the rightful King, and a song is now sung in heaven about the victory. The angels have defeated Satan *"by the blood of the Lamb"* (v. 11). This song then is yet another dramatic flashback. This chorale ponders the meaning of the Cross of Christ. We now know that in the death and Resurrection of Jesus Christ, more is involved than the fulfillment of the righteousness of the Law or the expression of holy love. Both are true, but now we know of a great battle that has been waged at the Cross. Now we see that Christ is the triumphant Lamb who has won the cosmic battle over the devil at the Cross. A battle was under way at Mount Calvary of which mankind was unaware. In this part of John's vision, the devil, who has been thrown down from heaven, now comes to earth in great fury because he knows that his "time is short" (v. 12).

But as violently as the dragon acts in rage and power to destroy the woman, it is nevertheless unable to harm her or her son. Even the earth helps her to survive. Therefore, the dragon sets out to stalk the rest of her offspring, which John defines as those who bear testimony to Jesus.

THE DRAGON'S ARMY

13:1 Then I stood on the sand of the sea. And I saw a beast rising up out of the sea, having seven heads and ten horns, and on his horns ten crowns, and on his heads a blasphemous name. ² Now the beast which I saw was like a leopard, his feet were like the feet of a bear, and his mouth like the mouth of a lion. The dragon gave him his power, his throne, and great authority. ³ And I saw one of his heads as if it had been mortally wounded, and his deadly wound was healed. And all the world marveled and followed the beast. ⁴ So they worshiped the dragon who gave authority to the beast; and they worshiped the beast, saying, "Who is like the beast? Who is able to make war with him?"

—Revelation 13:1–4

This chapter contains a portrayal of the violent servants of the devil which seek to do harm. Indeed, in this chapter their power appears total, except that it is a power that is allowed by God and which is under the restraint that he *"has a short time"* (12:12). The mysterious wound, *"as if it had been mortally wounded"* (13:3), is also a mixed sign of the vulnerability of this evil specter and yet also of its tenacity. This chapter is the narrative of the terrible reality of temptation to evil, of perverse distortion, and of blasphemy. It is a tragic chapter in that it tells of people who are willing and even enthusiastic to follow the twisted goals of evil; they will even worship the dragon. The show of power that wins their affection is accompanied with marvelous signs that astound the people and which conspire to complete the temptation. The haunting question of verse 4, *"Who is able to make war with him?"*, is like the cry of the intimidated person who is just at the breaking point. The power of evil seems so complete and sure; how can there possibly be any response? It is the feeling of both dread and fascination that Kurtz conveys to those around him in *Heart of Darkness* (Joseph Conrad) and the film *Apocalypse Now.* Evil is without match, apparently, and, therefore, in the face of such odds why not give way to its demands?

We know from the study of modern history that John's vision is socially and psychologically accurate not only in his own time but in our time as well. We human beings are often deceived by impressive and terrifying signs, and we are often manipulated by the show or the promise of power. There is an answer to the great question. The power of demonic power looks more fierce than it really is. But we must wait for the proof of this greater authority. At this point in the narrative we must be assured by mysterious signs such as the wound, and the fact that the dragon was not able to conquer the woman and her son.

THE TYRANNY OF THE BEAST

5 And he was given a mouth speaking great things and blasphemies, and he was given authority to continue for forty-two months. 6 Then he opened his mouth in blasphemy against God, to blaspheme His name, His tabernacle, and those who dwell in heaven. 7 It was granted to him to make war with the saints and to overcome them. And authority was given him over every tribe, tongue, and nation. 8 All who dwell on the earth will worship him, whose names have not been written in the Book of Life of the Lamb slain from the foundation of the world.

9 If anyone has an ear, let him hear. 10 He who leads into captivity shall go into captivity; he who kills with the sword

must be killed with the sword. Here is the patience and the faith of the saints.

—*Revelation 13:5–10*

The beast is haughty and blasphemous. Most interpreters have speculated that this symbol of the beast rising out of the sea, like its companion, the beast of the land, may be a hidden reference to Roman tyranny during the first century. At this point, it is important to understand the extent and nature of first-century Roman persecution of the church and also the extent and practice of emperor worship during the first century. Ramsey comments that "the shadow of the Roman Empire broods over the whole of the Apocalypse."[3]

At this point, let us try to understand the history of this period: Tiberius, A.D. 14–37, was a moderate ruler who did not encourage emperor worship, though temples were constructed to his honor in the province of Asia. His religious policy was one of tolerance, and there was no centralized religious persecution during this reign. Caligula, A.D. 37–41, was a psychologically unbalanced man who insisted upon the recognition of his own divine nature. He carried out an intense, though short-lived, persecution of Jews and Christians. Claudius, A.D. 41–54, reversed the policies of Caligula and was a moderate in religious questions. Toward the end of his reign he came under the influence of Agrippina, an ambitious woman. Claudius was finally poisoned by her. Nero, A.D. 54–68, was the Caesar who held power during these vital dates in New Testament history, and the intensity of his persecution was limited primarily to the area at and near the capital city of Rome.

Nero became emperor through the intrigue and plotting of his mother, Agrippina. The excesses of Nero's reign are a stain upon the history of the Roman Empire—a stain of terror, luxurious perversity, and inhuman brutality. Nero murdered his step-brother, Britannicus, who had been the rightful successor to his father Claudius. Nero murdered his wife, Poppaea Sabina. His teacher, the wise and moderate Seneca, was driven to suicide. The only voices of reason in Nero's government were Seneca and Burrus, who was also murdered by Nero. Finally, even Agrippina, Nero's own mother, was murdered at his command. His persecution of Christians following the fire of A.D. 64 was totally without mercy or precedent in Roman history up to that time. Finally Nero himself, after he was overthrown in A.D. 68, committed suicide.

Three emperors followed Nero in an eighteen-month period—Galba, Otto, and Vitellius. Those crucial eighteen months were a chaotic time in the empire. Vespasian, A.D. 69–79, reigned during the final days of the fall of Jerusalem. Titus, A.D. 79–81, had a brief reign. It was Domitian, A.D. 81–96, who was the most systematically brutal as a persecutor of the Jews and the Christians. He demanded that he be addressed worldwide as "Lord and God," and the persecution during his reign as Caesar was a program of the determined hunting down and destruction of the Christian church throughout the empire.

Because of the widespread extent of Domitian's persecution, most of the New Testament scholars have felt that it was within this late first-century period of persecution that the Book of Revelation was written, that is, between A.D. 81 and A.D. 96. One of the church fathers, Eusebius, held to that view, as did Jerome. Eusebius writes, "The Apostle and evangelist John related these things to the churches, when he had returned from exile on the island after the death of Domitian."

The development of emperor worship actually began before the beginning of the first century with the divine honors extended to Julius Caesar when Augustus, 27 B.C.—A.D. 14, had encouraged the worship of Julius Caesar who was his predecessor. Even prior to that time, temples had been built in one province of Asia to the Goddess of Rome. The intensity of this worship and, what is even more important, the demand for worship as a sign of loyalty, as we have noted, had an uneven history during the first century.

But the specter of Roman glory and power was always in the picture as a criterion and basis of the measurement throughout the Roman world and finally as a device for singling out those that were to be persecuted. The Jews and the Christians became those people who most often failed before the criterion and therefore were singled out for punishment. I think the strongest historical argument for the earlier date of authorship at the time near to or around A.D. 70 is precisely the fact that as John writes to the seven churches in the province of Asia, only the churches of Smyrna and Pergamum are singled out as those who are suffering what might be called intense religious persecution. Thyatira and Ephesus are honored for patient endurance, and Philadelphia is told of the hour of trial that is coming. Sardis and Laodicea are addressed as rich and prosperous. It seems to me that this is, therefore, not a portrayal of the systematic and full-scale persecution of Domitian but best describes the more erratic—sometimes hot, sometimes warm, sometimes intense, sometimes peaceful—period of the province of Asia during the time of Nero. But when John's vision confronts the tragedy of Nero's Rome, the story is different! We know from Tacitus that in Rome the Christians suffered beyond measure toward the end of Nero's reign.

> And so, to get rid of this rumor, Nero set up as the culprits and punished with the utmost refinement of cruelty a class hated for their abominations, who are commonly called Christians. Christus, from whom their name is derived, was executed at the hands of the procurator Pontius Pilate in the reign of Tiberius. Checked for the moment, this pernicious superstition again broke out, not only in Judea, the source of the evil, but even in Rome, that receptacle for everything that is sordid and degrading from every quarter of the globe, which there finds a following. Accordingly, arrest was first made of those who confessed (sc., to being Christians); then, on their evidence, an immense multitude was convicted, not so much on the charge of arson as because of hatred of the human race. Besides being put to death, they were made to serve as objects of amusement; they were clad in the hides of beasts and torn to death by dogs; others were crucified, others set on fire to serve to illuminate the night when daylight failed. Nero had thrown open his grounds for the display and was putting on a show in the circus, where he mingled with the people in the dress of a charioteer or drove about in his chariot. All this gave rise to a feeling of pity, even towards men whose guilt merited the most exemplary punishment; for it was felt that they were being destroyed not for the public good but to gratify the cruelty of an individual.[4]

This part of the second symphonic movement makes clear to us that the citizens of Nero's city cheered his excesses at first. It was only later, after the great fire, that the citizens of Rome had second thoughts. At the heart of this hard and difficult time, a word of exhortation comes to the saints, reminding them that, as their names are written in the Lamb's Book of Life, they must now, in this hard time, endure and keep the faith against all odds. Justice is the sure and real outer boundary. But now they must wait; they must survive; they must endure; and most of all, they must trust in the faithfulness of God and the Lamb.

THE BAD NUMBER *666*

11 Then I saw another beast coming up out of the earth, and he had two horns like a lamb and spoke like a dragon. 12 And he exercises all the authority of the first beast in his presence, and causes the earth and those who dwell in it to worship the first beast, whose deadly wound was healed. 13 He performs great signs, so that he even makes fire come down from heaven on the earth in the sight of men. 14 And he deceives those who dwell on the earth— by those signs which he was granted to do in the sight of the beast, telling those who dwell on the earth to make an image to the beast who was wounded by the sword and lived. 15 He was granted power to give breath to the image of the beast, that the image of the beast should both speak and cause as many as would not worship the image of the beast to be killed. 16 He causes all, both small and great, rich and poor, free and slave, to receive a mark on their right hand or on their foreheads, 17 and that no one may buy or sell except one who has the mark or the name of the beast, or the number of his name.

18 Here is wisdom. Let him who has understanding calculate the number of the beast, for it is the number of a man: His number is 666.

—Revelation 13:11–18

This chapter narrates the tragic account of the apparently unchecked reign of satanic power through its beasts. John closes this part of the visions with a cryptic reference which most ancient interpreters concluded was a hidden allusion to Nero. "This calls for wisdom: let him who has understanding reckon the number of the beast, for it is a human number, its number is six hundred and sixty-six" (v. 18, RSV). Irenaeus speculated that the number referred to the emperor Titus. Other early interpreters concluded that by 666 the Roman Empire itself was intended.

Another interpretive possibility was not so interested in counting the alphabet equivalents. Rather it noted that the number six falls short of the number seven, which, in the Old Testament, is the complete number that plays such a key role in the Revelation as the sign of full authority and completeness. In this view, the threefold repetition of the number six emphasizes the final shortfall of the power of these beasts in the devil's army.

It seems likely, in view of the subtle and guarded hiddenness of the final statement of verse 18, that John has in mind the oppressive reign of the Roman Empire during the cruel years of Nero, A.D. 54–68, and perhaps even Caligula, A.D. 37–41. The fascination with the cryptic number 666 in this chapter has produced a very wide assortment of speculations, most of which are more interesting than they are edifying or instructive. (J. M. Ford presents various speculations about the Babylonian Nimrod of Gen. 10:8 as the symbol of 666. She also tells of speculations concerning the second beast as Flavius Josephus, the Jewish historian.)

MOUNT ZION'S ARMY

14:1 Then I looked, and behold, a Lamb standing on Mount Zion, and with Him one hundred and forty-four thousand, having His Father's name written on their foreheads.
2 And I heard a voice from heaven, like the voice of many waters, and like the voice of loud thunder. And I heard the sound of harpists playing their harps. 3 They sang as it were a new song before the throne, before the four living creatures, and the elders; and no one could learn that song except the hundred and forty-four thousand who were redeemed from the earth. 4 These are the ones who were not defiled with women, for they are virgins. These are the ones who follow the Lamb wherever He goes. These were redeemed from among men, being firstfruits to God and to the Lamb. 5 And in their mouth was found no deceit, for they are without fault before the throne of God.

—Revelation 14:1–5

The specter of chapter 13 produces a feeling of desperate hopelessness with the worldwide power of the beasts who belong to the devil. Now over against that army of evil we see upon Mount Zion the Lamb with 144,000 who bear a new mark instead of the evil mark of the beast. They have the name upon their forehead of the Lamb and His Father.

Mount Zion is one of the hills upon which Jerusalem is built, and it is a term that is associated with King David and the triumph of his kingdom: "Mount Zion, on the sides of the north, the city of the great King. God is in her palaces; He is known as her refuge" (Ps. 48:2–3). The prophecy from Joel which Peter quoted in his sermon on the day of Pentecost concludes with a triumphant reference to Mount Zion: ". . . And it shall come to pass that whoever calls on the name of the LORD shall be saved. For in Mount Zion and in Jerusalem there shall be deliverance. . ." (Joel 2:32). This messianic meaning now prevails as our eyes are fastened upon the Lamb who stands upon His mountain and upon the great army at His side. The number 144,000, of which we first heard in Revelation 7:4, we now meet again. The number is probably symbolic of the vast and complete number of God's people. This people who are the obedient people of the Lamb—blameless, in that they are redeemed—comprise the army that is arrayed against the armies of the dragon.

This battle between the saints and the devil is not a new theme. The New Testament bears witness to this awesome contest in other places. Paul tells of the battle in Ephesians 6:10–20. "For we are not contending against flesh and blood" (Eph. 6:12, RSV). The weapons for the battle are the weapons of life, not the weapons of death. The devil is destroyed by new life in Christ. It is hope, faith, and love that conquer evil. Now we can understand Paul's surprising words at the close of his letter to the Romans: ". . . I want you to be wise in what is good, and simple concerning evil. And the God of peace will crush Satan under your feet shortly . . ." (Rom. 16:19–20).

John has seen something of the cosmic landscape wherein this battle against the evil one is being won. It is important to note that John is allowing a glimpse in this vision into the mysterious cosmic scale and landscape of the battle against the devil which the average Christian is waging on a day-to-day basis here and now. When we become Christians and decide to trust in the Lord Jesus Christ as our Savior and Lord, we are immediately engaged in this battle. Luther says the Christian "enters the warfare for God and takes up a new burden for God against the devil."[5] This means that our daily free choices for or against the temptation of evil are events of cosmic consequences.

THE ETERNAL GOSPEL

> [6] Then I saw another angel flying in the midst of heaven, having the everlasting gospel to preach to those who dwell on the earth to every nation, tribe, tongue, and people— [7] saying with a loud voice, "Fear God and give glory to Him, for the hour of His judgment has come; and worship Him who made heaven and earth, the sea and springs of water."
> —*Revelation 14:6–7*

In the midst of this scene another angel appears who proclaims the eternal gospel to every tribe, tongue, and people. This is the only place in the Book of Revelation where the word *"gospel"* appears, and its use here is decisive. Think of it! In the very middle of the scene of battle, the note of hope and good news is announced in a loud voice. It is the thrilling new possibility at the heart of darkness, at the place of broken dreams. It is not too late—even now—for the world to hear and repent and turn to the Lamb. This interlude of the gospel called out is theologically the companion theme to the holy restraint, the cease theme that we have observed throughout the great symphony. The restraint upon the powers of heaven and hell has signaled to us once again that Jesus Christ is Lord of history; He always is! Observe now that this loud proclamation of Good News states positively the same fact. Jesus Christ the Lamb proves His power most wonderfully in His power to forgive and heal precisely at the times when the options seemed closed and inopportune. This Good News interlude interrupts the darkness at the edge of the fearful judgment of God upon the earth.

BABYLON FALLEN

8 And another angel followed, saying, "Babylon is fallen, is fallen, that great city, because she has made all nations drink of the wine of the wrath of her fornication."

9 Then a third angel followed them, saying with a loud voice, "If anyone worships the beast and his image, and receives his mark on his forehead or on his hand, 10 he himself shall also drink of the wine of the wrath of God, which is poured out full strength into the cup of His indignation. He shall be tormented with fire and brimstone in the presence of the holy angels and in the presence of the Lamb. 11 And the smoke of their torment ascends forever and ever; and they have no rest day or night, who worship the beast and his image, and whoever receives the mark of his name."

12 Here is the patience of the saints; here are those who keep the commandments of God and the faith of Jesus.

13 Then I heard a voice from heaven saying to me, "Write: 'Blessed are the dead who die in the Lord from now on.'"

"Yes," says the Spirit, "that they may rest from their labors, and their works follow them."

14 Then I looked, and behold, a white cloud, and on the cloud sat One like the Son of Man, having on His head a golden crown, and in His hand a sharp sickle. 15 And another angel came out of the temple, crying with a loud voice to Him

who sat on the cloud, "Thrust in Your sickle and reap, for the time has come for You to reap, for the harvest of the earth is ripe." [16] So He who sat on the cloud thrust in His sickle on the earth, and the earth was reaped.

[17] Then another angel came out of the temple which is in heaven, he also having a sharp sickle.

[18] And another angel came out from the altar, who had power over fire, and he cried with a loud cry to him who had the sharp sickle, saying, "Thrust in your sharp sickle and gather the clusters of the vine of the earth, for her grapes are fully ripe." [19] So the angel thrust his sickle into the earth and gathered the vine of the earth, and threw it into the great winepress of the wrath of God. [20] And the winepress was trampled outside the city, and blood came out of the winepress, up to the horses'bridles, for one thousand six hundred furlongs.

—*Revelation 14:8–20*

The second angel announces the fall of Babylon the great (this name appears six times in the Book of Revelation: 16:19; 17:5; 18:2, 10, 21). The question is—what is the hidden significance of this name? The Babylon of the Old Testament was the place of captivity following the fall of Jerusalem in 586 B.C. But it is unlikely that John intends his readers to think here and now of the remote and distant territory of Babylon at the Euphrates River. We may rightly suspect that the word "Babylon" is used to refer to a more immediate danger that confronts the first-century Christians. John is not the only New Testament writer to make use of this name with a symbolic intention. The first letter of Peter contains a very interesting sentence in this regard, "By Silvenus, a faithful brother as I regard him, I have written briefly to you, exhorting and declaring that this is the true grace of God; stand fast in it. She who is at Babylon, who is likewise chosen, sends you greetings; and so does my son Mark" (1 Pet. 5:12–13, RSV).

It is clear that Peter intends a symbolic reference, and in the light of his and Mark's ministry at Rome, we conclude that the name of Babylon is used as a cryptic reference to Rome. Rome is not forever, in the same way that Babylon, though powerful, did not endure in the end. Rome, who has oppressed the earth, is to be brought down. That is the message of the second angel. The third angel tells of the judgment of God upon all who follow the evil of the beasts.

The disciples of the Lamb are called to remain obedient to the commandments (the holy will) of God and to trust in Jesus Christ.

Whether by life or by death, the people of the Lord are to know that they are blessed. The image of judgment that follows is that of angelic reapers who reap the grapes of wrath. It is a terrible picture of judgment and death. The battle against Satan has been won.

Verse 13 is a dramatic sentence, *"'Blessed are the dead who die in the Lord from now on.' 'Yes,' says the Spirit, . . ."* When we read these words, we hear echoes of the promise of Jesus Christ in the Sermon on the Mount: "Blessed are you when men revile you and persecute you and utter all kinds of evil against you falsely on my account. Rejoice and be glad, for your reward is great in heaven . . ." (Matt. 5:11–12, RSV). But we need to understand the biblical definition of blessed in order to make sense of the promise.

As mentioned in our discussion of Revelation 1:3, the Old Testament employs two words which are translated by the English word "blessed." *Bârak* is the Hebrew word used in such Psalms as 100 and 103, and it means literally "to bow before," or to kneel. Therefore, in sentences such as "Bless the Lord, O my soul . . ." (Ps. 103), the literal sense of the word is as follows: "Bow before the Lord," "Honor the Lord." A different Hebrew word commonly used in passages that refer to the blessing of a person is the word *'âshar,* which carries the literal meaning of "find the right path." In Psalm 1 we see this second word *'âshar:* "Blessed is the man who walks not in the counsel of the wicked . . ." It is clear that in this case, as in Psalm 119 and Proverbs 3, *blessed* means to find the right path in the face of false pathways. It is with this second sense of *'âshar* blessedness that Jesus begins the Sermon on the Mount (Matt. 5). It is also this sense of blessedness that the promise is now seen by John in its fulfillment. As Christians, we are blessed when we are on the right pathway. The pathway may be a joyous or a hard path, but it is the place of companionship with the Lord who made the promise.

This is how it is that a Christian is able to have peace in a tense place. It is not that danger is welcomed, but if I am where I know I should be, I can truthfully say—I feel blessed and I am grateful to be there. The time and the pathway may be tragic in every sense of the word and yet the reality of blessedness still hold true. One afternoon when our children were very young, a delivery truck struck our little dog; our son ran into the house screaming the terrible news. My wife, Shirley, was right there in seconds, and she and the children rushed the little dog to the vet. The children comforted Ruff Ruff with their hands as they drove. The vet was unable to save his life.

The event was tragic and nothing can change that fact, but it was a blessing that Shirley was there at that grave moment in the lives of our three small children and their dog. She was in the right place, and like salt and light she was able to stand alongside and help and pray and care and hug and cry. This is the missional sense of the word "blessing" in the Bible.

In the Bible, "blessing" is the word for success. The wondrous part of this biblical way of describing success is that the feeling of blessedness is not determined by the world's standards of success but by the standard of the gospel.

In Aleksandr Solzhenitsyn's brilliant novel *One Day in the Life of Ivan Denisovich,* the cynical Ivan mocks the faith and prayers of his young Baptist Christian friend, Alyoska. He doesn't see how the Christian prayers help Alyoska to get out of prison any faster than anyone else. Alyoska's response surprises Ivan; in effect he answers, "I don't pray for that—I pray to do the will of God. . . ." Alyoska recites to Ivan the "Our Father" prayer. There is not a word in that prayer about getting out of a Russian prison camp, but rather it is Alyoska's prayer to make it here and now in the twenty-four-hour cycle where everyone lives and to do the will of God in this part of His kingdom. What is impressive about Alyoska is that here is a man who has and knows he has meaning for his life in the midst of a hard pathway. He is blessed. Of course he wants out of prison like any human being wants to be free, but, nevertheless, he does not need to be out of prison in order to have faith, hope, and love; a mission; a deep sense of meaning; the rich sense of who he is as a human being. He is blessed here and now and wherever he is, even in death, he is blessed indeed because of the companionship of Jesus Christ. It is this unshakable blessing of God that John discovers in his great vision.

THE SONG OF MOSES AND THE LAMB

15:1 Then I saw another sign in heaven, great and marvelous: seven angels having the seven last plagues, for in them the wrath of God is complete.

² And I saw something like a sea of glass mingled with fire, and those who have the victory over the beast, over his image and over his mark and over the number of his name, standing on the sea of glass, having harps of God. ³ They sing the song of Moses, the servant of God, and the song of the Lamb, saying:

"Great and marvelous are Your works,
Lord God Almighty!

Just and true are Your ways,
O King of the saints!
⁴ Who shall not fear You, O Lord, and glorify Your name?
For You alone are holy.
For all nations shall come and worship before You,
For Your judgments have been manifested."
⁵ After these things I looked, and behold, the temple of the tabernacle of the testimony in heaven was opened. ⁶ And out of the temple came the seven angels having the seven plagues, clothed in pure bright linen, and having their chests girded with golden bands. ⁷ Then one of the four living creatures gave to the seven angels seven golden bowls full of the wrath of God who lives forever and ever. ⁸ The temple was filled with smoke from the glory of God and from His power, and no one was able to enter the temple till the seven plagues of the seven angels were completed.

—Revelation 15:1–8

Another sign now appears to John: seven angels who are to bring the seven plagues of punishment as the conclusion of the wrath of God toward evil. Just prior to those seven plagues, John hears a song that is sung by those in the triumphant army of the Lamb who have just conquered the beast.

We are told that these troops of the Lord now sing the song of Moses and the Lamb. The Old Testament's song of Moses is the great Psalm of Exodus 15. There are similarities in theme between that song of Exodus 15 and this song of Revelation 15: "I will sing to the Lord, for he has triumphed gloriously; the horse and his rider he has thrown into the sea. The Lord is my strength and my song, and He has become my salvation" (Ex. 15:1–2a, RSV).

The song of Moses is fulfilled in this chorale of Revelation 15. Moses and his army, like the army of the Lord in Revelation, have both won a victory, but Moses' song primarily exalts the Lord for the defeat of the foe; whereas, in the song of Revelation 15, the exaltation is larger and more far-reaching. God is not only the victor over Pharaoh, but He is King of the ages. All nations shall come to Him in worship. His mighty will has been revealed, and the whole created order shall experience the result.

Moses and Jesus Christ are united together in this scene in the same way that Jesus is united with David at the beginning of the battle scene in the image of Mount Zion. John's vision has thereby taught us that Jesus Christ rightly fulfills both Moses the deliverer and David the king. Here in Jesus Christ is the One who first called Moses at the burning bush, and here in Jesus Christ is the One great enough to be David's King.

The temple is opened, and the seven angels bring forth seven golden bowls filled with the wrath of God.

SEVEN PLAGUES

16:1 Then I heard a loud voice from the temple saying to the seven angels, "Go and pour out the bowls of the wrath of God on the earth."

2 So the first went and poured out his bowl upon the earth, and a foul and loathsome sore came upon the men who had the mark of the beast and those who worshiped his image.

3 Then the second angel poured out his bowl on the sea, and it became blood as of a dead man; and every living creature in the sea died.

4 Then the third angel poured out his bowl on the rivers and springs of water, and they became blood. 5 And I heard the angel of the waters saying:

"You are righteous, O Lord,
The One who is and who was and who is to be,
Because You have judged these things.
6 For they have shed the blood of saints and prophets,
And You have given them blood to drink.
For it is their just due."

7 And I heard another from the altar saying, "Even so, Lord God Almighty, true and righteous are Your judgments."

8 Then the fourth angel poured out his bowl on the sun, and power was given to him to scorch men with fire. 9 And men were scorched with great heat, and they blasphemed the name of God who has power over these plagues; and they did not repent and give Him glory.

10 Then the fifth angel poured out his bowl on the throne of the beast, and his kingdom became full of darkness; and they gnawed their tongues because of the pain. 11 They blasphemed the God of heaven because of their pains and their sores, and did not repent of their deeds.

12 Then the sixth angel poured out his bowl on the great river Euphrates, and its water was dried up, so that the way of the kings from the east might be prepared.

—Revelation 16:1–12

This chapter contains the most tragic part of the whole vision. We now read of the final judgment and conflict between God's just and holy wrath and those who are marked by the authority of the devil's beast. As the seven bowls of wrath are poured out, the restraint that was present in all of the previous visions is now seen in a new perspective. There is in this vision no apparent restraint on the punishment. It is not now a third of the sea that experiences destruction but *"every living creature in the sea died."*

The restraint is maintained, however, in one very important way. The people who are experiencing this punishment are not totally overwhelmed by God. They are permitted to curse God: "They cursed the name of God who had power over these plagues, and they did not repent and give him glory" (Rev. 16:9b, RSV). Therefore, in this one vital detail the restraint is still preserved. God will not destroy the freedom of the human being that He has created in His own image. Mankind is honored even in this tragic portrayal of total judgment. Even here, the human being is able to think and wonder and decide.

The reference to the great river Euphrates is probably once again a hidden reference to Rome and its sources of life and power, as it was the Euphrates River that nourished ancient Babylon.

ARMAGEDDON

13 And I saw three unclean spirits like frogs coming out of the mouth of the dragon, out of the mouth of the beast, and out of the mouth of the false prophet. 14 For they are spirits of demons, performing signs, which go out to the kings of the earth and of the whole world, to gather them to the battle of that great day of God Almighty.

15 "Behold, I am coming as a thief. Blessed is he who watches, and keeps his garments, lest he walk naked and they see his shame."

16 And they gathered them together to the place called in Hebrew, Armageddon.

17 Then the seventh angel poured out his bowl into the air, and a loud voice came out of the temple of heaven, from the throne, saying, "It is done!" 18 And there were noises and thunderings and lightnings; and there was a great earthquake, such a mighty and great earthquake as had not occurred since men were on the earth. 19 Now the great city was divided into three parts, and the cities of the nations fell. And great Babylon was remembered before God, to give her the cup of

the wine of the fierceness of His wrath. [20] Then every island fled away, and the mountains were not found. [21] And great hail from heaven fell upon men, each hailstone about the weight of a talent. Men blasphemed God because of the plague of the hail, since that plague was exceedingly great.

—Revelation 16:13–21

The final scene of John's judgment vision happens at a place which is called in Hebrew *Armageddon*. This word literally translated would be "Hill of Megiddo." A great battle in the history of Israel was once fought at Megiddo between King Josiah and King Neco of Egypt. This defeat paved the way for the downward destruction of the fortunes of Judah so that, in less than thirty years after the battle at Megiddo, Judah had fallen to the Neo-Babylonian empire of Nebuchadnezzar II. Megiddo is some sixty miles north of Jerusalem near Mount Carmel.

The reference to Megiddo would thus remind those who know Old Testament history of the defeat of Judah by Egypt, a defeat that set the stage for the fall of Judah to Babylon. There is a subtle portrayal by means of this place name of the balancing of the scales, so that this new Babylon—the Roman Empire—is to bear the judgment of God at the place where previously the old Babylon had been, in effect, the conqueror. But there is a larger context in this final judgment scene that goes beyond the judgment of the Roman tyranny. That larger setting, the major theme of this second symphonic movement, is the judgment of the devil, his armies, and his followers.

In the Book of the prophet Zechariah, there is a very moving reference to Megiddo that also helps us to feel some of the larger force of this scene. There are similarities between this account and the Zechariah text. Zechariah tells of a great battle, of a heavy stone, of the "cup of reeling" (Zech. 12:2) of a battle to which nations come arrayed against Jerusalem, and in the battle they are defeated. This apocalyptic prophecy of Zechariah closes with the following scene after the narrative of the triumph of God, "And I will pour out on the house of David and the inhabitants of Jerusalem a spirit of compassion and supplication, so that, when they look on Him whom they have pierced, they shall mourn for Him, as one mourns for an only child, and weep bitterly over Him, as one weeps over a first-born. On that day the mourning in Jerusalem will be as great as the mourning for Hadad-rimmon in the plain of Megiddo'" (Zech. 12:10–11, RSV). (Hadad-rimmon is a false god for which the Canaanites mourned.) Zechariah tells that at the close of the decisive victory over their enemies, the people of God will have compassion and will mourn; they will pray not for themselves but for the one who has been pierced. The question is, who is this one who has been pierced for their victory?

John, the writer of Revelation, quotes the Zechariah 12 prophecy in his own narrative of the death of Jesus Christ. John writes in his own Gospel record of the death of Jesus these words: "For these things took place that the scripture might be fulfilled, 'Not a bone of him shall be broken' (Ex. 12:46). And again another scripture says, 'They shall look on him whom they have pierced'" (John 19:36–37, RSV). In Revelation 1:7, this Zechariah text is quoted again. The text means very much to John. For John it is Jesus Christ who has won the battle, and the victory has been costly.

The result of Christ's victory for the disciples of Jesus is not a spirit of anger or vengeance towards those who are defeated but a spirit of sorrow, compassion, and earnest prayer because of the costly price that has been paid for the victory over evil.

The portrait then concludes with the account of hell's anger and cursing. Hell is self-imposed isolation from the realm of God into the realm of fear. Hell is that place where the last voice you hear is your own. ". . . Men cursed God for the plague of hail, so fearful was that plague" (Rev. 16:21, RSV).

The second movement ends on this lonely downward note. Because we know the Savior who was pierced on behalf of all humanity, even for these who now deny His love, the feeling on our part is not so much the exultation of victory but that mixture of feelings in Zechariah's vision: compassion, grief, and prayer.

This is the end of the second movement.

NOTES

1. Hans Lilje, *The Last Book of the Bible*, p. 286.

2. See her chapter, "The Bible and the Modern Reader" in *Christian Letters to a Post-Christian World* (Grand Rapids: Eerdmans, 1969), pp. 49ff. See also E. F. Palmer's discussion in *The Intimate Gospel*, pp. 32ff.

3. William Ramsey, *Letters to Seven Churches*, p. 93.

4. Tacitus, *Annales*, xv. 44.

5. Luther, *Commentary on Romans* (Grand Rapids: Zondervan, 1954), p. 100.

Movement III: The Triumph of God

Revelation 17:1—20:15

This third movement will offer a portrayal of the evil of Babylon in sweeping poetic strokes. The movement closes with the defeat of Babylon and of the imprisonment and then the final defeat of the devil. This movement is important theologically for its clear teaching that the devil is ultimately defeated by God, and this means that righteousness from God will outlast the tempting, accusing power of evil. It teaches that the universe is moral and that it is bounded in its entirety by God's authority. This movement expresses that boundary theology with dramatic forcefulness.

THE GREAT HARLOT

17:1 Then one of the seven angels who had the seven bowls came and talked with me, saying to me, "Come, I will show you the judgment of the great harlot who sits on many waters, [2] with whom the kings of the earth committed fornication, and the inhabitants of the earth were made drunk with the wine of her fornication."

[3] So he carried me away in the Spirit into the wilderness. And I saw a woman sitting on a scarlet beast which was full of names of blasphemy, having seven heads and ten horns. [4] The woman was arrayed in purple and scarlet, and adorned with gold and precious stones and pearls, having in her hand a golden cup full of abominations and the filthiness of her fornication. [5] And on her forehead a name was written:

MYSTERY,
BABYLON THE GREAT,
THE MOTHER OF HARLOTS AND OF THE ABOMINATIONS OF
THE EARTH.

[6] I saw the woman, drunk with the blood of the saints and with the blood of the martyrs of Jesus. And when I saw her, I marveled with great amazement.

[7] But the angel said to me, "Why did you marvel? I will tell you the mystery of the woman and of the beast that carries her, which has the seven heads and the ten horns. [8] The beast that you saw was, and is not, and will ascend out of the bottomless pit and go to perdition. And those who dwell on the earth will marvel, whose names are not written in the Book of Life from the foundation of the world, when they see the beast that was, and is not, and yet is.

[9] "Here is the mind which has wisdom: The seven heads are seven mountains on which the woman sits. [10] There are also seven kings. Five have fallen, one is, and the other has not yet come. And when he comes, he must continue a short time. [11] The beast that was, and is not, is himself also the eighth, and is of the seven, and is going to perdition.

[12] "The ten horns which you saw are ten kings who have received no kingdom as yet, but they receive authority for one hour as kings with the beast. [13] These are of one mind, and they will give their power and authority to the beast.

—Revelation 17:1–13

One of the angels calls to John to come and see the judgment of the great harlot. It becomes clearer than ever as John's vision unfolds that the imagery of Babylon and now the reference to the harlot are cryptic references to Rome and its empire. Roman writers themselves have given us a vivid record of the decadence of Roman society. Seneca called the city a "filthy sewer." Tacitus gives vivid descriptions of the perversity and sadistic cruelty of Nero.

John's descriptions of the Roman empire of the first century are poetically accurate.[1] The literary image of the harlot is familiar to those who know the Old Testament as the representation of rebellious Israel and also as a symbol of foreign, idolatrous peoples. Listen to Jeremiah as he speaks of Judah: ". . . Judah did not fear, but she too went and played the harlot . . . committing adultery with stone and tree" (Jer. 3:8, 9 RSV). Note that Judah's harlotry is a description of her idolatry. She abandoned God's love and chose idols for pay. Ezekiel accuses Jerusalem, "How lovesick is your heart, says the Lord God, seeing you did all these things, the deeds of a brazen harlot" (Ezek. 16:30, RSV). Isaiah accuses Tyre of being a harlot (Is. 23:15–17). The imagery of harlotry is not new to readers of the Bible.

Now in this passage Rome is described as a harlot who is seated upon a scarlet beast, beautifully dressed, wealthy, and impure. The mixture of descriptions gives the picture of garish, opulent excess—*"golden cup full of abominations"* (v. 4). The beauty of gold and pearls, jewels, and purple gowns now somehow turned luxurious and crude by its drunken chaos. But this harlot is drunk with the blood of those slain in the name of Jesus Christ. Tacitus has little sympathy for Christianity, but he was forced to note in his annals his own horror at the cruelty of Nero against Christians.[2]

At this point John gives several clues to his readers so that they will be able to discern the imagery. John must be exceedingly careful in this document because of the possible danger to the Christian churches if Roman authorities are able to fully understand its imagery. Much of the cryptic imagery of the seventeenth chapter is as opaque to us in the twenty-first century as it would have been to Roman intelligence officers of the first century.

COLLAPSE FROM WITHIN

[14] These will make war with the Lamb, and the Lamb will overcome them, for He is Lord of lords and King of kings; and those who are with Him are called, chosen, and faithful."

[15] Then he said to me, "The waters which you saw, where the harlot sits, are peoples, multitudes, nations, and tongues. [16] And the ten horns which you saw on the beast, these will hate the harlot, make her desolate and naked, eat her flesh and burn her with fire. [17] For God has put it into their hearts to fulfill His purpose, to be of one mind, and to give their kingdom to the beast, until the words of God are fulfilled. [18] And the woman whom you saw is that great city which reigns over the kings of the earth."

—*Revelation 17:14–18*

The chapter ends with the note of assurance that Jesus Christ remains Lord of lords and King of kings in spite of this powerful harlot.

Then John is told a further mystery. The harlot shall be devoured from within. Her own weapons shall be turned against her. It is God's will that makes this so. What we have here is a basic theological, historical principle taught in the Law and gospel. Because of the long-term, bedrock reality of God's righteousness, the human systems which depend upon injustice shall not endure. They are badly infected from within by their own fatal illness. The greed that gave them power, in time, shall destroy their power. The weapons by which they conquered will, in the end, conquer them. What they sowed they will reap.

This doctrine of long-term judgment is at the heart of the warnings against unrighteousness in the Old Testament wisdom literature. Listen to Solomon's advice to his son: "My son, if sinners entice you, do not consent. If they say 'Come with us let us lie in wait for blood, let us wantonly ambush the innocent. . . . My son, do not walk in the way with them . . . but these men lie in wait for their own blood, they set an ambush for their own lives. Such are the ways of all who get gain by violence; it takes away the life of its possessors" (Prov. 1:10–19, RSV).

The bedrock, holy reality that makes Solomon's counsel true is now reaffirmed in the vision of John. Rome will collapse from within long before the Germanic tribes from northern Europe will cross the Alps.

A POEM OF LAMENTATION

18:1 After these things I saw another angel coming down from heaven, having great authority, and the earth was illuminated with his glory. 2 And he cried mightily with a loud voice, saying, "Babylon the great is fallen, is fallen, and has become a dwelling place of demons, a prison for every foul spirit, and a cage for every unclean and hated bird! 3 For all the nations have drunk of the wine of the wrath of her fornication, the kings of the earth have committed fornication with her, and the merchants of the earth have become rich through the abundance of her luxury."

4 And I heard another voice from heaven saying, "Come out of her, my people, lest you share in her sins, and lest you receive of her plagues. 5 For her sins have reached to heaven, and God has remembered her iniquities. 6 Render to her just as she rendered to you, and repay her double according to her works; in the cup which she has mixed, mix double for her. 7 In the measure that she glorified herself and lived luxuriously, in the same measure give her torment and sorrow; for she says in her heart, 'I sit as queen, and am no widow, and will not see sorrow.' 8 Therefore her plagues will come in one day—death and mourning and famine. And she will be utterly burned with fire, for strong is the Lord God who judges her.

9 "The kings of the earth who committed fornication and lived luxuriously with her will weep and lament for her, when they see the smoke of her burning, 10 standing at a distance for fear of her torment, saying, 'Alas, alas, that great city Babylon, that mighty city! For in one hour your judgment has come.'

11 "And the merchants of the earth will weep and mourn over her, for no one buys their merchandise anymore: 12 merchandise of gold and silver, precious stones and pearls, fine linen and purple, silk and scarlet, every kind of citron wood, every kind of object of ivory, every kind of object of most precious wood, bronze, iron, and marble; 13 and cinnamon and incense, fragrant oil and frankincense, wine and oil, fine flour and wheat, cattle and sheep, horses and chariots, and bodies and souls of men. 14 The fruit that your soul longed for has gone from you, and all the things which are rich and splendid have gone from you, and you shall find them no more at all. 15 The merchants of these things, who became rich by her, will stand at a distance for fear of her torment, weeping and wailing, 16 and saying, 'Alas, alas, that great city that was clothed in fine linen, purple, and scarlet, and adorned with gold and precious stones and pearls! 17 For in one hour such great riches came to nothing.' Every shipmaster, all who travel by ship, sailors, and as many as trade on the sea, stood at a distance 18 and cried out when they saw the smoke of her burning, saying, 'What is like this great city?'

19 "They threw dust on their heads and cried out, weeping and wailing, and saying, 'Alas, alas, that great city, in which all who had ships on the sea became rich by her wealth! For in one hour she is made desolate.'

20 "Rejoice over her, O heaven, and you holy apostles and prophets, for God has avenged you on her!"
—*Revelation 18:1–20*

This long and detailed poem has many similarities to the description of the fall of Tyre in Ezekiel 26—27, and also Isaiah's song of doom regarding Babylon in Isaiah 13, 14, and 21. Wave upon wave of poetic image tells of the fall of Rome and its empire. There are frequent references to the luxurious and decadent Babylon. The vision of destruction is so total that there is no possibility of escape or help unless God Himself were to change the inevitable course of the collapse.

The saints, apostles, and prophets are told to rejoice that God has vindicated truth over against falsehood.

STILLNESS IN BABYLON

21 Then a mighty angel took up a stone like a great millstone and threw *it* into the sea, saying, "Thus with violence the great city Babylon shall be thrown down, and shall not be found anymore. 22 The sound of harpists, musicians, flutists, and trumpeters shall not be heard in you anymore. No craftsman of any craft shall be found in you anymore, and the sound of a millstone shall not be heard in you anymore. 23 The light of a lamp shall not shine in you anymore, and the voice of bridegroom and bride shall not be heard in you anymore. For your merchants were the great men of the earth, for by your sorcery all the nations were deceived. 24 And in her was found the blood of prophets and saints, and of all who were slain on the earth."

—Revelation 18:21–24

The final lines of the song of lamentation tell that as the city lay in collapse they found in her the *"blood of prophets and saints, and of all who were slain on the earth."*

The stern justice by which Babylon is destroyed was inevitable because the God who judges is the God of truth and love. Just as in the rubble of the Third Reich our generation found the terrible evidences of hatred for mankind represented in places like Auschwitz, so also Rome had done real harm upon the face of the earth. This poem calls out the song of doom so that mankind shall never forget that real harm and shall never forget that God judges all those who do harm. But in a deeper sense, mankind must never forget God's justice and love that made the fall of tyranny a necessity. The character of God stands behind the judgment.

How then are we to interpret these portrayals of the judgment of Rome? This is also a problem for the interpretation of Old Testament prophetic/apocalyptic books as well. In the Old Testament, nations and kings are also destroyed and the judgment of God is pronounced upon them. There are numerous examples in the Old Testament, for instance, the narratives in Genesis and Exodus concerning Egypt in the time of the Exodus. Certainly among Christians and Jews of the first century the judgments upon Egypt were well known because of the feasts that celebrated the memory of the Exodus.

There are many other examples as well: the judgment of God upon Sodom and Gomorrah as told in Genesis 18 and 19; the long, prophetic lamentations of doom that tell of God's judgment of Babylon (Jer. 50, 51); the Book of Amos beginning with a litany of the judgment of God against the nations that surround Judah, and the final judgment in that litany against Judah itself. Therefore, the question we must ask about the meaning for us today of these apocalyptic visions of judgment against Rome is the same question we must ask interpretively with regard to all the biblical pronouncements of judgment against nations.

What does it mean for us to read these texts in our century, since the cups of judgment have already been drained? Sodom and Gomorrah are destroyed cities that lie in ruin beneath the shallows of the Dead Sea. Babylon was destroyed at the time of Alexander the Great. Ancient Rome and its caesars are gone.

The answer is twofold. First, the Bible is a historical record as much as it is a theological affirmation. The Bible is the narrative about real people and real places. It tells of their journeys, and it tells of their yearnings. God reveals His character within the framework of history, not in the mythologies of magicians. The Exodus is a real event in the life of an enslaved people who were led out of Egypt by Yahweh. The Shema of Israel recalls that event. "Hear, O Israel . . . I am the Lord your God who brought you out of the land of Egypt" (Deut. 5:1, 6, RSV). Israel was to always remember that event and to ponder its meaning. God's love is not an idea or a story in the Bible; it is the event that happens. Because of this event orientation of the Bible, the Gospel narratives of the life of Jesus Christ are the narratives of events that actually happened. The Gospels are not novels about what God's love might look like if it had to do with people. God is able to speak for Himself, and He has spoken. His love has to do with people—real people like a man at the pool of Bethesda (John 5), a young couple who are newly married (John 2), a paralyzed youth lowered through a broken hole in a ceiling of a rich man's house at Capernaum (Luke 5). The Gospels tell about Jesus of Nazareth, about a Roman official Pilate and his fear of the crowd, about a real death on the Roman cross, about a real victory over death. The grave was empty!

As you can see, the whole of the Bible has an event perspective, and we learn the gospel first by watching the events and, secondly, by receiving into our lives by faith the living Lord of the events. When we human beings trust Jesus Christ, this becomes a new event that happens, and that new event, when it is united with other believers, is the birth of the Christian church in the world. The journeys of that church are the primary narrative concerns of all the books of the New Testament after the four Gospels.

Therefore, we must learn the Law and the gospel from the judgment narratives in Revelation in the same way that we learn the Law and the gospel from watching narratives of Amos and Jeremiah as they speak God's judgment and forgiveness in Israel's earlier history. We are watching God's justice and grace as an event.

The difference in vision literature is that the event of God's judgment is expressed by hidden language. When Jeremiah first speaks for God the news about the impending Assyrian attack of Samaria, his words are as follows: ". . . and I see a boiling cauldron facing away from the North." That hidden and symbolic language described as real a historical event as the invasion of Europe by the allies in 1944 which was signaled to the French underground with the hidden Code word *overlord.* These passages in the Revelation have importance for this very reason: They portray the event of judgment and the event of salvation. The judgments refer to a nation in first-century history, but the Code words and the time frame are mysterious. The historical fact is that judgment has happened against Roman tyranny—and what is even more important—against evil at the cosmic order of the creation as well as the devil.

There is another answer to the question of interpretation. There is a timeless relevance to everything that God has revealed about Himself. That timeless relevance stretches beyond the historical context of Jeremiah's century or the first century. When Jesus breaks through the barrier of racial prejudice in His gracious encounter with the woman at the well (John 4), we are rightly interpreting that event when we seek to understand what Jesus Christ has revealed about His own character and His will for human life in that unique historical situation. The scenes in themselves are historical and important, yet they point beyond themselves to the self-disclosure of Jesus Christ.

John calls the event at the wedding at Cana just such a sign. The surprising miracle of water turned to wine was a joyous experience for the wedding crowd, but it also had greater meaning. It showed the glory of Jesus Christ. This same fact is true of the Exodus event. It is very important as an event in the journey of Israel, and yet it also is a signpost that points beyond itself to the self-disclosure of God's character.

Therefore, in these texts in the Revelation we discover more than simply the narratives of Rome and its lusts and its fall. These texts of judgment and hope teach us about the theology of power, of accountability, of the eternal measuring of human institutions, of the hope that is rooted in God's character.

One has the picture in this 18th chapter of a grieving John walking among the now silent wasteland of human arrogance. Everything has collapsed in the crashing sounds of chapter 18. The lamps are out, voices are silent, the flutes and minstrels are no longer playing. The scene is stark and hopeless. The city was powerful, rich, and cruel, and now it has all come to this. "This is how the world ends, this is how the world ends, this is how the world ends, not with a bang but a whimper" (T. S. Eliot, *The Hollow Men).* But from the distance, there gradually swells a new source of sound so that John's eyes and ears are caught up again by a surprising new song.

THE SONG TO THE SALVATION OF GOD

19:1 After these things I heard a loud voice of a great multitude in heaven, saying, "Alleluia! Salvation and glory and honor and power belong to the Lord our God! 2 For true and righteous are His judgments, because He has judged the great harlot who corrupted the earth with her fornication; and He has avenged on her the blood of His servants shed by her." 3 Again they said, "Alleluia! Her smoke rises up forever and ever!" 4 And the twenty-four elders and the four living creatures fell down and worshiped God who sat on the throne, saying, "Amen! Alleluia!" 5 Then a voice came from the throne, saying, "Praise our God, all you His servants and those who fear Him, both small and great!"

—*Revelation 19:1–5*

The first word he hears is the word "alleluia," which is a transliteration of the Hebrew, literally *haleel,* "praise *Yahweh"*—God. In the Old Testament English Bible, this Hebrew phrase is translated into English by the phrase, "praise the Lord" (e.g., Ps. 113:1). It is interesting that the transliterated word "alleluia" ("Hallelujah," RSV) is found only in the Book of Revelation.

Salvation, glory, and power belong to God. The song continues to praise God for His true and righteous judgment against the harlot. We are reminded once again of the song of Moses in Exodus 15 and the closing lines of the song of Moses in Deuteronomy 32, "Praise his people O you nations; for he avenges the blood of his servants, and takes vengeance on his adversaries . . ." (Deut. 32:43, RSV).

This is a song of salvation, and the principle theological content is the praise of God for the triumph of His justice and the judgment that must go with justice. This grappling with evil is an essential part of the theology of salvation. The promise of forgiveness does not mean anything without the felt sense of need and guilt. If evil is not judged, then the promises of grace have a hollow ring about them, in that there is no solid measuring rod against which a real discovery of who I am has occurred. That real measuring is so essential that without it, instead of grace and forgiveness of sin, what is left in its place is indifference. But these visions in Revelation have shown that God is not indifferent to human suffering—to tyranny—to idolatry. Everything in the life of mankind is grappled with by God. This grappling is the judgment of the God who cares.

Now the heavenly chorus sings praise to God for that faithful judgment. They praise God because the foundation cornerstone of truth has won the battle against the storm of the devil. Therefore, the promises are founded upon a sure foundation. That is the importance of this song. The river has broken its banks and fallen upon the house, but the house has withstood the storm (Matt. 7).

MARRIAGE OF THE LAMB

6 And I heard, as it were, the voice of a great multitude, as the sound of many waters and as the sound of mighty thunderings, saying, "Alleluia! For the Lord God Omnipotent reigns! 7 Let us be glad and rejoice and give Him glory, for the marriage of the Lamb has come, and His wife has made herself ready." 8 And to her it was granted to be arrayed in fine linen, clean and bright, for the fine linen is the righteous acts of the saints.

9 Then he said to me, "Write: 'Blessed are those who are called to the marriage supper of the Lamb!'" And he said to me, "These are the true sayings of God." 10 And I fell at his feet to worship him. But he said to me, "See that you do not do that! I am your fellow servant, and of your brethren who have the testimony of Jesus. Worship God! For the testimony of Jesus is the spirit of prophecy."

—*Revelation 19:6–10*

The second half of the song is the invitation to the marriage of the Lamb and the bride who shall be clothed in the pure bright linen of righteousness. The church of Jesus Christ is this bride, as the later references in the Revelation will make clear. This image for the church and for God's people as a bride is common in both the Old and New Testaments. The songs of chapter 19 are, first, the song of praise for the righteous judgment of God and, second, praise to God for the privilege of relationship with the Lamb as His bride. It is not enough to know the truth of God. We are welcomed into His family as His beloved bride.

John, in his enthusiasm, falls down to worship the angel who has shared with him the news of the joyous wedding. But the angel refuses the worship of John. *"See that you do not do that! I am your fellow servant . . . !"* Only God deserves human worship. We are to worship nothing in heaven or earth—only the eternal Lord.

THE LORD OF THE WHITE HORSE

[11] Now I saw heaven opened, and behold, a white horse. And He who sat on him was called Faithful and True, and in righteousness He judges and makes war. [12] His eyes were like a flame of fire, and on His head were many crowns. He had a name written that no one knew except Himself. [13] He was clothed with a robe dipped in blood, and His name is called The Word of God. [14] And the armies in heaven, clothed in fine linen, white and clean, followed Him on white horses. [15] Now out of His mouth goes a sharp sword, that with it He should strike the nations. And He Himself will rule them with a rod of iron. He Himself treads the winepress of the fierceness and wrath of Almighty God. [16] And He has on His robe and on His thigh a name written:

KING OF KINGS AND LORD OF LORDS.

[17] Then I saw an angel standing in the sun; and he cried with a loud voice, saying to all the birds that fly in the midst of heaven, "Come and gather together for the supper of the great God, [18] that you may eat the flesh of kings, the flesh of captains, the flesh of mighty men, the flesh of horses and of those who sit on them, and the flesh of all people, free and slave, both small and great."

[19] And I saw the beast, the kings of the earth, and their armies, gathered together to make war against Him who sat on the horse and against His army. [20] Then the beast was cap-

tured, and with him the false prophet who worked signs in his presence, by which he deceived those who received the mark of the beast and those who worshiped his image. These two were cast alive into the lake of fire burning with brimstone. 21 And the rest were killed with the sword which proceeded from the mouth of Him who sat on the horse. And all the birds were filled with their flesh.

—Revelation 19:11–21

Now follows a dramatic vision of a white horse with a majestic rider who is called faithful, true, the righteous warrior, judge, the *Word of God.* Many features of this vision of Jesus Christ are similar to the first vision of the book. Now, instead of being called the Alpha and Omega, He is called the Word of God. He is God speaking for Himself, making Himself known in authority and truth.

Another scene of judgment against the armies of the devil is portrayed. John is shown the terrible finality of condemnation to a lake of fire. This lake of fire portrayal, would be a familiar reference to hell for a first-century reader. Jewish and Christian writings both refer to the place of punishment as a place of burning, Gehenna.

THE THOUSAND YEARS

20:1 Then I saw an angel coming down from heaven, having the key to the bottomless pit and a great chain in his hand. 2 He laid hold of the dragon, that serpent of old, who is the Devil and Satan, and bound him for a thousand years; 3 and he cast him into the bottomless pit, and shut him up, and set a seal on him, so that he should deceive the nations no more till the thousand years were finished. But after these things he must be released for a little while.

4 And I saw thrones, and they sat on them, and judgment was committed to them. Then I saw the souls of those who had been beheaded for their witness to Jesus and for the word of God, who had not worshiped the beast or his image, and had not received his mark on their foreheads or on their hands. And they lived and reigned with Christ for a thousand years. 5 But the rest of the dead did not live again until the thousand years were finished. This is the first resurrection. 6 Blessed and holy is he who has part in the first resurrection. Over such the second death has no power, but they shall be

priests of God and of Christ, and shall reign with Him a thousand years.

—*Revelation 20:1–6*

The judgment vision now comes to its last part. The dragon (the devil) is thrown into the bottomless pit for a thousand years. The number 1,000 as a significant unit of time is given attention in two other places in the Bible. Psalm 90:4 is a famous example, "For a thousand years in thy sight are but as yesterday when it is past, or as a watch in the night." An important New Testament passage is 2 Peter 3:8: "But, beloved, do not forget this one thing that with the Lord one day is as a thousand years, and a thousand years as one day." Now in this Revelation vision John is presented with the same number. Those who had remained loyal to Jesus Christ unto death were resurrected. (In this vision, up to verse five, the past tenses are used.) They reign as priests with Jesus Christ in this thousand-year time. We recall the promise made to the Christians in the church of Smyrna who were promised that they had nothing to fear of the "second death." This promise is now repeated, and in this chapter we will discover that the second death means punishment in the lake of fire. In this narrative we learn about the two resurrections as well as the two deaths.

How are we to correctly interpret this narrative of the thousand-year reign of the saints with Jesus Christ? There is a sense of cosmic fulfillment that echoes within this remarkable passage. Those who have been faithful to Jesus Christ shall be raised up and reign with him for a thousand years. There is no mention of earth as the place of that reign; therefore, the wonder of the promise is all the more impressive. We catch here the vision of the tremendous importance of the Christians and their lives. Paul, in his letter to the Ephesians, has an understanding of this amazing destiny (Eph. 1:3–10). Paul tells the Ephesian Christians that they were loved and chosen before the foundation of the world and destined in love to discover the mystery of God's will "as a plan for the fullness of time, to unite all things in him, things in heaven and things on earth" (v. 10, RSV).

This promise of the thousand-year reign must be honored and gratefully received by the Christian, but the promise should not be carelessly handled or carelessly interpreted. We should stand back with respect and wonder at the sheer scale and extent of the promise. The details of this destiny shall be fulfilled and worked out according to God's will, and it is enough that Christians realize that we shall have tasks and work to do after the first boundary of our earthly pilgrimage. We shall be with Jesus Christ, and we shall reign with Him.

THE LAST BATTLE

[7] Now when the thousand years have expired, Satan will be released from his prison [8] and will go out to deceive the nations which are in the four corners of the earth, Gog and Magog, to gather them together to battle, whose number is as the sand of the sea. [9] They went up on the breadth of the earth and surrounded the camp of the saints and the beloved city. And fire came down from God out of heaven and devoured them. [10] The devil, who deceived them, was cast into the lake of fire and brimstone where the beast and the false prophet are. And they will be tormented day and night forever and ever.

—Revelation 20:7–10

Following this vision of the priestly reign of those who had died as martyrs and who had not worshiped the beast, the final vision tells of the release of Satan from his prison following the thousand years, so that he and all of his followers may be gathered together for the last judgment. Gog and Magog comprise that army of followers.

Gog and Magog, in this context, appear to be a symbol for the hosts of the wicked. In Jewish apocalyptic writing, Gog and Magog represent forces of evil.[3] In Ezekiel 38, 39, the same evil connotation prevails.[4]

THE FINAL JUDGMENT

[11] Then I saw a great white throne and Him who sat on it, from whose face the earth and the heaven fled away. And there was found no place for them. [12] And I saw the dead, small and great, standing before God, and books were opened. And another book was opened, which is the Book of Life. And the dead were judged according to their works, by the things which were written in the books. [13] The sea gave up the dead who were in it, and Death and Hades delivered up the dead who were in them. And they were judged, each one according to his works. [14] Then Death and Hades were cast into the lake

of fire. This is the second death. [15] And anyone not found
written in the Book of Life was cast into the lake of fire.
—*Revelation 20:11–15*

There follows now the final judgment of the army of Satan and
then one more scene. This part of the vision literature of the Book
of Revelation has been the most difficult to interpret with confidence. The opinions differ among Christian interpreters, and Leon
Morris's counsel is very helpful in his commentary on this millen-
nial text. He writes: "There have been endless disputes, some of
them very bitter, over the way to understand this chapter. Evangeli-
cals have divided from one another and sometimes have been quite
intolerant of views other than those of their own group. It is necessary to approach the chapter with humility and charity."[5]

It is my view that this thousand-year portrayal is a mysterious
reminder to the Christians of all time who read this letter. Its message is that our shepherd Lord both treasures His people and that
His people share with Him in the holy task of sharing the gospel
of Jesus Christ in the world. It is a priestly reign that the loyal followers of the Lamb are granted. The text is mysterious in that it is
not said that this is a reign on earth or in heaven, but a priestly
reign it is—and that means a task that the Lord's people are
enabled to do in the companionship of the Lamb. Wherever the
disciples of Jesus Christ are—whether alive or dead—we belong to
the Lamb and His task is our task. This amazing text has now preserved the mystery of it all.

The readers of John's letter must have had a strange feeling at
this point in the book as they realized the cosmic and far-reaching extent of their lives and ministries. The very term "a thousand
years" stretches far beyond any lifespan that we can expect. As a
symbol, therefore, this has the effect of affirming to us just how
important God's people are to Him—and especially those who
have suffered in His name. It becomes a first glimpse of the eternal life that awaits God's people.

The final scene in this movement is that of the white throne of
God, and before the throne the great and the small standing before
God as books were opened. The judgment is made upon each one of
these who have been drawn up (resurrected) from all time to stand
before God and hear of the result of the reading of the books. The
most important book is the Book of *Life.* This term was first used in
Revelation in the letter to the church of Sardis. In the Gospel of Luke
our Lord also promised such a living record to His disciples, ". . . do

not rejoice in this, that the spirits are subject to you; but rather rejoice because your names are written in heaven" (Luke 10:20). No further evidence is given to us with regard to the means and ways of this judgment, except that the God of justice and grace is the One who decides. Everything is out of our hands in this vision. It is the vision of the singular justice and kindness of God Himself.

This moment is a very serious and awesome moment, as even death itself is ended by the judgment of God. But it is a good moment too because God is that judge. The third symphonic movement ends with this scene of Holy decision about the destiny of every living being. There is a quietness about the moment of supreme truth.

NOTES

1. See William Barclay's discussion of first-century Rome.

2. *Annales* 25:44.

3. Jubilees 8:25; Sibylline Oracles 3:31; also in the Targums.

4. See discussion by L. Morris, *The Revelation,* p. 239, and J. M. Ford *Revelation (Anchor),* p. 356.

MOVEMENT IV: A NEW HEAVEN AND A NEW EARTH

REVELATION 21:1—22:5

THE DWELLING OF GOD WITH US

21:1 Now I saw a new heaven and a new earth, for the first heaven and the first earth had passed away. Also there was no more sea. ² Then I, John, saw the holy city, New Jerusalem, coming down out of heaven from God, prepared as a bride adorned for her husband. ³ And I heard a loud voice from heaven saying, "Behold, the tabernacle of God is with men, and He will dwell with them, and they shall be His people. God Himself will be with them and be their God. ⁴ And God will wipe away every tear from their eyes; there shall be no more death, nor sorrow, nor crying. There shall be no more pain, for the former things have passed away."

—Revelation 21:1–4

The earth and heaven and the sea have *"passed away."* The language of the fourth movement is fulfillment language which means that the old orders have been fulfilled by the new. God promises all things new, and yet the first *"new"* we meet is a new city with an old name. Jerusalem is a new city with an old name. Jerusalem is the city that David first founded; it now becomes new. The vision is of Jerusalem fulfilled and now made into the city that it was originally intended.

The same shall happen for the earth, heaven, and the seas; they pass away not toward oblivion but toward this new completion of God's fulfilled design. Therefore, in the order that John describes to us in this fourth movement of the grand symphony, we hear about the fulfillment of what we already know. Water, mountains, trees, fruit, metals, people, food; even distances are recorded and doorways counted in the vision of the new order. In other words, the symbolism of the new heaven and new earth is the language of completion, not absorption. The central and most fundamental language of this new fulfilled order is *relationship language.* Notice how impressive and far-reaching is the theology of relationship as taught in this vision.

The new Jerusalem is not described first of all as a geographical phenomenon but as a bride. This is the most intimate relationship language of all, as much so in the first century as today. There is a tenderness and joyousness in the marriage image. That symbol is to become our very first impression of God's new order. It is not the splendor of the wealth of God's new order. It is not the splendor of the wealth of God that first confronts John in his vision of the new heaven and new earth. Rather, first he sees God's beloved bride. We are shown first of all that of which the Lamb is proudest. It would be like visiting the estate of a great man who, as you first enter his estate, proudly introduces you to his family, his bride, his children; everything else is secondary in his mind. So it is in God's eternal new order.

We are so conditioned to think of ourselves in deprecatory terms that we have a hard time really believing this vision. This is the "weight of glory" of which C. S. Lewis speaks. Even the spiritual problem of pride is usually a cover-up for the person who, if he or she were really known, at heart feels unacceptable. Whether proud or depressed, the human personality has a hard time accepting the gift of importance that this vision has conferred upon our lives. We share the center stage of this great scene with the Lamb. Think of it! The seven struggling churches of the province of Asia, made up of ordinary Christians, together with ordinary men and women like them throughout all time, are the beloved bride. What an experience for John as he looks in upon this great vision of his own future destiny! He sees in God's new heaven and new earth the people that he knows.

For me in this twenty-first century, it is difficult to take it all in—to think that also I and my family know some of those who make up this joyous company. Christians of our own life's journey are there—Dallas and Mary Birch, Peter Adler, Sally Scheid, Hanna Warner, Henrietta Mears, L. David Cowie, Bob Griffin, Larry Christenson, Dick Jacobson. We who believe in the Lamb are the bride. No one has been forced to come to the marriage. The grace of the Lamb is triumphant, but that grace has not compelled men and women to believe. His grace woos us but does not cancel us out (C. S. Lewis). The freedom to believe or not believe has been preserved throughout this whole book, and that freedom is now fulfilled in the image of the bride. It is not a slave brought to the king as the spoils of war, but the bride who will dwell with her husband in love.

The imagery of relationship continues with a sentence that is a restatement of the new covenant promise in Ezekiel, "My dwelling place shall be with them, and I will be their God, and they shall be my people" (Ezek. 37:27, RSV). The new covenant promise in Jeremiah had made the same promise: "They shall be My people, and I will be their God . . . I will make with them an everlasting covenant . . ." (Jer. 32:38, 40, RSV).

The language of relationship continues with the promise that God cares about the deep concerns that are on the hearts of His people. Once again in these verses, the Old Testament prophetic hopes for God's care are quoted (Is. 25:8; 35:10). These deep yearnings of the prophets are now fulfilled.

ALL THINGS NEW

5 Then He who sat on the throne said, "Behold, I make all things new." And He said to me, "Write, for these words are true and faithful."

6 And He said to me, "It is done! I am the Alpha and the Omega, the Beginning and the End. I will give of the fountain of the water of life freely to him who thirsts. 7 He who overcomes shall inherit all things, and I will be his God and he shall be My son. 8 But the cowardly, unbelieving, abominable, murderers, sexually immoral, sorcerers, idolaters, and all liars shall have their part in the lake which burns with fire and brimstone, which is the second death."

—*Revelation 2 1:5–8*

The *"all things new"* is this very fulfillment of the real presence of God with His people.

The phrase *"He who overcomes,"* which we saw at the close of each of the seven letters to the seven churches, now appears again in a way that unites this vision with those seven letters. It is our repentance and faith that make us conquerors.

Another relationship promise is announced: *"I will be His God and he shall be My son."* We are now called the children of God. This is the description Paul gives to the Christians in his Romans 8 promise of the ministry of the Holy Spirit. When we are assured of Christ as our Savior and Lord, we are enabled to say, *"Abba, Father"* (Rom. 8:12–17).

The final part of the second paragraph (vv. 5–8) reminds the viewer of this vision that repentance and faith are necessary to enter into this fellowship with the One who is the Alpha and Omega. There follows another list of sinful attributes that are examples of the arrogance and hurtfulness of sin which go against the will of God for life and thus cannot endure the fellowship of

God. Their destiny is destruction, not life. This list is something like a postscript attached to this relationship portrait. It shows by negative contrast what in the positive sense is the will of God— not fearfulness, but faith; not distortion, but truth; not murder, but life; not sexual chaos, but wholeness; not mysticism, but relationship; not idols, but encounter with the living God; not deception, but the open face of trust.

THE NEW CITY

9 Then one of the seven angels who had the seven bowls filled with the seven last plagues came to me and talked with me, saying, "Come, I will show you the bride, the Lamb's wife." 10 And he carried me away in the Spirit to a great and high mountain, and showed me the great city, the holy Jerusalem, descending out of heaven from God, 11 having the glory of God. Her light was like a most precious stone, like a jasper stone, clear as crystal. 12 Also she had a great and high wall with twelve gates, and twelve angels at the gates, and names written on them, which are the names of the twelve tribes of the children of Israel: 13 three gates on the east, three gates on the north, three gates on the south, and three gates on the west.
14 Now the wall of the city had twelve foundations, and on them were the names of the twelve apostles of the Lamb.
—Revelation 21:9–14

This text contains the description of the new Jerusalem. The most important question we must ask is this: what is the theological significance of this most precise and elaborate part of the vision of Revelation? The principle concern of this description is to show that the Christian church is the true fulfillment of the people Israel: that people established as twelve tribes and made a nation in David's city, Jerusalem. The vision makes clear this vital connection between the original holy history of Israel and the expanded Israel of all those who believe in Israel's Messiah. The description of the twelve foundations of the temple have inscribed upon them not the names of Dan or Benjamin but the names of the twelve apostles of the Lamb.

A GREAT CITY

15 And he who talked with me had a gold reed to measure the city, its gates, and its wall. 16 The city is laid out as a

square; its length is as great as its breadth. And he measured the city with the reed: twelve thousand furlongs. Its length, breadth, and height are equal. [17] Then he measured its wall: one hundred and forty-four cubits, according to the measure of a man, that is, of an angel. [18] The construction of its wall was of jasper; and the city was pure gold, like clear glass. [19] The foundations of the wall of the city were adorned with all kinds of precious stones: the first foundation was jasper, the second sapphire, the third chalcedony, the fourth emerald, [20] the fifth sardonyx, the sixth sardius, the seventh chrysolite, the eighth beryl, the ninth topaz, the tenth chrysoprase, the eleventh jacinth, and the twelfth amethyst. [21] The twelve gates were twelve pearls: each individual gate was of one pearl. And the street of the city was pure gold, like transparent glass.

—*Revelation 21:15–21*

Another important feature in the description of the new Jerusalem is the immensity of the dimensions. It is a perfect cube, twelve thousand stadia in length, height, and width. This means, in terms of miles, that the city is 1,500 miles in each direction. Even in an era of supersonic speeds, this is a city that takes our breath away. Images now compound beyond our ability accurately to describe. For example, we are told of pure gold that is as transparent as glass. The foundations are adorned with every jewel.

The list of jewels has posed a fascinating puzzle for interpreters of this vision. John has given a list in basically the reverse order of the instructions in Exodus 28:17–21 for the arrangement of jewels on the high priestly breastplate. His order of jewels is also the reverse order of the stones associated, according to Josephus *(Ant* 3:186) and Philo *(Vit Mos* 2:124–6), with the signs of the zodiac by which the ancient world traced the times and seasons of the year.

I believe this reversal is significant. It shows that all of the jewels are there, but they are placed in the new authoritative order of the Lamb. I take this to mean that nothing has been wasted in God's design, whether stars or jewels or colors or mountains. Everything is accounted for, and in this vision everything is fulfilled by the sovereign decision of God. And furthermore, there are surprises even in the arrangement of that fulfillment.

THE UNIVERSAL CITY

[22] But I saw no temple in it, for the Lord God Almighty and the Lamb are its temple. [23] The city had no need of the

sun or of the moon to shine in it, for the glory of God illuminated it. The Lamb is its light. [24] And the nations of those who
are saved shall walk in its light, and the kings of the earth
bring their glory and honor into it. [25] Its gates shall not be
shut at all by day (there shall be no night there). [26] And they
shall bring the glory and the honor of the nations into it.
[27] But there shall by no means enter it anything that defiles, or
causes an abomination or a lie, but only those who are written
in the Lamb's Book of Life.

—Revelation 21:22–27

The universal nature of the new Jerusalem is clearly stated in
the last paragraph of chapter 21, *"kings of earth shall bring their
glory the glory and honor of the nations."* Those who make up
this new Jerusalem are those whose names are written in the
Lamb's Book of Life. The old distinctions are no longer barriers
between people. But the uniqueness of each person and tribe is
preserved as part of their glory just as the unique colors of the jewels are preserved as part of their glory. In this vision, we do not
have the blurring of uniqueness or memory or relationships but
rather the fulfillment of the ways in which we have been originally created and the ways in which we have lived out our created
individuality. But the surprise is that the uniqueness does not iso-
late us from each other. The *ethnos* (nations) of the world are
honored and set free from the old competitions and fears, but the
gift that each tribe and family and individual person has to bring
is not the orchestrated "amen" or *"sieg heil"* of a Nurenberg Nazi
rally with every voice identical. No, the jasper does not become a
diamond, nor the pearl a sapphire. Each voice is heard in conver-
sation like that of a bride with her lover—not the lock-stepped
zombie adoration that has so characterized the cults and political
tyrannies of our time.

Teilhard is right in his letter to his atheist friend, Julian Huxley,
when he tells him that the problem of humanism is its
shortsightedness. He informs Huxley that his own intention as a
Christian paleontologist is to continue his scientific research on
into eternity. Why not! The vision in Romans 8 and here in
Revelation 21 is that of the fulfillment of what has been started in
the order of creation, not its obliteration as in the case of the Greek
hope of immortality. Greek spiritualization really amounted to the
absorption of the human spirit into the vague tapioca pudding of
eternity.

The vision in Revelation is much more dynamic. Yes, by all means, work hard in your research into the wonders of plasma physics, and plan on continuing that study into the new order. That research is part of the glory and honor of your *ethnos*. So are your relationships with children, parents, friends; so are your hobbies and avocations—as also is the color of your skin and eyes. When Paul says, "The mortal puts on immortality" (1 Cor. 15:54), he does not have in mind a Greek vision of absorption but the Christian hope of resurrection. God who made us and redeemed us will raise us up again. He will fulfill us and the whole created order too (Rom. 8:18–25).

THE TREE OF HEALING

22:1 And he showed me a pure river of water of life, clear as crystal, proceeding from the throne of God and of the Lamb. 2 In the middle of its street, and on either side of the river, was the tree of life, which bore twelve fruits, each tree yielding its fruit every month. The leaves of the tree were for the healing of the nations. 3 And there shall be no more curse, but the throne of God and of the Lamb shall be in it, and His servants shall serve Him. 4 They shall see His face, and His name shall be on their foreheads. 5 There shall be no night there: They need no lamp nor light of the sun, for the Lord God gives them light. And they shall reign forever and ever.

—Revelation 22:1–5

The last vision is the best. At the center of the city is the presence of Almighty God and the Lamb. John's eye is then drawn to the river of life and a tree with leaves for the healing of the nations. This means that John's final discovery is that of the redemption that flows from the throne of God and the Lamb.

The last sign is the sign of hope. Jesus Christ is able to forgive and heal; the One who heals is the One who also reigns and, therefore, the healing of this Lamb has authority. It lasts. Jesus Christ, the Lamb/Shepherd, is able to keep His sheep to sustain them for all time.

This conviction is what gives to the Christian church our real authority in the world. Just as the authority of a university professor in a class meeting is not established by his academic title but by the truth of his lecture, so, in the same way, the authority of the church depends upon the authority and truth of our gospel about Jesus Christ and His promises. John has closed the fourth movement with his narrative of the vision of that ultimate authority. This has very practical implications: the reason a Christian does not despair in the midst of the sinfulness and confusion of our own generation is because of the tree that heals. Because of that living hope, there is no person or situation that is hopeless. Drug addiction, racial hatreds, luxurious selfishness . . . self-righteousness.

These and all other sins are variations on a theme, and each one of them can be healed by the Redeemer Jesus Christ.

But what is equally important is that His healing lasts for all time. The only sin that cannot be healed is the aloneness-sin that does not want the forgiveness of the Lamb. "The one principal of Hell is . . . I am my own" (George MacDonald). But if we repent and if we open the door of our heart, then the Lamb will come in and will sup with us and we with Him. Now in the vision of His dining room, we have discovered what a party it is! The journey of the Bible is a journey from the Word of God to the Word of God . . . from the Garden of Eden to the City of God.

This is the end of the Great Symphony!

CHAPTER SIX—EPILOGUE
REVELATION 22:6–21

Scripture Outline

Holy Colony (22:6–11)

Come, Lord Jesus (22:12–16)

All Who Are Thirsty (22:17–21)

HOLY COLONY

⁶ Then he said to me, "These words are faithful and true." And the Lord God of the holy prophets sent His angel to show His servants the things which must shortly take place.

⁷ "Behold, I am coming quickly! Blessed is he who keeps the words of the prophecy of this book."

⁸ Now I, John, saw and heard these things. And when I heard and saw, I fell down to worship before the feet of the angel who showed me these things.

⁹ Then he said to me, "See that you do not do that. For I am your fellow servant, and of your brethren the prophets, and of those who keep the words of this book. Worship God." ¹⁰ And he said to me, "Do not seal the words of the prophecy of this book, for the time is at hand. ¹¹ He who is unjust, let him be unjust still; he who is filthy, let him be filthy still; he who is righteous, let him be righteous still; he who is holy, let him be holy still."

—Revelation 22:6–11

The angel assures John of the trustworthiness of what he has experienced. That commendation is then extended to those who will read and obey the words of the prophecy of this book. Following this endorsement, a blessing is extended. They who follow the will of God are blessed. Prophecy in the Old Testament is always the proclamation of the will of God for His people. This sentence of blessing thus represents the same form and contextual understanding of blessing as we find throughout the Old Testament prophetic literature. It has not changed. There is an essential continuity, and God's people have always found the right way (blessing) when they have followed the will of God. That is the sense of this passage.

Once again, John, in his respect for the angel, falls down to worship him because of what the angel had shown John. Once again, the angel rebukes John for worship misplaced. The angel defines himself to John as a fellow servant. John's double experience of misplaced worship has the effect of strongly impressing upon his readers the pastoral and theological importance of worship as the rightful human expression toward God alone. John's worship of the angel is a form of temptation which the angel resists by remembering two things: First, he remembers his solidarity with John and John's companions in faith. The angel is under orders as they are under orders. Second, he reminds John of the great theological fact which the Ten Commandments had long ago stated: only God alone deserves worship. Worship is as dangerous a human act as it is a wondrous. When worship is given to any part of the human created order, it becomes both a temptation to evil for those who receive such adoration and an act of idolatry for those who offer such adoration. This double experience of John has doubly warned the readers of this possibility.

John is told not to seal the notes that he has written of his vision but to share them with the churches because of the critical moment that is at hand.

The next sentence is very powerful: "Let the evildoers still do evil, and the filthy still be filthy, and the righteous still do right and the holy still be holy" (v. 11, RSV). What does this sentence mean in its own setting and for us today?

First, the text is clearly not teaching that the times are so far gone that there is no hope for the filthy or the evildoer and, therefore, that God's people should ignore them. In a very few sentences John will call upon those who are thirsty to come to the waters. What, then, is the meaning of the angel's words?

The text is a statement of strategic realism for the Christians in the world. The Christian is not to wait until an ideal time and place in which to live out his faith, love, and hope. Christians are to live their witness to the truth of the gospel here and now in the less-than-ideal setting of their cities. They are not encouraged to escape to a place of refuge but to stay where they are and be what they are, wherever they are. There is no denying the difficulty they face in their cities with the gross excesses of Graeco-Roman mystery cult religions and the intensifying persecution from Rome. But they are to be the light of the world in those cities, and this text teaches that they will be able to do just that! This is a very hopeful promise, because the Christians are, in fact, granted a strategy for the decadent cities of Asia Minor. They are to model hope in those cities.

Solzhenitsyn has captured the theological force of this text in his novel *One Day in the Life of Ivan Denisovich*. Alyoska, the young Christian, is in the bunkhouse with the rest of the prisoners; he has the same ten-year sentence as the rest; he works on the same work crew, but he "reads his Gospels facing the light bulb." Russian epic novelists favor just such symbolism as is represented by such a simple line. The fact is that Alyoska has found meaning for life in the midst of the same twenty-four-hour cycle as the other men in that work camp. Bad as it is, harsh as it is, lonely as it is, Alyoska is a person who is modeling the hope that comes from God. The Christians are not encouraged to flail the wind in panic because of the decadence of Roman culture. They are rather to face up to the sinfulness; they are encouraged to try to understand its many causes and then to develop a strategy for the gospel in the very middle of it all.

This book has equipped them for a fourfold strategy if they read it closely. It is the strategy of *models;* it is the strategy of *light;* it is the strategy of *nourishment;* it is the strategy of *love.*

Models—God's strategy is primarily His people placed in the cities as a holy colony. They are a network of support to each other and a community that reaches out to neighbors and invites them in to find Jesus Christ. This Book of Revelation is a book that begins and ends, as we will see, with the colony—the seven churches—real people in real places who are God's people in those places and for all time.

It is the strategy of the light. This is the significance of the terms "righteousness" and "holy." The people of God are the people of God's character, of His truth to which they belong. We who make up the colony are to model our obedience to the will of God in the twenty-four-hour cycle—"to read the Gospels facing the light bulb." That light bulb gives to God's colony pastoral sensitivity toward the people in the cities where we live. One of the important teaching roles that the Book of Revelation fulfills is its very perceptive insight into the reasons behind the idolatry, immorality, and despair that are the sources of most sins. The light bulb of biblical understanding of personality enables God's people to understand the setting into which we have been planted.

It is the strategy of food and water. Sooner or later the false gods give way. It happens to people every day, and, when it does, God's people must be in the place where people are so that we may share with them the authentic food of the gospel. But this takes time; it is a fact of life demonstrated throughout the Bible that people must be hungry and thirsty before the food of the gospel is welcomed. When they are—we need to be there. The best antidote to false foods is good food, and the best cure for spiritual malnutrition is the healthy food of the gospel. It is important that we as Christians realize how nutritious to the whole person is the gospel of Jesus Christ. We should listen again to Lewis: "The best safeguard against bad literature is a full experience of good; just as a real and affectionate acquaintance with honest people gives better protection against rogues than a habitual distrust of everyone."[1] I am convinced that the strategy of nourishment is vitally needed in our generation. The best ways to protect a person against cultism are not grim warnings about cultic excess so much as a healthy and nourishing diet of the lasting relationships and values of the gospel. Most people desperately reach out to the false promises because of exhaustion and depletion. Therefore, what we need more than anything in our own day is food to keep us sound and growing. What we need for ourselves is what the world needs.

It is the strategy of love. It was the love of Jesus Christ that first found us and healed us. It is that strong love that motivates the bride to join with the Holy Spirit in welcoming those who are thirsty (v. 17). The last sentence of this book will remember the love of the Lord Jesus Christ. The first letter in this book to the church of Ephesus warned that the church must not forget the central importance of God's love in its life and also in its strategy. Love is the gift we have to offer to the world that will completely take it by surprise. When people experience real love, they become very thirsty for its source.

COME, LORD JESUS

12 "And behold, I am coming quickly, and My reward is with Me, to give to every one according to his work. 13 I am the Alpha and the Omega, the Beginning and the End, the First and the Last."

14 Blessed are those who do His commandments, that they may have the right to the tree of life, and may enter through the gates into the city. 15 But outside are dogs and

sorcerers and sexually immoral and murderers and idolaters, and whoever loves and practices a lie.

16 "I, Jesus, have sent My angel to testify to you these things in the churches. I am the Root and the Offspring of David, the Bright and Morning Star."

—*Revelation 22:12–16*

Once again, Jesus Christ speaks to John. He will come soon as judge. The term used in that text is, literally, the one who brings "wages." He comes as the One who is the beginning and the end. This teaching of the Second Coming of Jesus Christ is taught in other places in the New Testament as well as in the Book of Revelation.

The Thursday evening discourse of Jesus contains the promise of His Second Coming: "And when I go and prepare a place for you, I will come again and will take you to myself, that where I am you may be also" (John 14:3, RSV).

Luke tells us in the opening of the Book of Acts of the promise made to the disciples on the day of the Ascension of Christ: "Men of Galilee, why do you stand gazing up into heaven? This same Jesus, who was taken up from you into heaven, will so come in like manner as you have seen Him go into heaven" (Acts 1:11). Throughout the New Testament letters, the expectation of the return of Christ is expressed in immediate terms: The apostle Paul writes of the soon return of Christ. That coming will be by surprise, he tells us, "For you yourselves know well that the day of the Lord will come like a thief in the night" (1 Thess. 5:2, RSV). Paul longs for that triumphant return as he expresses his expectation in the final greeting of 1 Corinthians 16:22 ". . . O Lord, come!"[2]

Paul is concerned about the Christians who are confused on this question, "Now concerning the coming of our Lord Jesus Christ, . . . we beg you, brethren, not to be quickly shaken in mind or excited" (2 Thess. 2:1, 2, RSV). Evidently, there were those at Thessalonica who were confused about this question and, as a result, they had withdrawn from their obligations to work and live daily as responsible disciples. Paul teaches that the expectation of the soon return of Jesus Christ gives more meaning and, indeed, more importance to our life and ministry here and now.

A question that inevitably emerges in the study of the New Testament Second-Coming expectation is this: how soon is soon? To answer this question, we must be careful not to measure the eschaton of God by an earthly, chronological measuring rod. We have witnessed in these passages, on the one hand, the prophetic shortening of time; but, also, we have been introduced to the prophetic/apocalyptic mystery of time.

There is no way really to develop a chronological time-measurement scale for the language of Paul's eschatology—"in a moment, in the twinkling of an eye . . ." (1 Cor. 15:52). The same is true of the eschatological language for time in John's vision in Revelation. God's time is not captive to the measurement frame of the solar system. The zodiac jewels are reversed in John's vision. Time is a much more complicated reality that an hourglass or a stopwatch would suggest. The mathematician-physicist Albert Einstein has found a witness to this fact in his discovery that time, even as we know and experience it, is altered by the speeds and gravitational fields of the created order.

Time itself is a baffling mystery, and the vision of John has borne witness to that mystery, but not in a way that confuses or distorts reality. His vision has helped us to see history meaningfully. All of time, as all of creation, belongs to its Lord. "We live each day as if it were our last, and each day as if there were to be a great future."[3]

For most people, the compulsory abandonment of planning for the future means that they are forced back into living just for the moment, irresponsibly, frivolously, or resignedly; some few dream longingly of better times to come, and try to forget the present. We find both these courses equally impossible, and there remains for us only the very narrow way, often extremely difficult to find, of living every day as if it were our last, and yet living in faith and responsibility as though there were to be a great future: "Houses and fields and vineyards shall again be bought in this land," proclaims Jeremiah (32:15), in paradoxical contrast to his prophecies of woe, just before the destruction of the holy city. It is a sign from God and a pledge of a fresh start and a great future, just when all seems black.

This is the New Testament conviction about time. "Soon" is the best word, the most accurate word, to describe the return of Christ as Lord because we have already received the companionship here and now of the Lord of the beginning and the end. The Holy Spirit has already confirmed and granted that living presence to everyone who trusts Jesus Christ here and now. We have the down payment—the earnest money of what eternity will be.

The central importance of the doctrine of the second coming of Jesus Christ is that Jesus Christ stands at the end of history "writ large." He holds in His hand the destiny of the whole. Jesus Christ also stands at the end of history "writ small"—the destiny of my own life. History does not trail off into emptiness, nor does it endlessly repeat its themes, like a vast confined circle. History from the biblical perspective has a meaningful beginning through the decision of God. History has the decisive center which is the radical intervention of God—the eternal Word and event Jesus Christ. History moves toward the decisive fulfillment. The same Jesus Christ who stands at its beginning and at its center also stands to greet us at its end.

We have in the Epilogue the Lord Jesus Christ once again proclaimed to us in the images that we have earlier discovered in this book and have come to understand. He is the Alpha/Omega, the root of David, the bright morning star.

ALL WHO ARE THIRSTY

17 And the Spirit and the bride say, "Come!" And let him who hears say, "Come!" And let him who thirsts come. Whoever desires, let him take the water of life freely.

18 For I testify to everyone who hears the words of the prophecy of this book: If anyone adds to these things, God will add to him the plagues that are written in this book; 19 and if anyone takes away from the words of the book of this prophecy, God shall take away his part from the Book of Life, from the holy city, and from the things which are written in this book

20 He who testifies to these things says, "Surely I am coming quickly."

Amen. Even so, come, Lord Jesus!

21 The grace of our Lord Jesus Christ be with you all. Amen.

—Revelation 22:17–21

"The Spirit and the bride say, 'Come!'" I interpret these great invitations as evangelistic encouragement to any who may read this book and who now desire to meet the Lamb. The Holy Spirit is joined with the church in calling out the words of generous encouragement to all who are thirsty. The Isaiah prophecy is recalled: "Ho, everyone who thirsts, come to the waters; and he who has no money, come, buy and eat!" (Is. 55:1, RSV). These words of grace are the last words to the world.

The book closes now with a postscript which contains a warning to the readers. I am reminded by this postscript of the fact that a Christian marriage service ends with a similar postscript just prior to the benediction. That postscript is also a warning. The warning does not destroy the joy and wonder of the wedding vows and prayers, but it has the effect of reminding people of how meaningful and important to God is the event of that wedding. The warning goes as follows: "Whom God has joined together let no man put asunder." That warning just prior to the benediction and the kiss of the bride and groom is both good and necessary. It is a warning in our behalf. It is a woe pronounced by the prophet of the Lord against any who would tamper with the vows and promises, the love and commitment that have been sealed between the man and woman in marriage.

This book concludes with a warning of the same kind. We the readers are warned not to tamper with the record of these visions, either by subtraction or addition. We are to stand reverently before and beneath God's Word. We do not look over the Bible's shoulder to correct its theology; it is rather that the Bible corrects our theology. Karl Barth summarizes it well:

> Once and for all, theology has . . . its position *beneath* that of the biblical scriptures. While it is aware of all their human and conditioned character, it still knows and considers that the writings with which it deals are *holy* writings. These writings are selected and separated; they deserve and demand respect and attention of an extraordinary order, since they have a direct relationship to God's work and word. If theology seeks to learn of prophecy and the apostolate, it can only and ever learn from the prophetic and apostolic witnesses. It must learn not this or that important truth but the one thing that is necessary—and with respect to this one thing on which all else depends, the biblical witnesses are better informed than are the theologians. For this reason theology must agree to let *them* look over its shoulder and correct its notebooks."[4]

The warning is a statement of criterion. Christians are the people under the Gospel. We are biblical Christians. Finally, "*The grace of the Lord Jesus be with all the saints. Amen.*"

The book ends as it began—with the first love that comes from the Lord Jesus Christ. The book ends with the assurance of the faithfulness of that love. Amen! Here is the rock upon which to build your life: the faithfulness of the love of Jesus Christ. It will last.

NOTES

1. Lewis, *An Experiment in Criticism,* p. 94.

2. The Greek word is *maranatha,* a transliteration into Greek from two Aramaic words. It was probably a common saying among the early Christians.

3. Bonhoeffer, *Letters and Papers,* p. 15.

4. Karl Barth, *Evangelical Theology* (New York: Holt, Rinehart and Winston, 1963), p. 32.

BIBLIOGRAPHY

Barclay, William. *The Letters of John.* Edinburgh: St. Andrew's Press, 1958.

Barmen Declaration, Article I. *Book of Confessions,* 2nd ed. United Presbyterian Church in the U.S.A., 1970.

Barth, Karl. *Dogmatics in Outline.* New York: Harper, 1959.

_____. *Evangelical Theology.* New York: Holt, Rinehart and Winston, 1963.

Bonhoeffer, Dietrich. *Letters and Papers from Prison.* New York: Macmillan, 1967, 1972.

_____. *Life Together.* New York: Harper & Bros., 1954.

Bruce, F. F. *Answers to Questions.* Grand Rapids: Zondervan Publishing House, 1972.

Bulletin of the American Schools for Oriental Research, 1958, 1959, 1966.

Bunyan, John. *The Pilgrim's Progress.* London: J. M. Dent & Sons, 1954.

Calvin, John. *Institutes of the Christian Religion,* Beveridge trans. 2 vols. Grand Rapids: Eerdmans, 1953.

Colson, Charles. *Life Sentence.* Lincoln, Va.: Chosen Books, 1979.

Ford, J. M. *The Anchor Bible: Revelation.* New York: Doubleday, 1980.

Houlden, J. L. *A Commentary on the Johannine Epistles.* New York: Harper, 1973.

Irenaeus, "Against Heresies." In *Early Christian Fathers,* ed. C. C. Richardson. New York: Macmillan, 1970.

Kittel, Gerhard, and Friedrich, Gerhard. *Theological Dictionary of the New Testament.* 10 vols. Grand Rapids: Eerdmans, 1964.

Koestler, Arthur. *Darkness at Noon.* New York: Macmillan, 1941.

Lewis, C. S. *An Experiment in Criticism.* New York: Cambridge University Press, 1961.

_____. *Four Loves.* New York: Harcourt Brace, 1960.

_____. *Miracles.* New York: Macmillan, 1947.

_____. *Screwtape Letters.* New York: Fontana Books, 1942.

Lilje, Hans. *The Last Book of the Bible.* Philadelphia: Fortress Press, 1967.

Luther, Martin. *Lectures on Romans.* St. Louis: Concordia Press, 1972.

Morris, Leon. *I Believe in Revelation.* Grand Rapids: Eerdmans, 1976.

Palmer, Earl F. *The Intimate Gospel.* Waco, Tex.: Word Books, 1978.

_____. *Love Has Its Reasons.* Waco, Tex.: Word Books, 1977.

Pliny the Younger. Correspondence to Trajan. Quoted in H. Bettenson, ed., *Documents of the Christian Church.* London: Oxford University Press, 1943.

Ramsey, William. *Letters to Seven Churches.* 1904.

Sayers, Dorothy. "The Bible and the Modern Reader." In *Christian Letters to a Post-Christian World.* Grand Rapids: Eerdmans, 1969.

Scofield, C. I. *Holy Bible: Scofield Reference Edition,* p. 1331.

Stott, J. R. W. *The Epistles of John.* Grand Rapids: Eerdmans, 1960.

Tacitus, Cornelius. *Annales,* xv. 44.

Vanauken, Sheldon. *A Severe Mercy.* New York: Harper & Row, 1977.

Van Unnik, W. C. *Newly Discovered Gnostic Writings.* London: SCM Press, 1960.

Westcott, B. F. *The First Epistle of John.* Grand Rapids: Eerdmans, 1952.